O9-BTM-769

Politics And The Muse

Politics And The Muse: Studies in the Politics of Recent American Literature

Edited
by
Adam J.Sorkin

MIDDLEBURY COLLEGE LIBRARY

Bowling Green State University Popular Press
Bowling Green, Ohio 43403

Copyright© 1989 by Bowling Green State University Popular Press

Library of Congress Catalogue Card No.: 88—64054

ISBN: 087972-447-1 cb
    087972-448-x pb

Cover design by Gary Dumm

Contents

Introduction

Politics and the Muse:
Voices and Visions at the Crossroads

Adam J. Sorkin

That the Muse traditionally invoked by the writer is not, or not just, the handmaiden of beauty, inspirer of art and true knowledge, goddess of song and story, but is political, is a recognition whose time has come in the last decades of the twentieth century. The present collection of fourteen new essays on the politics of literature investigates aspects of our understanding of the political Muse, with a focus on American writing since World War II.

The term "political," of course, can have numerous senses. This volume takes it broadly, and hospitably, to refer to power relations among groups of a variety of kinds, e.g., classes, races, genders, nations and so forth, including less objectively defined categories of society such as those who perceive themselves as haves or have-nots, as participating in or excluded from the dominant culture, as propelled naturally to social status and economic success or impelled necessarily to resist oppression. What is political, then, points to not just formal systems and practical arrangements of order and social hierarchy but also concepts of, and values underlying, these power relations, from the officially legislated and the institutionalized to the ignored, implicit and denied. The concept embraces as well the sentiments and emotions that attend these relations. It is my belief that at its furthest extension for literature, the political thus infuses what both writer and reader see, believe, think, feel and say.

The interpenetration of the political and the literary is an idea that has grown in prominence over the last two centuries, perhaps partially in protest to the privileging of writing-as-art, *belles letters,* as a special category and tradition separate from other kinds of writing. Concomitantly, there has been continuing and sometimes strident dispute about the relations between politics and literature. In an overview of the connections between the two, Matei Calinescu singles out "the problem of commitment and the various theories of literary discourse

1

that are implicit in this notion" as having been, "since the dawn of Romanticism...one of the most sensitive and controversial issues that modern aesthetic consciousness has had to face" (123-24). But commitment is merely one question that criticism must still actively confront as it attempts to understand culture and the arts (from high to low or popular). The challenge issued a decade ago by Judith Fetterley at the beginning of her introduction to *The Resisting Reader* is one that remains with us: "Literature is political. It is painful to have to insist on this fact, but the necessity of such insistence indicates the dimensions of the problem" (xi).

One aspect of the problem is that when this fact is accepted, the political character of literature is frequently thought of as a disjunction, a yoking or clash of opposites, and therefore described in highly dramatic ways. For example, in his classic essay, "Reality in America," Lionel Trilling speaks in a bold and suggestive metaphor of "the dark and bloody crossroads where literature and politics meet" (8).[1] Using a forceful image with similar hints of physical conflict, the novelist Stendhal presents in *The Red and the Black* a dichotomy between, on one side, politics conceived of as an inappropriate, interjection of raw event into, or a significant disruption of, what on the other side is literary performance construed essentially as novelistic integrity and craftsmanship. Stendhal's authorial interpolation into the story is well known: "Politics in the midst of imaginative activity is like a pistol shot in the middle of a concert" (304), he proclaims, although in the novelist's works, politics quietly imbues the imagined ordinary behavior and everyday private life of the characters, too. Irving Howe uses a version of Stendhal's epigrammatic pronouncement to open the first chapter of his influential 1957 volume, *Politics and the Novel*. But to me, the presence of the political in the aesthetic is less the "violent intrusion" Howe at one point calls it (15), or "shattering" in Stendhal's words,[2] than an unavoidable crossing of paths in a merging of imaginary and real-life concerns and journeys, both for writers and for readers.

Beyond evoking an aggressive and frightful side of life that politics can bring into literature, the notion of dimly illuminated crossroads obliquely betokens other kinds of tense and paradoxical relation between them. On the one hand, imaginary or fictive experience, if (in one figure among many) a made-up game, is personally engaging for the individual reader, implicates powerful emotions, and, though private and subjective, is empirically repeatable. On the other hand, politics, whether belief, commitment, system or public historical occurrence, while potentially having profound impact on people's lives separately and in groups, is anything but made-up, artificial; yet its real-world, time-bound events can seem contingent, feel distant, and occur impersonally, abstractly, as if arbitrarily. This is, it goes without saying, a reflection of the old truism that art serves to heighten, to clarify, to validate, to intensify the ordinary and familiar, making the common and everyday appear more real. Additionally, the interrelation of literature and politics is complicated further by the homely truth that many readers rely on literature for factual knowledge, turning not to the social sciences, history or philosophy but to imaginative writing for specific understanding of the actual politics in their lives. Mary McCarthy, countering a claim that American novels fail at being political, notes that "indeed, Americans, I think, tend to get their political education through fiction" (1). Despite such domestication of the problem, however, controversy about the immanence of the political in the literary continues.

Disagreement about this problem is less than heated, to be sure, when the topic is some conventionally or obviously politicized aspect of literature such as, say, a writer's explicit commentary on powerful individuals in public life or on groups or trends in society, or, similarly, the articulation of partisan opinions in literary works. Further, while the material forms writing takes as manufactured object are usually neglected in literary studies, it is hardly polemical to observe *prima facie* political overtones to the roles writing plays in a consumer economy and mass culture as a market commodity that is produced, distributed and sold. And likewise, little protest is generated at an author's or an interpreter's construing as political the rendering of humanity in and of society, including the concrete mimetic representation that constitutes a major socio-political content of literature—although it should be added that many scholars and teachers tend to view this as the thematic inclusion of concerns that are more properly social, political, economic and historical, and therefore the unavoidable introduction of something extrinsic to the basic nature of literature. Such a conception is at base formalistic, so it is not surprising that, in spite of these areas of apparent general consensus, the counter-argument of programmatic aestheticism, which rejects the concept of verbal art as anything but imagination and consciousness raised to an autonomous formal structure of words, has wide appeal. A strong statement of this ostensibly apolitical or anti-political position, not from the customarily cited Wilde or Valéry but, instead, a contemporary American fictionalist and philosopher, can be found in a catechistic passage from William H. Gass's essay, "The Artist and Society": "Why are works or art so socially important?" Gass asks rhetorically and then answers, "Not for the messages...but because they insist...on their own reality: because of the absolute way in which they exist" (282).

Except for the proponents of art for pure art's sake, who deny the political entirely, or the advocates of the other side of the same absolutist coin, anti-art for anti-art's—and Calinescu notes that writers in both wings of the party of self-conscious literariness have historically been close to an anarchist ethos, if not doctrinal adherents (123), there is ongoing dispute about interpretations of art that take for granted its inherent political character. The insistent critical problem some readers (Fetterley, for instance) have noted pertains most of all to the undramatic ways in which the Muse incarnates the literary and the political as one. But while there continues to be antipathy to the idea that all writing has intrinsic political substance and scope, there is the growing pressure of a body of work by recent analysts—too many to begin to cite here, and not just Marxist thinkers[3]—who accept as a starting point the idea that art emotionally mediates, in both directions, between consciousness and what the individual perceives as the real world. Thus not only the organization and appearance of reality but also the structure and content of thought have incontrovertible political dimensions. This dual outlook provides much clear light upon the dark crossing of politics and literature.

In this prospect, writing always expresses—overtly, in parallel unconsciously, and at the same time even resistantly—a range of political assumptions, an ideology. Ideology is itself a hotly debated concept that is broader in its reference than just political content. I shall sidestep the plethora of formulations by adapting Janet Wolff's "carefully agnostic" version (50),[4] for it is enough to remark here that ideology, as ideas, beliefs, values, is reflective of the actual material conditions of existence and, more importantly for this argument, of the culture which determines, or at least leaves a dominant imprint on, many of its attributes and which, far from monolithic, can itself contain inconsistency and contradiction. For writing, aspects of the ideological are discernible as much in what a text leaves out or refrains from comment on or fails to notice as in its words and images and allusions. Prior attitudinal givens inhere, additionally, in the reception of writing, cutting across from readers' responses to literature that are mistakenly put down as naive, direct, escapist, merely emotive, to those, the favored approaches in higher education, that derive from the sophisticated attention of professors and other trained critical readers. A central contention of one of the most important recent books to discuss the politics of literary expression, Peter J. Rabinowitz's *Before Reading*, is thus that scholars and theorists need to understand the contexts from which readers derive presuppositions about world and word. Rabinowitz demonstrates convincingly that readers are conditioned in their reading and judgment of narratives by their "prior knowledge of conventions of reading," a knowledge he insists is infused with political assumptions and content. Thinking about literature has thus come far in the direction of perceiving the interconnections of writing and politics. But nevertheless Rabinowitz, too, notes that there is dismay at the general position—still "more controversial than it ought to be"—that not only is literature political but "the very act of interpretation is inevitably a political act" (3-4).

To contend that the Muse has always been in essence political, however, we need not enter directly into the last few decades' growing reaction to the now disintegrating academic hegemony of the New Criticism, with its theory of autotelic works of art that are dehistoricized, depoliticized, deracinated, detraditionalized and at times deauthored.[5] A look at the Muse herself reiterates this point, as the poet and maverick scholar of religious mythology, Robert Graves, concludes in his introduction to *The Greek Myths*, where he asserts the in itself not uncommon view that "a large part of Greek myth is politico-religious history" (17). The stories associated with the Muses remind us of the innately political situation and deep political content of the arts. This is a truth that is somewhat masked in the standard view of nine Muses who each conveniently and oh so gracefully preside over some particular art or science, a late classical codification quaintly familiar from polite bowdlerizations like Bulfinch's *The Age of Fable*. But in early stories, there were initially only three Muses, mountain goddesses of obscure origin, instead of the nine we have come to know as the daughters of Zeus and Mnemosyne (memory), and the female trinity dwelled not on Mount Helicon but on Mount Pieria, north of Olympus (Tripp 385-86; Graves, *White Goddess* 427-28). The Muses with which we are acquainted, Graves proposes, derive from what was first of all a set of "orgiastic priestesses" and the equivalent (indeed, the direct antecedent) of witches (*White Goddess* 178, 428). He argues that the removal of the Muses from their early haunts and the eventual reduction in their exalted status were part and parcel of the triumph of invaders and their world view. The patriarchal consciousness of these northern and Asian outsiders disrupted early Europe and led to the development of patrilinear, classical, logical Apollonian culture, which Graves disparages as "intellectual homosexuality," over the magic of the Moon-goddess or "White Goddess, or Muse, the Mother of All Living, the ancient power of fright and lust." This "triple muse" of "true poetry" was an aspect of the divine female focus of aboriginal European fertility cults, a religion unchallenged in power and prestige and based on man's offering to woman not only sexual homage but also spiritual appeasement and adoration (*White Goddess* vi-viii, 12, 424). Thus the Muses, later in effect captured again by Apollo who in Virgil's *Georgics*, which Graves cites in *The White Goddess*, vows to transplant them once more, this time to Delphi on Mount Parnassus, places sacred to himself (424), fell victim to "the revolutionary institution of fatherhood, imported into Europe from the East," in a political decline in status and function as "the social status of woman altered" and the male god Apollo won power and eventually became the patron of the Muses (431-33).[6]

But even discounting Graves's somewhat conjectural reconstruction, it is highly suggestive that in other stories the Muses were first located and worshiped by the rebellious twin giants Otus and Ephialtes who piled mountain upon mountain to storm the ancient heavens (Tripp 437; Graves, *Greek Myths* 136-38). It would be hard for a modern reader— or any sensitive receiver of the tale—not to take note that in this fable of revolt it is the interlopers, the disloyal opposition, who first find the Muses; the brothers' discovery of the patronesses of the arts and knowledge symbolically underscores their political nature and social potency. "Greek mythology was no more mysterious in content than are modern election cartoons" (Graves, *Greek Myths* 22). The giants' locating the Muses gives quintessential narrative recognition to the complex relations between the arts and whatever powers be, relations that in contemporary eras we know all too well can vary, often not at all subtly, between the poles of advocacy and alienation, collaboration and confrontation, victimization and resistance. Indeed, a critic need be at most an armchair deconstructionist to suppose that perhaps the gigantic twin nine-year-old rebels lost heaven *because* they lost the control of the story: thus they will forever be not heroes but merely big bad boys!

The political Muse, then, is no Tenth Muse (Lately Sprung Up in the Twentieth Century, to echo the title of Anne Bradstreet's 1650 book of poems), but always was, and is. I need no multiplication or reductionist "departmentalization" of the ancient nine (Graves, *White Goddess* 433) to suggest that the title, *The Political Muse*, under which I have grouped these studies of the coming together of politics and literature, implies that literature is richly, vibrantly, significantly political. It is political in its choice and representation of its material, in both the subjective, emotional, inward side of human experience and the outward, the social, the historical, the concretely circumstantial. It is political in its styles, its forms and structures, its history, genres and themes; in authorial interests, assumptions, intents, achievement. It is political as commodity and artifact, in its distribution, in the uses to which it is put. It is political in its relationship to the culture it comes out of and to explicit, assumed and subliminal cultural values, in its innate implications inseparable from its linguistic medium, in its privileging of certain voices, forms of expression and concerns and its disregard or dismissal of others. It is political in its reception, in its reflection of readership constituencies, in as it were its dialogue with readers. It is political in the attitudes of its readers, the expectations, considerations, hopes and fears they bring to the literary experience, their understandings and misunderstandings about their lives, their fellow beings, their world present and past. Indeed literature is political in just about every way imaginable, and this inescapable truth about the

Muse has been bodied forth by American writing since World War II both comprehensively and deeply.

The voices and visions in this volume comprise a broad range of approaches to the Muse and politics, reflecting many of these facets of the political nature and situation of literature I cite above, and then some. To close these introductory reflections, I should like to return one last time to the Greek narratives of the Muses in the course of hinting at my personal motivation behind intellectual and scholarly inquiry into the relations between literature and politics. I find it enlightening that, among the many classical traditions, it was the Muses who taught the riddle to the Sphinx. Today we don't need the cursed wisdom of an Oedipus (who had his own problems with crossroads) to see that the great riddle is still as the Muses taught: man, humankind. In a world of great inequality and in danger of blowing itself higher than the pinnacle of Mount Pelion piled on top of Mount Ossa, which the twin giants accomplished in their futile assault of the Olympic heavens, humanity is the conundrum, the essence of the problematic. But human understanding, values, self-criticism and knowledge must shape the answer as well, and if anything is to change, must create the mode for change. In a familiar truism of the past century, George A. Panichas notes that "we have come to rely a great deal on the writer to help us understand a world in the midst of"_____ (xxix)—fill in the blank with every darkness that needs illumination, every ill and danger that require solution.[7] One idealistic mental traveler looking at the important juncture of literature and politics, Jay Cantor, has envisioned humanity imaginatively connecting over "the space between" and creating a "turning" that is both "revolution" and "verse," for "art and politics are of the same metaphysical substance" (15, 12). Perhaps, indeed, one approach to the riddle is to remind ourselves that, yes, if literature is political, and if we turn to it to delineate the nature and causes of our suffering and to understand the limitations and constraining structures of our condition, it is also playful, fabulous, dream-laden, celebratory, and can imaginatively transform human experience in such a way that writers and readers might realize the salvation that is a better world in all its_____.

Exactly because the Muse touches upon both literature and politics, the Muse can better help us fill in both blanks and rise above their riddling emptiness.

Notes

[1]Trilling's phrase was picked up recently as the title of a designedly partisan neoconservative account by Norman Podhoretz; my use of it has nothing to do with Podhoretz's. Trilling's metaphor evokes a disturbing, tragic side to the relationship

between not only literature and politics but politics and the world. The relation is one that in the twentieth century has often been truly bloody, although some of the essays in this collection in effect question concomitant judgments such as Howe's, in his recent epilogue to the third edition of *Politics and the Novel*, that "the political fiction written after the Second World War" takes character as "a literature of blockage, a literature of impasse" (252).

[2]Stendhal goes on to add "without being forceful" and calls politics "a millstone hung on the neck of literature" (304). I should add that Howe's book as a whole stresses not politics as interruption but political ideas and the political milieu as definitive of the political novel.

[3]Insights derived from feminist perspectives in particular propel many critics and scholars in this direction. Fetterley's book is just one of a multitude of examples. To this, besides a plethora of modern Marxists, whose views reach great critical sophistication, we can add structuralists, post-structuralists, deconstructionists, subjectivists, neoconservatives, various adherents of the theories and practice of a number of French intellectuals, and others.

[4]See Chapter 3, "Art as Ideology" (49-70), where Wolff also usefully reviews a variety of theoretical positions.

[5]See Rabinowitz for a succinct summary of the debate (4-8).

[6]This early political history is summarized by Graves in the Introduction to *The Greek Myths*, 11-20; a brief overview of Graves's re-reading of the history of the Greek Muses appears in *The White Goddess*, 436-37.

[7]For the curious, Panichas completes the prepositional phrase abstractly with "ideological turmoil and cultural fragmentation."

Works Cited

Bulfinch, Thomas. *The Age of Fable, or Stories of Gods and Heroes. Bulfinch's Mythology: The Age of Fable, The Age of Chivalry, Legends of Charlemagne.* 1855. New York: Modern Library-Random House, n.d. 1-295.

Calinescu, Matei. "Literature and Politics." *Interrelations of Literature.* Ed. Jean-Pierre Barricelli and Joseph Gibaldi. New York: Modern Language Association, 1982. 123-49.

Cantor, Jay. *The Space Between: Literature and Politics.* Baltimore: Johns Hopkins UP, 1981.

Fetterley, Judith. *The Resisting Reader: A Feminist Approach to American Fiction.* Bloomington: Indiana UP, 1978.

Gass, William H. "The Artist and Society," *Fiction and the Figures of Life.* Boston: Nonpareil-David R. Godine, 1980. 276-88.

Graves, Robert. *The Greek Myths.* Vol. 1. Baltimore: Penguin, 1961.

———. *The White Goddess: A Historical Grammar of Poetic Myth.* Amended and enlarged ed. New York: Vintage, 1959.

Howe, Irving. *Politics and the Novel: With a New Epilogue.* New York: Meridian-New American Library, 1987.

McCarthy, Mary. "The Lasting Power of the Political Novel." *New York Times Book Review* 1 Jan. 1984: 1+.

Panichas, George A. "The Writer and Society: Some Reflections." *The Politics of Twentieth-Century Novelists.* Ed. Panichas. New York: Hawthorn, 1971. xxiii-liv.

Podhoretz, Norman. *The Bloody Crossroads: Where Literature and Politics Meet.* New York: Simon and Schuster, 1986.

Rabinowitz, Peter J. *Before Reading: Narrative Conventions and the Politics of Interpretation.* Ithaca: Cornell UP, 1987.

Stendhal. *Red and Black.* Trans. and ed. Robert M. Adams. Norton Critical Edition. New York: Norton, 1969.

Trilling, Lionel. "Reality in America." *The Liberal Imagination: Essays on Literature and Society.* Garden City: Doubleday Anchor, 1950. 1-19.

Tripp, Edward. *Crowell's Handbook of Classical Mythology.* New York: Thomas Y. Crowell, 1970.

Wolff, Janet. *The Social Production of Art.* New York: New York UP, 1987.

American Literature, Politics and
the Last Good War

Joseph J. Waldmeir

It was politics which made World War II a good war—that is a moral, a just, a righteous war—just as it has been politics that have defined the two wars since 1945 (two and one half, perhaps, if we count Nicaragua) in terms of degrees of badness ranging from questionable to reprehensible to evil. It isn't that the politics have been very different; indeed, they are quite similar, so similar in fact that one might argue that at basis the politics which inform the ideology of the wars since 1945 are the logical inheritance of the politics of World War II. There has been the fear of an inimical ideology using force or threats of force to extend its sphere of influence or its boundaries. There has been the old-liberal determination that the world should never again allow itself to be blackmailed into an appeasement of that ideology à la Munich. And most importantly, there has been the old-liberal argument for acceptance of responsibility to prevent either the appeasement or the extension of that ideology.

What made the perception of the three post-World War II wars so radically different, then? I believe it was the growing belief on the part of most Americans, whether liberal or conservative (excluding those in the extremities in either direction), that there was no real political conviction in the wars; that their pursuit was motivated by a kind of pragmatic (read "political," which gradually became a dirty word) insincerity. That we, and the other side as well, had no firm, unshakeable ideological certainty behind our actions. That, as a matter of fact, we were simply playing politics, perhaps—especially at the peace tables— only for the sake of the game.

This was not the case with World War II. We went into that war pretty much ideologically convinced that it was right and proper to fight it; and as the war proceeded, the conviction grew that we were in the right, at least in Europe, and in the Pacific as well since Japan had allied herself with the European enemy. And it is in this conviction that World War II is distinguished from the wars since then, including the threatening rumbles in Nicaragua, as the last good war.

This conviction is clearly expressed in the fiction of the second World War, or in that part of it which might be called ideological if not political, and which is the subject of this paper. It is most clearly understood historically, in terms of the crusading social-critical literature of the 1930s out of which it logically grows—of which it is the logical extension as well as its culmination. Such protest writers as John Steinbeck, Richard Wright, Clifford Odets, and a myriad other major and minor talents who chronicled the depression years, identified the social ills and inequities which they attacked as manifestations of varying degrees of rightist ideology, and the reforms which they proposed or threatened reflected equally varying degrees of leftist thought. By the end of the decade, most of the social evils which had occupied liberal reformers for ten years—poverty, racism, cops, factory and farmer owner-exploiters—had become particular aspects of Fascism, a universal moral illness merely epitomized or personified in the regimes of Fascist countries. It was the evil itself, wherever found, which had to be combated. And most of the reformer combatants, still leftist but not really politically liberal—not Communist, since the evils of Stalinism ranging from the betrayal of Spain, the Stalinist purges, and the Nazi-Soviet Pact of August 1939 were pills far too bitter for the reformers to swallow easily—directed their energies toward the exposure and destruction of the rightist enemy. Their approach was basically negative, anti-Fascist. Because they were not committed to a specific political ideology, they offered very little to replace the inimical ideology which they wished to supplant. They weren't far enough left to supply a viable alternative to the extreme right except to argue for its destruction. To fight against something is hardly the same as fighting for something; and winning only in a negative sense, especially if the fight is fundamentally political, may be to leave a vacuum as dangerous as the defeated ideology. Indeed, a vacuum is good breeding ground for a resurgence of the enemy, Fascism, itself.

It was with these issues that the ideological war novelists were primarily concerned.[1] Between 1945 and 1965, the years in which most of the novels were published, they constituted the one group of writers to maintain consistently a social critical posture intimately related to the 1930s; and Nazi-Fascism as the ultimate ideological enemy was for most of them such an immediate and overpowering evil that the war against it, vicious and barbaric though it was, was justified in the novels as at least necessary if not actively good. The German or Italian Fascist was a neat, easily identifiable enemy who performed evil deeds in the name of a politico-economic system. And luckily, the war simplified the solution to the moral and ethical problem he presented: It allowed the anti-Fascist legally to punish him.

The American Fascists in the novels were another animal entirely, and had to be dealt with in an entirely different manner—if indeed they could be dealt with at all. But many of the novelists in order to make their ideological points perfectly clear could and did deal with actual German and Italian villains to illustrate their anti-Fascism. Chief among these are Stefan Heym in *The Crusaders* (1948), Irwin Shaw in *The Young Lions* (1948), and Alfred Hayes in *All Thy Conquests* (1946). Their foreign enemies are consummately villainous, and the authors take great delight in punishing them accordingly. Obersturmbannfuhrer Pettinger in *The Crusaders*, cold, calculating, ruthless, is the complete Nazi. He rose through the rise of Naziism from "dirt and disease and decay in a gutter," and he knew that even in the bad days of 1943-44, there was hope for the future of the Party. "The men who yammered and were depressed by a few defeats went to pieces...because their horizon had the approximate reach of a toilet seat" (135). He knows that the imminent chaos of defeat can and must be controlled. For this reason, he conceives of and sells the General Staff on a scorched earth policy, and as the policy's enforcer, he uses not only propaganda techniques but force as well: Germans unwilling to destroy their homes and villages are forced at gunpoint to do so. When the people of Ensdorf hole up in an abandoned mineshaft rather than leave, Pettinger cold-bloodedly orders their suffocation by sealing the mine with dynamite.

"The mass migrations," he reasons, "the destruction of home and town, the creation of a new type of man—the barracks man...were the guarantees of ultimate National-Socialist victory, regardless of the issue of battle. And the Allies, the fools, were helping this new world on its way, by their invasion that turned Europe into a battlefield...let them try to set up once more a world as they knew it. It was impossible" (132). After the war has ended, he advises the Allied-appointed mayor of Kremmen to "play along" with the Allies. "Preserve for us what can be maintained. Because, beaten and defeated, we still hold the balance of power. But we must know where we're going!... We must have a leadership...through what government the occupants permit us, through business, schools, the Church..." (528).

A Europe destroyed, a population without roots, an expediently hypocritical leadership—these are both the means and ends of Pettinger's Nazi ideology which can and must fill the vacuum created by defeat.

The industrial half of the complex of which Pettinger represents the military half is as important a contributing factor to Pettinger's evil potential as it was to Hitler's. The pragmatism of business and industry rejects ideology, or uses it willy-nilly to serve its own ends. Delacroix and Cie. is the French mining and steel industry which is the economic (hence ideological, in pragmatic terms) cohort of the German Rintelen Works. Pettinger, as the commanding officer of Major Dehn, the heir apparent of the Rintelen Works, acts as go-between to protect the reciprocal interests of the two companies. And when Dehn is captured at the Bulge and commits suicide, Pettinger assumes his identity—with the connivance of the Rintelen family and the aforementioned mayor of Kremmen, the city in which the Works is located.

Thus in Pettinger are combined the dangers of that military-industrial complex which Eisenhower warned of some twelve years after *The Crusaders* was published, and in addition he embodies all of the evils of Nazi-Fascism and of real-life individual Nazis. And Stefan Heym gives him an appropriate retribution. Unmasked, Pettinger escapes only as far as an air raid shelter in Kremmen; he is armed and dangerous, and rather than risk casualties, the American officers order his exits sealed with dynamite, thus entombing him alive as he had entombed the citizens of Ensdorf in the coal mine.

Sgt. Christian Diestl and Lt. Hardenburg in *The Young Lions* are also committed Nazis with a cold, even sadistic ruthlessness akin to Pettinger's. However, Diestl begins as a youthful German idealist who gradually develops into an Nazi idealogue through the teachings of Hardenburg, his political mentor. Hardenburg, sado-masochist grotesque whose face had been destroyed by Allied bombing while on retreat in Africa, lectures Diestl in his sickroom, "a combination of lecture room and confessional" where Christian learns that his mistake had been his idealism which the Lieutenant replaces with the hard, practical facts of Nazi-Fascism. "After this one is over, we must leap into another war," he preaches. "Against the Japanese. It is always necessary to subdue your allies.... And after that, it will be necessary to permit some nation, somewhere, to grow strong, so that we can always have an enemy who will be difficult to beat. To be great, a nation must always be stretched to the limits of its endurance.... The fruits of war can only be enjoyed in future war, or you lose everything..." (288).

Hardenburg assumes that, despite the loss of Africa, Germany will be victorious; but the idea that the vacuum is essential to the health of the Nazi-Fascist State still runs through his lectures. "For the purpose of our country we need an empty Europe," he argues. "It is a mathematical problem and the equalizing sign is slaughter.... Wherever we go everyone must realize that we are quick to kill" (290). Christian must be disabused of that idealism which sees peace and prosperity as the fruits of victory: "We can be prosperous only if all Europe is a pauper," Hardenburg continues. "Do I want the illiterate Pole, drunk on potato alcohol in the winter mud of his village, to be prosperous?... Do I want a fat

Greek homosexual to teach Law at Heidelburg? Why? I want servants, not competitors. And failing that, I want corpses" (291).

So run Hardenburg's lectures, and Christian learns his lessons well. His discovery, upon taking leave to Berlin, of the decadence and corruption at the heart of German society, and the suicide of Hardenburg with a penknife, ironically only serve to strengthen his newly learned Nazi resolve. And by the end of the novel, he has become the cold-blooded götterdammerung killer prophesied by Hardenburg. As the war is ending in defeat, he turns in to the Gestapo an artist friend who had deserted. "better friends than Brandt had died beside him for four years," he reasons, "should Brandt be left alive to suck on Hardenburg's bones?" (579). Finally, in an attempt to reach the German lines which no longer even exist, he is trapped in a woods outside a concentration camp being liberated by the American infantry company which contains the two Americans, Noah Ackerman and Michael Whitaker, to whose story half of the novel is devoted. In a futile, senseless gesture, Diestl kills Ackerman from ambush. The symbolic significance of the fact that Ackerman is a Jew is underscored by the fact that Christian does not know it. Of even greater significance is Whitaker's stalking of Diestl through the woods, catching him helpless with a jammed gun, and shooting him cold-bloodedly point-blank as Christian "watched the American lift his gun and press the trigger" (689).

Alfred Hayes' *All Thy Conquests* is one of the most powerful ideological novels to come out of the European war. It is a frame novel at the heart of which is the war crimes trial, before an Italian tribunal, of the Fascist Questore of Rome. He is being tried for murder because, upon the order of the German officer in command of the city, he had submitted a list of 350 innocent Italian civilians—ten for each of thirty-five members of a German patrol wiped out by the underground—for retaliatory execution. The 350 men, women, and children had been machine-gunned to death in a sandpit at the outskirts of Rome. The Questore's defense is that he had merely followed orders; and as at Nuerenberg, the defense is disallowed and he is convicted. But not before Hayes has given us a history of Fascism from its birth to its death, through both the slow-witted inarticulateness of the party hack and the pointed responses of the Prosecutor. "Inside me there was this heaviness, the lack of something always,..." thinks the Questore (198), clarifying the Prosecutor's earlier comment that "His very defects as a human being contribute to his success as a Fascist" (108). But he points out, too, that not simply a psychological quirk or intellectual inadequacy had caused the birth and growth of Fascism; environment also had played a major role. After the first World War, Italy was economically and socially depressed, and her citizens were restless for change. The prosecutor sees that the ex-soldier misanthrope "is poor; he is discouraged; he is bitter; he sleeps badly. He is ripe for politics" (107). He is ripe for Mussolini just as Pettinger and Hardenburg, the articulate intellectual Germans had been ripe for Hitler.

"There is a dynasty of superiors to whom one is answerable, who give the orders and accept the responsibility. That is how it must be," argues the defense (198). But the Prosecutor asks for the death penalty: "Twenty years, signori; twenty years we have endured these careers. Twenty years we have bled from such authorizations.... And who knows what terrible surgery may be needed before we are healed?" (109).

But before sentence can be handed down, the Roman people explode. A mob invades the court and drags the Questore away. They beat him, stone him, and drop him from a bridge into the Tiber. A boat full of young men is rowed out, and they pound on the struggling victim until finally he sinks and drowns.[2]

Upon the frame of this trial and execution, Hayes hangs the stories of three Italians and two American soldiers. He makes no explicit connections between the stories and the frame; nor does he, as do Heym and Shaw, use the novel as a Jeremiad warning of the resurgence of Fascism in the vacuum of defeat. His Italian and American characters represent little more than themselves and the immediate reactions of people caught up in a suddenly post-war world—hope, fear, vanity, a sense of loss.

But many of the novelists, harking back to 1930s social-critical political literature, suggest or draw explicit parallels between Fascism as a foreign ideology and whatever is insidious on the right of the American socio-political spectrum. Nazi-Fascism is, for the novelists, the epitome of all that is morally and ethically evil. It justifies amoral means by materialistic ends; it permits the individual to deny responsibility for his actions though he may with impunity enjoy the fruits of them; it subscribes to the simple, single solution to physical and ideological conflicts—to the final solution. And the novelists believe that anything or anyone that reflects these tendencies, even in part, is potentially as evil as Fascism itself. They also believe, most importantly for their ideology, that the immanence of the whole is present in its parts, that the tendency toward evil casts the shadow of its epitome.

They find the tendency and the shadow within many Americans and Americanism—within 100% patriotism; within the businessman's morality; within the complacency which encourages a world view based on good guys versus bad guys and which results so often in an aggressive paranoia; and within that other kind of complacency which recognizes the tendency, sees the shadow, and contrives pragmatically to use them to further its own ends.

But the American Fascist (for this is implicitly how he is identified) does not represent the organized ideological evil of his German and Italian counterpart. Furthermore, his side won the war. Thus the novelists cannot punish him in the same manner and with as much satisfaction as they can a Pettinger, a Questore, a Hardenburg and Diestl. Indeed, winning the war is proof that he need not be punished at all; ironically, his existence is justified by the destruction of his German and Italian prototype. Success does not shake the confidence of the complacent. Rather it entrenches confidence, feeds it, even arms it. Thus, willy-nilly, American Fascism threatened to flourish in the post-war world. America was not physically harmed, so the vacuum to be filled was politico-economic; and because of the combination of complacency and the spoils of victory, the novelists saw and warned that the ideology which might fill the vacuum was more subtly dangerous than it might be as a last gasp hangover in Pettinger's or Hardenburg's Germany. And seeing and warning amounted often to fearful prophecy.

There are two types of American Fascists in the novels. They correspond roughly to the two wings of German and Italian Fascism—the ideologues and the blindly patriotic brown-blackshirts. Usually, both American types see themselves as pure and patriotic Americans, and usually neither type is committed to a political ideology though the first espouses and practices conservative, right-wing, capitalism.

Alfred Hayes does not deal with American Fascism in either of its manifestations in *All They Conquests*, but Stefan Heym does, and so does Irwin Shaw. Heym clearly draws a parallel between ugly Americanism and Fascism. Dondolo, the Mess Sergeant in *The Crusaders*, along with Captain Loomis are sadistic brutes and criminals. Both deal in the black market, each rapes or attempts to rape, both cause physical and spiritual death with their sadism. In addition, Dondolo is almost violently anti-semitic; his opening gambit to all Jews is "Vot ees it?" and he tells Sgt. Bing, one of the novel's main characters, a naturalized American of German-Jewish parentage: "It's because of people like you I had to leave my kids. If anything happens to them, I'll kill you. Bunch of Jews get themselves into trouble, and the whole American Army swims across the ocean" (37).

Other of the novelists pick up on anti-semitism as an obvious characteristic of American Fascism. General Mallon in Ned Calmer's *The Strange Land* mentally labels a war correspondent named Marks a "Jew-boy" and "Jew-red," and calls his newspaper a "red rag." And a correspondent named Wexel in the same novel thinks, "Maybe you can't expect to see too much cooperation from soldiers commanded by a Jew.... It's almost as bad as expecting white men to be led into battle by a Negro. It won't work, that's all. Hitler knows that. It's one of the things he's right about'' (73).

Unfortunately, the novelist often feeds such superficial portrayals of American Fascism into his novel just to make a quick point, and consequently, they are often a bit too pat and one-dimensional. Irwin Shaw flirts with such superficiality in *The Young Lions*, and barely avoids it by expanding and enlarging upon the analogy between the two Fascisms. He creates an entire company of American anti-semites, typified by Sgt. Rickett, a lisping Southerner who says to Noah Ackerman: "Ah'll tell yuh, heah an' now. Ah ain't got no use for Niggerth, Jewth, Mexicans, or Chinamen, an' from now on you're going' to have a powerful rough row to hoe in this here company.... Now get you ass inside and keep it there... Move, Iki, Ah'm tahd of lookin' at your ugly face" (302). The persistence of this attitude in the company, coupled with the anti-intellectualism of his officers (they take *Ullyses* from his footlocker as a response to his Jewish left-wing intellectualism) and extended to include a severe beating administered to him anonymously in the darkened company street, prompts Noah to issue a vainglorious challenge to fight each of the men one at a time. He wins only the last fight, then he deserts, and upon his capture he is placed under psychiatric care. The fights help him eventually to win the right to his self-respect and dignity, but at the expense of a badly battered body and mind—and at the expense of his life as well, for at the moment when he finally feels himself liberated with the liberation of the Jews from the concentration camp, as he grandly proclaims his new freedom and selfhood to Michael Whitaker, at that moment Christian Diestl pulls the trigger. The analogy is thus made clear, and despite the formulaic patness of it, the potential for superficiality is mitigated by the sheer drama of the situation.

Shaw does not deal with an ideological wing of American Fascism; he does not create an American equivalent of Lt. Hardenburg. But Stefan Heym does so deal and so create. Col. Willoughby in *The Crusaders* is the alter ego of the Nazi Col. Pettinger. A Wall Street wheeler-dealer in civilian life, Willoughby forms the same connections with French and German steel and armament interests; and though they are operating unbeknownst to one another, it is clear that Willoughby is unconsciously conspiring with Pettinger to resurrect Fascism. Pettinger is, like Lt. Hardenburg, overtly political; Willoughby is apolitical as well as amoral, and he lets neither ethics nor morality stand in the way of business.[3] But the analogy reaches the political level with the realization that Willoughby is a syncophant to General Farrish (a thinly disguised portrayal of General Patton), who openly uses ex-Nazis to help put the occupied territory under his command back into peacetime operation, and who also has political ambitions.

Farrish is ideologically dangerous because his ambition is coupled with single-mindedness and a need to simplify problems and solutions. "There's too much democracy in the Army, and that doesn't work," he says. When asked what he means by democracy, he responds: "What I said. Talk, inefficiency, politics, double-crossing, stealing my gas. A war has got to be run on the basis of dictatorship. . . ." And to disapproval of this sentiment, he replies: "You can't get around it old man. Afterwards, when there's peace, they can have it all back—the politicians their politics, and the crooks their graft. We've got to take our lesson from the enemy— much as we might hate doing it. God, if one tenth of the gas sold in Paris had been stolen on *their* side, hundreds of them would be lined up against the wall, and justly so!" And to the charge that this is Fascistic, Farrish answers, "I don't care what you call it. As long as it works" (258).

Willoughby assists Farrish in putting Kremmen—the city of the Rintelen Works and Pettinger's cover—back into smooth operation, back, as Heym comments, into "a setup in which everybody has his place— the Chamber of Commerce men running their businesses, and the other people working for them" (551). And it matters not at all either to Willoughby or to Farrish that these were the same men who ran things under the Nazis. In a classic oversimplification, Farrish says that "In our country we have two Parties, and I haven't asked a single one of my officers and men whether he's a Democrat or a Republican. To me, a man is a man first; whatever else he is, comes after." This statement is made in response to Mayor Lammlein, Pettinger's cohort, who has asked "Shall we judge a man by a label, or by what he has done?" (553).

Farrish's naiveté is abetted by Willoughby's cunning. Willoughby takes control of Farrish first, because he truly sees the General as a potential political force; and secondly, because his proximity to Farrish is good cover for his "plunge into international cartelization" with the French and German steel empires—the same cartel with which Pettinger is involved. A lawyer in civilian life, Willoughby has assumed the task of tying the steel interests together to the advantage of his law firm, and ultimately to his own advantage within the firm. He protects the head of the French firm from charges of collaboration; he protects Pettinger, though he knows that he is only posing as the Widow Rintelen's son in law. "Democracy is purely a matter of form," he argues. The question is, will it be people of know-how who control the industry, "Or will it be a committee of the great unwashed, men from the DP

camp, perhaps, you know only one thing—to work with their hands?''
(292).

The American anti-Fascists—Whitacre in *The Young Lions*, Sgt.
Bing, Major DeWitt, and Lt. Yates in *The Crusaders*—handle the foreign
enemy with dispatch. Whitacre guns down Diestl, and it is Yates who
orders the burial alive of Pettinger. But they are largely bewildered and
impotent when it comes to dealing with the enemy in their midst. Except
for befriending Ackerman, Whitacre does nothing about the anti-semitism
of the Company; and it is only through the sacrificial death of Bing
that Yates is converted to sufficient commitment to destroy Pettinger
and to expose the graft and corruption which characterize the leadership
of Col. Willoughby and Sgt. Dondolo. But he cannot expose the political/
ideological corruption because it is implicit, unconscious. One can't
accuse the Dondolos, the Farrishes, the Willoughbys of Fascism; they
are, in their own minds, and at least partly in truth, 100% Americans.
"The war, after all, had been a good investment," Willoughby muses
after his exposure. "He had always maintained that war was like peace;
except that in war the stakes were bigger, the opportunities greater..."
(598).

Yates wins, but his victory is ironic at best. Dondolo keeps his black
market profits and his anti-Americanism and is transferred to the rear;
Willoughby is shipped stateside with his cartel in his pocket and an
assured successful future in his law firm intact. Discredited, defeated,
cast out—each ends better off than be began. Thus, Heym lets them
stand as a warning that their potential for evil is greater at war's end
than it was at the start, greater after the death of Pettinger and the collapse
of Nazism than it was before or during the crusade against them. To
the spoils belongs the victor, Scott Fitzgerald said, and Heym would
argue that there were many American victors who, like their counterparts
in the Berlin that Christian Diestl visits, welcomed the corruption that
accompanied victory.

But an even more explicit construction of the equation between
American Fascism and Fascism as a foreign ideology occurs in Norman
Mailer's *The Naked and the Dead*. Mailer, like many of the novelists
whose war experience was not in the ETO, but who wanted to write
an ideological/political novel, faced a peculiar problem. The Japanese
enemy was not Fascistic: indeed, through most of the war, we didn't
understand what their ideology was. We knew that they were an empire,
and that they had a strong-man militaristic government, but we saw
them as almost totally a physical, not a political enemy—unlike the
way we could perceive the Germans or Italians. Thus Mailer and other
PTO novelists (Martin Dibner, for instance, and Herman Wouk) did
not have the advantage of creating actual ideological enemy villains that

Shaw, Heym, and Hayes had. Instead, they had to invent Americans who were clearly fascistic and fight the ideological war within our own ranks.

But in the case of Mailer, this is only a minor part of the reason. He clearly wanted to portray and attack American Fascism and Fascists; there is every reason to suspect that, had *The Naked and the Dead* been set in Europe, the major villains would still have been American. German and Italian Nazi-Fascism was an accepted, agreed-upon evil. The real danger lay in American tendencies toward the evil, and it is these that Mailer—and Stefan Heym—are most concerned with. Their novels amount to exposures and prophecies, therefore.

Artistic and ideological dangers abound in the situation faced by the anti-Fascist novelist of the Pacific Theater. Martin Dibner falls victim to both in his abortive attempt to tie Japan and the Western world together ideologically through his exaggerated portrayal of the Fascistic executive officer of the *Atlantis* who, at the novel's climax, commits hara-kiri. And Captain Queeg in Wouk's *The Caine Mutiny* loses his command upon exposure of his Fascist paranoia and consequent over-reaction to frustration; but Wouk inflicts a reversal of intention upon the situation that flies in the face of the ideological evidence, and at best puzzles the reader, or at worst, as in my case, chagrins him. Mailer on the other hand, manages to meet squarely every danger—exaggerated character-ization, doubtful or oversimple motivation, the tendency to editorialize, patriotic dishonesty—which faced the ideological novelist in the Pacific, and by a combination of sheer writing ability and great sincerity, pulls free of nearly all of them.

Again, both wings of Fascism, the ideological and the brownshirt, are present in the novel. And again, the liberal response is largely impotent against either wing.

Sgt. Croft and Pvt. Gallagher represent the brownshirt, physical threat of American Fascism. Gallagher is an Irish Catholic from Boston who fears and hates anything or anyone different from or better than himself, particularly Jews and "liberals" whom he identifies as Communist. He is not at all ideological; he is a vicious fool whose danger will remain merely potential until it can be controlled and directed—perhaps after the war, Mailer suggests, by an ideologue. Croft on the other hand is a non-intellectual, semi-literate sadist who hates "EVERYTHING WHICH IS NOT IN MYSELF" (164), who is not even nominally political, who is an excellent soldier (as Diestl had been) whose singular desire is to command, and who will go to any lengths to keep command.

As Dondolo had been Willoughby's alter ego, Croft is Major General George Cummings'. But Cummings resembles more closely Lt. Hardenburg than Col. Willoughby, both ideologically and methodologically. From the outset of the novel, he works to educate his aide, Lt. Robert Hearn, a right-thinking though ineffectual liberal—quite different from Christian Diestl, Hardenburg's receptive pupil—whose arguments stand at once as an exciting challenge to Cummings' Fascistic intellectualism and as a straightman for his sophistries. Hearn's arguments have neither the strength nor the self-assurance of Cummings'. While Hearn is feeling his way through an overly simple, emotional liberalism, the General has thought his way carefully to what the 1930s liberals such as Hearn would label Fascistic conclusions and beliefs.

"The root of the liberals' ineffectiveness comes right spang out of the desperate suspension in which they have to hold their minds," Cummings tells Hearn in the first of three ideological confrontations between the two. Again he says: "We have the highest standard of living in the world and...the worst individual fighting soldiers of any big power.... They're comparatively wealthy, they're spoiled, and as Americans.... They have an exaggerated idea of the rights due themselves as individuals and no idea at all of the rights due others." And again: "The Army functions best when you're afraid of the man above you, and contemptuous of your subordinates" (174-75).

At a later confrontation, after the less articulate Hearn has reacted childishly to Cummings' verbal facility by stubbing a cigarette out on the General's tent floor, Cummings decides to punish by assuming and asserting absolute control over the rebel. "The longer you tarried with resistance," he says to himself, "the greater it became. It has to be destroyed." His approach is rhetorically oblique. "Have you ever wondered, Robert, why we're fighting this war?" he asks. "I suppose there's an objective right on our side," Hearn answers. "That is, in Europe. Over here...it's an imperialist tossup." But immediately after this, Mailer begins to tie the European and Pacific wars together ideologically. "There's an osmosis in war," Hearn says; "call it what you will but the victors always tend to assume the...eh, trappings of the loser. We might easily go Fascist after we win, and then the answer's really a problem" (319-20).

Cummings' lecture-like retort carries the analogy between the two wars and the two Fascisms to their logical extreme. He proceeds to "explain the war" to Hearn:

"I like to call it a process of historical energy. There are countries which have latent powers, latent resources, they are full of potential energy, so to speak. And there are great concepts which can unlock that, express it. As kinetic energy a country is organization, co-ordinated effort, in your epithet, fascism." He moved his chair slightly. "Historically, the purpose of this war is to translate America's potential into kinetic energy. The concept of facism, far sounder than communism if you consider it, for it's grounded firmly in men's actual natures, merely started in the wrong country, in a country which did not have enough intrinsic potential power to develop completely. In Germany with that basic frustration of limited physical means there were bound to be excesses. But the dream, the concept was sound enough." Cummings wiped his mouth. "As you put it, Robert, not too badly, there's a process of osmosis. America is going to absorb that dream, it's in the business of doing it now. When you've created power, materials, armies, they don't wither of their own accord. Our vacuum as a nation is filled with released power, and I can tell you that we're out of the backwaters of history now." (321)

The quotation is long—indeed, it is only part of a much larger lecture by the General—but it is worth giving in full since it effectively summarizes most of what this paper has been about.[4] Hearns' liberalism is largely negative anti-Fascism. Though he had for a time flirted with Communism while a student at Harvard, his lack of true ideological commitment had caused the Party to reject his membership. He is accordingly weak to the point of inarticulate impotence when confronted with Cummings' "Fascistic" certainty. Thus, after the lecture, at the General's order, he picks up the cigarette butt. Then, ashamed of what he sees as his cowardice, be vaingloriously demands to be transferred to combat duty. Unwittingly, Cummings seals his doom by giving him command over Sgt. Croft's platoon. Croft, Cummings' brown-shirt alter ego, rescues his command by holding back scouting information about a Japanese machine gun emplacement and letting Hearn walk into an ambush.

But, before his execution, Hearn ponders the liberal quandary as the war draws to a close:

If the world turned Fascist, if Cummings had his century, there was a little thing he could do. There was always terrorism. But a neat terrorism with nothing sloppy about it, no machine guns, no grenades, no bombs, nothing messy, no indiscriminate killing. Merely the knife and the garrote, a few trained men, and a list of fifty bastards to be knocked off, and then another fifty.

A plan for concerted action, comrades. He grinned sourly. There would always be another fifty, that wasn't the idea. It had no use. It was just something to keep you occupied, keep you happy. Tonight we strike at Generalissimo Cummings.

And Hearn concludes with the final, damning expression of his impotence—"Aaah, horseshit" (585).

The ineffectual liberals, the Hearns, the Bings, the Ackermans, even the Yates and the Whitacres, lose, as they must since they have no weapons except invective and cigarette butts. But in the losing, they stand as a warning by Mailer and Heym and Shaw, a warning that is almost a Jeremiad, that the Cummings and Willoughbys and the inheritors of the Pettingers and the Hardenburgs—the League of Omnipotent Men as Hearn labels the neo-Fascists—were on the verge of having their century. The vacuum was there for them to fill.

Most of the novelists, with the exception of those like Herman Wouk and James Gould Cozzens *(Guard of Honor)* who did not believe in the danger of an American Fascism, felt that what was needed to fight back against the League was a politico-ideological commitment similar to that which was aborning in the 1930s until political disenchantment set in. It was a commitment which, despite the disenchantment, they gave to the struggle against Fascism wherever it appeared. It was a commitment which was softened, diluted as the war was won. The year 1948 saw an attempt to revivify it in Henry Wallace's Progressive Party, supported by Mailer among other of the ideological war novelists. The attempt was aborted by a strange combination of apathy and activism— the apathy of the liberal/left and the activism of the militant right. The combination seems not so strange if one recalls it was just that which war novelists such as Mailer and Heym were warning of. McCarthyism should have come as no surprise to the reader of *The Crusaders* or *The Naked and the Dead*.

Finally, and most significantly, it was a commitment which has not been felt or believed in in any of the wars since—not in Korea, nor in Vietnam, nor in Nicaragua. But that is the subject for another essay. Suffice to say here, in conclusion, that it *was* a commitment which has allowed us to identify World War II as the last, good war.

Notes

[1] I am indebted to my own book, *American Novels of the Second World War*, for much in this essay concerned with the ideological aspect of the literature of that war.

[2] Suffocation, mutilation, torture, murder—as I said above, the novelists delight in meting out harsh, even cruel justice for physical crimes which also bear strong political overtones. And the reader is constantly reminded that these villains are Fascists or Nazi-Fascists.

[3] Willoughby is a sort of Milo Minderbinder portrayed seriously and with indignation. He and his antics may be funny in 1961 in Heller's *Catch-22*; they are not in 1948—the blood is still too warm.

[4] It also points up both the novel's strengths and its weaknesses. its strength comes from the ideological conviction and honesty which motivated Mailer to put the lecture in Cummings' mouth. Its weakness, ironically, comes from the fact that the speech *is* a lecture—by Mailer to the reader.

Works Cited

Calmer, Ned. *The Strange Land*. New York: Charles Scribners Sons, 1950.

Cozzens, James Gould. *Guard of Honor*. New York: Harcourt, Brace and Co., 1948.

Dibner, Martin. *The Deep Six*. New York: Permabooks, 1955.

Hayes, Alfred. *All Thy Conquests*. New York: Howell, Soskin, 1946.

Heym, Stefan. *The Crusaders*. Boston: Little, Brown and Co., 1948.

Mailer, Norman. *The Naked and the Dead*. New York: Rinehart & Co., Inc., 1945.

Shaw, Irwin. *The Young Lions*. New York: Random House, 1948.

Waldmeir, Joseph. *American Novels of the Second World War*. The Hague [The Netherlands]: Mouton, 1969.

Wouk, Herman. *The Caine Mutiny*. New York: Doubleday and Company, 1951.

The Literary Art
of the
Hollywood Ten

Ruth Prigozy

The words, "the Hollywood Ten," suggest historically the HUAC, the McCarthy era, the early days of the Cold War, the blacklist, and the personal tragedies that befell those caught up in the anti-Communist mania from the late 1940s through the 50s. To many today, the words, "the Hollywood Ten," have come to symbolize courage, dignity, decency, self-respect, and self-sacrifice. Several members of the group have written that those who considered their behavior treasonable as well as those who, then and now, consider it heroic, are judging the actions subjectively. For the Ten, in Ring Lardner's words, "once we were the targets chosen, by what seems to have been a rather haphazard process, we had no acceptable alternative to doing what we did" *The Lardners* (321-22).[1]

As Larry Ceplair and Steven Englund reported several years ago in *The Inquisition in Hollywood*, "They did not then, not do most of them now, hold themselves forth as martyrs" (437). Whatever the historical accuracy may be, the Hollywood Ten *are* symbols, for many of us, of a courageous resistance to those who would destroy our constitutional freedoms. However important symbols may be, and however much we admire those to whom we give the status of symbol, individual identities and achievements are necessarily sacrificed to the larger meaning. Thus, what the three words, "the Hollywood Ten," do not, historically or symbolically, signify immediately is artistry—the artistry of extraordinarily gifted writers and directors whose contributions to the cultural life of America had, long before the three words came to describe the group, achieved recognition for them as artists. Paradoxically, then, the historical title, "the Hollywood Ten," while it connotes at once exemplary qualities of character, at the same time subsumes the individual identity, and more important, the achievements of each member of the group.

25

Six of the ten were writers: Samuel Ornitz, Alvah Bessie, Dalton Trumbo, Albert Maltz, and John Howard Lawson had been successful writers of novels, stories, and plays before turning to screenwriting. The sixth, Ring Lardner, Jr., whose screenplay for *Woman Of the Year* had earned an Academy Award in 1942, began a brilliant satirical novel, *The Ecstasy of Owen Muir*, while serving his prison sentence for contempt of Congress. Lardner, youngest of the group, is also perhaps the best known, for his second Academy Award-winning screenplay *M*A*S*H* in 1970.

Had they not been among the Hollywood Ten, their achievements simply as writers would have earned them individual recognition. Indeed, the works of several had been widely praised when they were first published, years before the Committee began its inquiries. But their participation in one of the most traumatic moments in our history blurred the memory of their original calling. Although Lardner's novel has achieved a cult status among some contemporary academics, and indeed, was favorably reviewed in the fifties, he was unable to find a major publisher willing to touch it. Ceplair and Englund note that "radical screenwriters and directors receive short shrift from critical or aesthetic surveys of Hollywood if they are mentioned at all." They go on, "If we focus only on the Ten, we find, outside of [Richard] Corliss' book, no other retrospective, critical or otherwise, which discusses a member of the Ten" (333). Ceplair and England hypothesize that the group has been ignored either because of their "politics" or their "lack" of "great talent." As they note, "It has long been fashionable among those who write about this period of Hollywood history to disparage the artistic capabilities of the Ten—without supplying a persuasive analysis of their scripts..." (332). Of their other literary endeavors, there is silence, save for a survey of Albert Maltz's writings. The author of that book notes that Maltz has come to be remembered as one of the Hollywood Ten— "a writer who defied the House Committee on Un-American Activities, was sentenced to prison, then was blacklisted, and for almost twenty years was unable to put his own name on his work. But to remember Maltz solely in this way is to do him a great injustice" (Salzman 139). Indeed, they have all been doubly victimized: not only have their artistic contributions been virtually ignored, but with the exception of Lardner (whom Richard Corliss admires), the scantiest critical deliberation has decided, in the phrases of various commentators, that "their story is a failure of promise," or even worse, that they were simply "High-priced hacks" (qtd. in Ceplair and Englund 332).

Bernard Dick, the literary and film scholar, is now at work on a major reassessment of the ten writers and directors. I propose here, more briefly, to help us remember that the Hollywood Ten were persecuted because they were exceptional artists as well as political activists. By looking at a small sample of the work of six writers, I shall at least begin the task of adding a third dimension to the historical and symbolic significance of the words, "the Hollywood Ten."

In their works as well as in their lives, the writers accepted politics as a normal, even inevitable and inseparable part of everyday life. Although their individual backgrounds differed, historical events of the 1920s and 1930s tended to politicize art; whether left or right-wing, writers became acutely conscious of the role played by social and economic forces in contemporary American life. The writers among the Ten, by virtue of their personal histories, were, more than most, sensitive to political and social forces that were reshaping America during the years when working-class struggle developed into Depression-era radicalism. Politics, for them, was a natural subject for literature, and all of the writers among the Ten were political writers, molded and directed by their responses to such phenomena as the development of labor unions, the Spanish Civil War, the Depression, the Second World War, and McCarthyism, to which they all fell victim. In the following pages, I shall explore the literary efforts of the Hollywood Ten as expressions of deeply political sensibilities, and assess, when possible, the influence of politics on the artistry of each writer. (I am using the word "politics" in its broadest sense: the social and political orientation of the writer as it governs his work.)

I will consider Samuel Ornitz's remarkable 1923 immigrant novel, *Haunch, Paunch and Jowl* (recently reissued[2]); Dalton Trumbo's harrowing anti-war fiction, *Johnny Got His Gun*; Alvah Bessie's deeply moving Depression novel, *Bread and a Stone*, as well as his Hollywood novel, *The Symbol*; John Howard Lawson's expressionist dramas, *Roger Bloomer* and *Processional*, both major influences on the American theater; from Albert Maltz's prolific career as short story writer, dramatist, and novelist his war novel, *The Cross and the Arrow*; and finally, the comic, ironic novel by Ring Lardner, Jr., *The Ecstasy of Owen Muir*, a beautifully sustained narrative that hinted at the 1970 film that would introduce a new kind of cool, hip humor to the American filmgoing public.

Samuel Ornitz, the oldest of the Ten, published his first and probably his best novel in 1923, *Haunch, Paunch and Jowl*. A corrosive account of a first-generation Jewish boy's rise to wealth and power in New York City, the novel was denounced by rabbis and relished by readers who bought over 100,000 copies. Conceived as the autobiography of a judge, the novel was published anonymously, and readers believed that it was based on the life of a prominent public figure who had died five years earlier. It is certainly unlike most of the novels about Jewish immigrant life, and even today, it is remarkable in its vitality and freshness. Written in the first-person and narrated in short, active sentences in the present tense, Ornitz's novel creates a sense of immediacy that recreates the excitement of turn-of-the-century city street life. Like Stephen Crane's description of the tenement in *Maggie*, Ornitz's picture of the meeting of boys' gangs suggests a surrealistic hysteria: "And boys are careening in all directions, their forms seeming to leap skyward with the flames" (35). Along with the standard subjects of early immigrant fiction—poverty, sex, social injustice, religion, political corruption, money, socialism, labor unions, and reformers. Ornitz describes the life of Meyer Hirsch, who learns as a boy to follow only one policy: "to make every situation return a profit" (31). Escaping from the harsh punishment and narrow superstitions of the *cheder*, he finds his real education a capitalist's credo in the city streets, "Even in the beginning when I started to play the game of life, I found it was better and safer to use my wits and let the other fellow do the manual or risky share of the job—the dirty work" (30).

But Hirsch is the corruption of the immigrant dream, and not for a moment does Ornitz let the reader forget the values that have been buried under the feverish battle for survival. Although others felt, like Hirsch, "transient, impatient aliens in our parents' homes" (30), not everyone spent a lifetime rejecting the claims of family, faith, and compassion. *Haunch, Paunch and Jowl* offers a firm alternative to Hirsch's conviction that "you are nothing but what people think you are...I am convinced that is the big thing in life, there is nothing else" (74). Like Farrell's Studs Lonigan, who dreams of Lucy until he dies, Meyer Hirsch's better self resides in Esther, his boyhood ideal who ironically, marries Hirsch's bitterest political enemy, the social idealist Finn, a *goy* and a millionaire by inheritance.

The best of the novel is its rich canvas of immigrant city life, the streets, the brothels, the night clubs, the political back room, the factories, the labor battles, and the language that employs Yiddishisms, soaring socialist incantations, street slang, and always, the smug, yet sad voice of Meyer Hirsch, who ends his days fat, successful, but depressed, living on "Allrightniks Row, Riverside Drive." *Haunch, Paunch and Jowl* is a fine social novel, its politics skillfully woven into its rich tapestry of Jewish life. Samuel Ornitz should be remembered as its author.

John Howard Lawson had a long and distinguished literary career both before and after his skillful and profitable work as screenwriter. Indeed, he is cited briefly in most surveys of American theatre, as well as in theoretical studies of film and drama. (There is one book on Lawson, a published Ph.D. dissertation on his screenwriting,[3] as well as two or three dissertations on his plays.) I would like to focus here on his two early dramas, *Roger Bloomer* (1923) and *Processional* (1925), which demonstrate his use of expressionist techniques to develop an increasingly radical criticism of American life. *Roger Bloomer* is about a young Midwestern boy who rebels against the conformity and complacency of his parents' existence—a true illustration of the "revolt from the village"— and seeks answers in New York City to his questions about the meaning of a mature life in America apart from the traditional passage from parents to prestigious college to business, power and money. The play would be forgettable were it not for Lawson's effective dramatic technique, which, as one critic has noted, is expressionistic throughout, unlike O'Neill's which blends expressionism with realism in such plays as *The Hairy Ape* and *The Emperor Jones* (Carr 2). In the jail scene at the end of the play, Lawson's expressionism is most evident and most effective. As Roger lies down, the prison walls open, revealing a shrouded body lying in a wide green place. Roger rises, speaks. " 'In the open at last...here's a space for dreams...space....' [*He knows that a nightmare has taken him and that he belongs to it*]" (195). Lawson's stage directions for the next scene indicate his method (and it should be mentioned that this play preceded Elmer Rice's noted *The Adding Machine* by eighteen days):

ROGER's dream is a nightmare of pursuit. This follows technique of a very rapid ballet, with accompaniment of words half changed. Playing time is extremely short, for it is done at great speed, like a piece of very exciting music. There are three movements or strophes. FIRST STROPHE: All the figures of the play, representing the conventions and proprieties, surround ROGER threateningly in grotesque black. SECOND STROPHE: In ROGER's fevered imagination, the grotesque figures become a mocking orgy of Sex and obscenity. Behind all the respectabilities, there is obscenity and fear of Death. ROGER defies the taunting ghosts, they rush upon him to kill him. THIRD STROPHE: LOUISE, "the dream will not die," life force, rises radiant to protect him, dispersing the bloody ghosts that surround him, leaving him alone, ready for manhood. (196)

In the drama sequence that follows, figures from Roger's past confront him, accompanied by female figures representing death. Through the help of Louise, the working-class girl whom he loved, for whose suicide he has been imprisoned, he is released from the confining ghosts of his past, enabling him to face the morning, and to hear the "tread of marching people singing a new song" (225). What is unusual about this play is Lawson's firm commitment to his new method, his determination to realize his social protest in a uniquely new form.

Processional is a much better play, for here, the language is equal to the playwright's techniques and ideas. It has been called by John Gassner "a jazz symphony of American life and class tensions" (qtd. in Gould 192) and it is no less than an extraordinary blend of Yiddish theatre, ethnic racial stereotypes from vaudeville, popular musical comedy; and domestic melodrama. Its subjects, again, reveal Lawson's concern with social issues: Wall Street, strikes and strikebreakers, the KKK, and against these, forces of history, sex and marriage. In his Introduction to the published version of the play, Lawson calls for a new theatre, a theatre that rejects both the commercial and the art theatre of the period, a new theatre that will use the popular forms closest to the people (like vaudeville and farce) as its base. Lawson introduces music throughout the play: jazz, blues, popular pieces like "Running Wild," sentimental songs like "Dear Old Mother of Mine," and a folk ballad suggestive of Woody Guthrie's "This Land Is Your Land." He balances tragedy and farce with firm control, and ends the play with a "jazz wedding," in the form of a vaudeville show, attended by the Ku Klux Klan. The finale is parody—not, as has been suggested, a forced happy ending. Popular domestic drama and films do end with marriage—but here, the bride is six-months pregnant and the groom has had his eyes gouged out by the KKK. The play concludes in a grand procession marching triumphantly through the audience, an ironic celebration of peace in the strike and the marriage of the decidedly unromantic principals. In *Processional*, Lawson's fusion of message and technique is complete; indeed, by allowing his sympathies to find expression within the extreme stylization of expressionism, he achieves, paradoxically, his social ends more effectively than much of the social realism of the thirties proletarian drama.

When Alvah Bessie was called before the Committee in 1947, his career in Hollywood was just beginning. He had completed only four screenplays (one, *Objective Burma*, had been nominated for an Academy Award), and thus found it impossible, upon release from prison, to find even black-market writing assignments. His second novel, *Bread and a Stone*, had been published in 1941, a month before Pearl Harbor; in the ensuing turmoil, the public was indifferent to a belated proletarian novel, no matter how good the reviews. Now Bessie's career as a screenwriter was effectively finished (later, for twelve years he served as the lighting technician at the hungry i nightclub in San Francisco). In 1965, Macmillan published *Inquisition in Eden*, an anguished account of the trial and its effect on his life. A year later, the sixty-three year old Bessie published his finest work and achieved a belated, if muted success. *The Symbol*, a fictional account of the life of Marilyn Monroe, received mixed reviews, and was subsequently adapted—in a garbled version— for television.[4]

Alvah Bessie seems to me to have been the most serious casualty among the Hollywood Ten. His promise as a young novelist was perhaps the greatest, his rejection by Hollywood was firm and unrelenting, and his consequent bitterness was so fierce and enduring that it finally clouded his creative vision. The two novels, *Bread and a Stone* from pre-HUAC days, and later *The Symbol*, stand as testimony to the brilliant novelist whose truncated career is poignant evidence of the artistic devastation wrought by the Committee.

Bread and a Stone is the story of Ed Sloan—an archetypical Depression-era victim: rootless, alone, mistrustful, vulnerable, his need for a home and family inexorably leading to a tragedy as compelling as those of Dreiser's Clyde Griffith and Wright's Bigger Thomas. Although Bessie at the outset seems to be setting up a typical proletarian-novel situation—a working-class loser, raw and uneducated, is victimized by the system—the novel discards its propagandistic overlay as soon as Bessie begins to explore Ed Sloan's life, feelings, and even ideas. Structurally, the novel is daring: a murder has been committed before the action begins, and there is never any doubt that Sloan is the murderer. The book is then divided into sections that treat the same events from different perspectives, principally Ed's and Norah's (his wife of nine months). In these sections, through flashbacks, Bessie gradually strips away Sloan's tough exterior to reveal a sensitive, moral, childlike, and hopelessly needy man, caught in the grinding poverty that is at constant war with his need to assert his independence and manhood. Norah, Bessie's liberal intellectual heroine, is also his propaganda mouthpiece, and as such is the weakest aspect of the novel, spouting sentimental idealizations of the working class: "I'm really a simple gal. I've always got along better with simple people, working people, people with no booklearning, no education. They're not complicated the way we are; I've always felt like a fish out of water trying to keep up with you brainy boys" (107). And despite Norah's typical Depression faith in the ability of the environment to mold character, the novel transcends its facile sermonizing simply by allowing Ed Sloan to dominate the work, as its probes the confusions, complexities, and contradictions within this "simple" man.

Bessie follows the Party line, as his tortured attempt to justify isolationism in the face of Hitler's aggression demonstrates, and as the testimony of Dr. Pincus for the defense illustrates:

Well, I think you know I'm not a pacifist; Hitler has got to be stopped. I supported Spain and I support China, and I think I'd support any war that was a real anti-fascist war. The German people will have to take care of Hitler in the end, but it won't be easy. They'll have to get some help from people who really want to help. (177)

He's not to be condemned. Criticism should be leveled at those who have failed to provide him with emotional training, and I think society in general—which is accountable largely for the failure to develop those qualities that most of us have at birth—is culpable throughout. (256)

These are, however, stilted and unconvincing intrusions into a study of American isolation. In creating Ed Sloan, Bessie has drawn a victim who goes to his death with the awareness that renders him a genuinely tragic figure. Despite the highly politicized days just before World War II when this book was written, Bessie turns what might have been a hackneyed proletarian novel into an affecting exploration of human isolation. In the last line of the novel, appropriately Sloan's thoughts, there is no cant, nothing but the simple ring of the character's truth: "You been dead all your life since you was born, he thought, except for maybe a little time between nine months, and now you're dead" (346).

To this day, *The Symbol* remains one of the finest Hollywood novels, and certainly the best work ever written on the short, tragic life of Marilyn Monroe. As in *Bread and a Stone* Bessie achieves an intensity of vision that keeps the reader at all times within the limited perspective of its subject, the actress Wanda Oliver. Alternating between Wanda's monologues, all from 1957, are sections labeled "Scenes," dating from 1943 to 1957, the year of her suicide. By confining his narrative to a limited third-person, Bessie never wavers in his focus, and the actress's gradual emotional disintegration achieves a raw dramatic intensity that all of the recent accounts of the actress's life—despite their sensational revelations—lack. The narrative captures that breathlessly naive quality so characteristic of Monroe, reflecting Wanda's sensitivity as well as her rudimentary education. His narrative picks up her thoughts: "When men would whistle at her, 'She would pay them no mind, it made her no nevermind.' " Wanda is another American wanderer, and despite her worldly success, another failure, unable to establish who she is in a system that is deaf to the inarticulate yearning of people like her and Ed Sloan. Here again, within the framework of a literary sub-genre, Bessie takes the Hollywood novel and turns it into a rich evocation of the inner life of a lonely and lost soul, part of the landscape of American despair. Hollywood is still under scrutiny, but Wanda-Marilyn is at the center of this intensely human story.

The novel is more than a *roman à clef:* it is a penetrating and devastating portrait of Hollywood—no new subject to fiction, certainly. But perhaps because of its poignant evocations of Marilyn Monroe, it becomes a compassionate study of the exploitation of one woman, and by extension, all women who travel from starlet to sex symbol on the path marked out by a ruthless, male-dominated industry.

Dalton Trumbo was the highest-paid screenwriter in Hollywood and author of a famous National Book Award anti-war novel, *Johnny Got His Gun* (1939), when the events of the cold war caught up with him. Because of his successful screenwriting career, he was able to sell his work (for a fraction of his normal fee) on the black market during the years of the blacklist. We may remember that he won an Academy Award for Best Motion Picture Story in 1956 for *The Brave One* under the name of Robert Rich. He was also the first of the Ten to break the blacklist when in 1960 Otto Preminger assigned him to the screenplay for *Exodus*. As a literary figure, Trumbo's fame rests on *Johnny Got His Gun*, which, despite its many flaws—chiefly sentimentality and long passages of inflated anti-war polemic—is still a powerful novel.

Trumbo's genuine achievement is the creation of a state of terror worthy of Poe: the terror of premature burial. The narrator, a wounded soldier, is imprisoned within the remnant of his own body— without limbs, eyes, mouth, ears; only his brain survives intact, and so memory and desire fill his waking moments. Trumbo's conception is forcefully conveyed to the reader who shares the narrator's gradual comprehension of his own condition. With the revelation to the soldier that he is doomed to darkness and isolation comes the choking claustrophobia that marks Poe's tales of terror. Trumbo's narrative is relentless, for the soldier's morse-code head-tapping breakthrough proves ultimately futile. The absurd question from the doctors, "What do you want?" conveys the essential hopelessness and horror of his condition. Trumbo would have been wise to end the novel at this point; the final warnings and visions of a new war are redundant, for the case has already been made, beyond rhetoric. Paradoxically, although the novel received acclaim on publication for its strong anti-war message, it is strongest in its central idea and in the soldier's gradual rebirth. The politics of the novel are so insistent, the rhetoric so inflamed, that the horror is vitiated by the last paragraph. It is ironic that of the Ten, Trumbo had made the best reputation as a writer, and was certainly the best paid, both before and after his prison term. Undoubtedly his best writing went into his screenplays.

Unlike Trumbo, who was primarily a screenwriter, Albert Maltz, from the age of twenty-two when his first literary effort, "Merry Go Round" (1932), a melodrama that exposed political corruption and police brutality, opened at the Provincetown Theatre, saw himself as a creative writer first, and screenwriter second. During the next ten years, Maltz moved from drama to fiction, in 1938 winning first prize in the O. Henry Memorial Awards for his short story, "The Happiest Man on Earth," over second and third prize winners Richard Wright and John Steinbeck. The story, about an unemployed linotype worker who accepts a job driving a truck filled with nitroglycerin to be used in oil drilling, even though the prospects for his survival are minimal, conveys the joy of a man at last able to pay—even with his life—for a pair of shoes, candy for his children, a night at the movies. The story is unsentimental, without polemic; in such short stories Maltz is, as Mike Gold described him, "a nerve along which crept all the vast sufferings of the poor" (qtd. in Salzman 44).

Albert Maltz's fiction deserves more than passing words. He was an extremely talented American writer of social protest fiction who despite the inquisition, prison, years of blacklist, and final brief re-entry into the world of the Hollywood screenwriter, never stopped writing.

Of all the writers among the Ten, Maltz was always most able to embody ideology in viable fictional form. Indeed, his characters are often less compelling than the ideas they represent, the social and political issue they dramatize. Unlike Bessie, whose work attains its power when it is most independent of ideology, Maltz uses ideology as the source of his creative energy. Thus his important novel about Germany during World War II, *The Cross and the Arrow* (1944), was prompted by Maltz's concern over the issue of Vansittartism (Baron Robert Gilbert Vansittart, an English diplomat, first articulated the doctrine which then took his name): "the German people as a race were addicted to war; from the time of the Franco-Prussian war they had supported, and continued to support the militaristic and aggressive policies of their leaders. It was [he held] essential therefore, that the German people be forced to undergo a corrective program which would educate them to be a less military people. Should this program fail, it would then be necessary to exterminate them" (Salzman 74-75). Maltz was disturbed that Vansittartism, which he branded as another form of racism, was finding adherents among people who should have known better, including some Marxists. Maltz's approach to German history was historical; each of the three wars Vinsittart used as illustrations, Maltz held, had a different origin—none in a "war-like virus in the German bloodstream" (Salzman 75). He looked for an explanation of the problem of German militarism through his novel, *The Cross and the Arrow*, the story of a German worker, Willi Wegler, who, before the action begins, has lit an arrow of hay pointing to a German tank factory at the very moment that British planes were flying overhead. The question for the Germans investigating the incident, and for the reader, is, who is Willi Wegler, and why did this apparent patriot (who the previous day had received an award as outstanding factory worker) signal the enemy?

The major part of the novel, "The Investigation," answers that question, from the German point of view, as well as from Maltz's. And his conclusion is the antithesis of Vansittart's theory. For Maltz, "there is no fixed destiny to any people" (398), or as he later stated, the human being "is born neither good nor evil, but can, by circumstances or pressures, be led in varied directions" (Salzman 75).

Maltz works out his ideas through skillful series of introductions and revelations. We meet members of the German investigation team, the factory doctor, the Gestapo commissar, Willie's mistress; and we meet Willi, as he was as a dutiful young German worker in the twenties and as he has become, a despairing German who must perform one action that will serve as unequivocal statement of man's humanity in a time of barbarism.

The novel is immensely readable and still remarkably stirring. Although it was widely praised at the time by both left-wing and mainstream critics as a work of "breadth" and "scope," it is nevertheless less interesting today for its faith in the triumph of human dignity and decency than for its suspenseful plotting, its clever orchestration of dramatic incidents, and its compelling delineation of the horrors of Nazi Germany. For Albert Maltz, politics, literature, and life are indissolubly linked; literature without clear political ideology is unthinkable. For him, at least, politics makes fiction possible.[5]

Ring Lardner, Jr's brilliant absurdist novel, *The Ecstasy of Owen Muir* (1954),[6] is a sharp satire of Catholicism and the operations of the Catholic church in contemporary America. But Catholicism is not the only subject of Lardner's novel. Along the way, he dissects pacifism, penology, fascism, capitalism, advertising and marketing, economics, psychoanalysis, business corruption, and a subject he knew well from personal experience, the practice of informing. (Indeed, the rationale for the FBI informant who operates within the Communist Party and informs on his mother is a biting parody of the excuses offered by the parade of informers in Hollywood).

From the opening lines, the ironic, self-possessed narrative voice flays the absurdities of American life and the fanatical innocent, Owen Muir, who must embrace ideology, political or religious, in its minutest demand. Lardner's Candide, Owen Muir, is a relentless thinker who demonstrates that when one accepts an initial absurd premise, all ensuing actions will follow with the determinism of pure logic. For example, having realized, in his pacifist period, that his refusal to register for the draft was going unnoticed, Owen worried that notifying his draft board of his intentions might be regarded as cooperating with the same powers that he was protesting. "It occurred to him that by using the mails he was collaborating with the processes of a government which had no moral right to exist, but the alternative of sending a private courier the two hundred and fourteen miles to East Point seemed a trifle ostentatious" (12).

The first half of the book consists of a number of situations that are comparable to the most hilariously involuted theorizing of Joseph Heller's hero, Yossarian. Indeed, Heller's *Catch-22*, published a little over half a decade later, would seem to take up where Owen Muir left off. For example, when, in prison for his pacifist stand, Owen has collapsed from the rigors of hard physical labor, the medical assistant who is to treat him finds no reason for his blacking out. When Owen again faints, banging his head on the floor, the technician is elated: "Blood streamed from the resulting gash, furnishing the MTA the kind of concrete symptom with which he could cope" (21). Lardner's irony never falters, and like Heller, he can deliver an immortal one-liner: as part of his punishment, Owen must chop trees, "A tree not wholly lost to fatalism would have shuddered at his approach" (21). Again, as in *Catch-22*, the reasoning of illogic prevails: the affluent criminals (income tax evaders, bank embezzlers, stock swindlers, corrupt public officials) are given short prison sentences, and are regarded as good parole risks, whereas petty thieves, who presumably stole from necessity, are not. The latter could be expected to resume their criminals activities out of need.

Again, with logic reminiscent of *Catch-22*, the American Nazi, Mulvaney, extemporizes: "Any Jew who knew Hitler's attitude toward them would have been insane not to be against him. You could pick them out at random and be sure you had either a hopeless imbecile or an enemy of the state. Whichever it turned out to be, you couldn't let them run around loose" (28).

Mr. Muir, Owen's father, delivers many lectures on the virtues of capitalism, his credo, that "By the way our economy works, no occasion when money changes hands is useless" (97). By the second part of the novel, Lardner establishes the connection between the picaresque adventures of the first section and the account of Owen's love for April, a Catholic, and his absorption into the tortuous permutations of Catholic theological argumentation. Everything up to this point has been preparation for Lardner's brilliant satire on the operations of American Catholic functionaries, from the highest to lowest orders. In particular, the Church's position on abortion and Owen's attempts to justify his love for April with the proscriptions of his adopted faith are among the sharpest, yet most poignant, moments in this extraordinary novel.

The Ecstasy of Owen Muir ends unforgettably, comparable only to Huxley's *After Many a Summer Dies the Swan*. Ring Lardner, Jr.'s great 1954 novel, really the first evidence of sixties black humor, points directly to *M*A*S*H*, his screenplay which, like the novel, expresses the sensibility of a new era.

If Bessie is the most natural writer in the group, Lawson the most innovative, Maltz the most professional, Ornitz the most evocative, and Trumbo the most commercially successful, then surely Lardner is the cleverest, a witty satirist whose blistering attack on fifties America is perhaps the best example of politics in the service of art. As Sorkin demonstrates, this work "examines the period...with a direct and unambiguous political perspective and illustrates for us vicious, corrupt and repressive aspects of American society with a brightness and a detail beyond those provided by most other works of the period" (59).

In this brief survey of the literary efforts of the Hollywood Ten, I have tried to show that, with varying degrees of success, their works reflect their passionate social concerns, their idealism, their creative efforts on behalf of the deep commitments that resulted in their incarceration. All of them believed that their lives were inseparable from their work. Often their ideology resulted in sentimentality or tendentiousness, but there is no doubt that they became writers and continued to write because of their deeply held beliefs. For this small group of American writers, fiction without social purpose was meaningless, and they have left us a body of work that forces us to respond to them not simply as symbols, but as genuine creative artists.

Notes

[1]See also Dalton Trumbo, *The Time of the Toad: A Study of Inquisition in America and Two Related Pamphlets* (especially 138).

[2]This paperback reprint, with a fine introduction by Gabriel Miller, was published under the title *Allrightniks Row: "Haunch, Paunch and Jowl."* New York: Markus Wiener, 1986.

[3]See Gary Carr, *The Left Side of Paradise: The Screenwriting of John Howard Lawson.*

[4]For a detailed analysis of the novel and the problems in adapting it to television, see Gabriel Miller's excellent essay, "The Sex Symbol: Marilyn, Prime Time, and the Nielsens."

[5]Maltz would shortly confront the problem of politics and literature in a heated public discussion (much of it in *New Masses*) about whether or not art was to be employed as a weapon in the class struggle. See Jack Salzman, *Albert Maltz* (85-95), for a summary of the argument.

[6]For a brilliant and thorough analysis of the role of politics in *The Ecstasy of Owen Muir*, see Adam Sorkin, "Politics, Privatism and the Fifties: Ring Lardner Jr.'s *The Ecstasy of Owen Muir*." Sorkin's is the definitive essay on the novel.

Works Cited

Bessie, Alvah. *Bread and a Stone*. New York: Modern Age Books, 1949.
———. *Inquisition in Eden*. New York: Macmillan, 1965.
———. *The Symbol*. New York: Random House, 1966.

Carr, Gary. *The Left Side of Paradise: The Screenwriting of John Howard Lawson.* Ann Arbor: UMI Research Press, 1984.

Ceplair, Larry and Steven Englund. *The Inquisition in Hollywood: Politics in the Film Community, 1930-1960.* Berkeley: U of California P, 1980.

Gould, Jean. *Modern American Playwrights.* New York: Dodd, Mead, 1966.

Heller, Joseph. *Catch-22.* New York: Simon & Schuster, 1961.

Lardner, Ring Jr. *The Ecstasy of Owen Muir.* 2nd ed. New York: Cameron and Kahn.

_____ *The Lardners.* New York: Harper and Row, 1976.

Lawson, John Howard. *Roger Bloomer.* New York: Thomas Seltzer, 1923.

_____ *Processional.* New York: Thomas Seltzer, 1925.

Maltz, Albert. *The Cross and the Arrow.* Boston: Little Brown, 1945.

_____ *Afternoon In the Jungle: The Selected Short Stories of Albert Maltz.* New York: Liveright, 1976.

Miller, Gabriel. "The Sex Symbol: Marilyn, Prime Time, and the Nielsens." *Literature/Film Quarterly* 12 (1984): 257-70.

Ornitz, Samuel. *Haunch, Paunch and Jowl: An Anonymous Autobiography.* New York: Boni & Liveright, 1923.

Salzman, Jack. *Albert Maltz,* Boston: Twayne, 1978.

Sorkin, Adam J. "Politics, Privatism and the Fifties: Ring Lardner Jr.'s *The Ecstasy of Owen Muir,*" *Journal of American Culture* 8.3 (1985): 59-73.

Trumbo, Dalton. *Johnny Got His Gun.* New York: Lippincott, 1939.

_____ *The Time of the Toad: A Study of the Inquisition in America and Two Related Pamphlets.* New York: Harper and Row, 1972.

The Plight of the Left-Wing Screenwriter

Tom Dardis

1

By "Plight of the Left-Wing Screenwriter," I mean the fate of the blacklisted Hollywood writers who tried to keep themselves alive when no one would hire them. I am talking about the infamous blacklisting system that was a characteristic of "The Great Fear," the title of David Caute's account of a nightmarish episode in American history. In the years 1947 through about 1962, the original "Hollywood Ten" were followed by scores of other writers who found themselves unemployable and with no legal recourse to fight the discrimination being practiced against them. It is a period some choose to forget, but I believe we should not forget the events of these years, nor should we try to be neutral about them. When Elie Weisel accepted his Nobel Peace Prize in Oslo in 1986, he made it clear that one must

never be silent whenever human beings endure suffering and humiliation. We must always take sides. Neutrality helps the oppressor, never the victim. Silence encourages the tormentor, never the tormented. ("Weisel's Speech" A12)

After the first onslaught of the House Committee on Un-American Activities in 1947, it was the studio executives, acting in concert, who issued the famous Waldorf Declaration which deprived the "Hollywood Ten" of their contractual rights of employment. By 1951, when the second and far more thoroughgoing witch-hunt began, the people and individuals who might have been expected to fight for and defend the writers under attack—their agents, their unions, and their lawyers—had become so terrified of the fire storm effect of the Hearings that all of them turned their backs. By 1953 the Screenwriters Guild decided not to fight the black list and endorsed that decision by a vote of nine to one. A writer who had incurred the wrath of the House Committee became a social pariah, a non-person without constitutional rights and absolutely unemployable in the film industry. No matter how strong your case, if you attempted to fight the blacklist by resorting to the courts, as long

39

as the issue was in any way concerned with Communism, you could not win it.

To even begin to think of regaining employment in the industry, it became necessary for "contaminated" individuals to purify themselves publicly in two ways. The first was by writing self-debasing letters to the editors of journals like *The American Legion Magazine* designed to demonstrate not only the writers' errors of judgment in the past but also their reawakened patriotic feelings, not omitting their sudden warm regard for the Committee that had left them jobless. The purpose of these clearance letters was, of course, to break the spirit of the rebels who had strayed from the true path. Their missives had to strike just the right note of groveling contrition or they were considered unacceptable; some writers and performers had to compose several to achieve clearance. The second part of the purification process was the supreme all-or-nothing test for the redeemable writer: would he or she *name names*—the names of people the writer knew to be members of the Communist Party or people he or she had at least *seen* at meetings. The fact that the Committee members, as well as the FBI, knew these names so well by then that they could recite them in their sleep, made no difference. It was the principle of the thing, the *act* of betrayal that counted in this self-degradation process. Only by once again hearing a recital of these familiar names could people on the Committee and in the industry feel sure about the new purity of these exiles. The systematic betrayal of one's friends and colleagues soon became an accepted way of regaining lost jobs in Hollywood, or in some cases of advancing a career on the basis of one's prowess as an informer.

It was truly an infamous period—*Scoundrel Time*, Lillian Hellman called it—and its excesses penetrated into the academic world as well, a place that one might have thought would have remained impervious to such attacks on constitutional freedom. For example, the former Librarian of Congress, Daniel Boorstin, denounced five of his colleagues at Harvard.

Although the House Committee summoned nineteen individuals in 1947, only eleven testified; all but Bertolt Brecht were found guilty of contempt and were sentenced to one year jail sentences. After 1951, hundreds of other people in the film industry were thrown into permanent unemployment through the testimony of informers, a process that was identified morally by Brecht in his ballad "What Keeps a Man Alive?" in *The Threepenny Opera* when he answers his question with "He lives on others" and refers to the "stifling, silencing and oppression of millions." He concludes with

A man just keeps alive by completely
Being able to forget that he's a human being too. (Brecht, 6)

When it became clear that no studio would ever hire them again, some of the writers attempted to resume their careers as novelists and playwrights, careers which had been interrupted by the call to Hollywood. In these endeavors they were rarely successful. One of the most prominent of the informers, Mr. Budd Schulberg, while insisting that what he had done wasn't all that bad (he named only people that other informers had named), also claimed that "These people, if they had it in them, could have written books or plays. There was not a blacklist in publishing" (Navasky 243). But there was, and I present some evidence that proves him wrong in his assertion. Before getting to that, however, it is important to point out that Schulberg's naming of names, along with the similar actions of Elia Kazan, have been defended by them as their personal contribution in the fight against the peril of Communism. The facts don't bear them out: both men knew perfectly well that the Communist Party in the United States was a weak and absurd organization and in no sense a threat to American security or freedom. Secondly, both men came forth to testify against their former friends *only* when they themselves had been named by previous informers. It is clear that Schulberg (who named fifteen) and Kazan (eleven) informed in order to protect themselves from what they regarded as a threat to their careers, careers which flourished verdantly when the two men got together to make the film *On the Waterfront*, a picture that endorses and glamourizes the act of informing.

2

John Sanford is eighty-two and the author of eight novels, four volumes devoted to American history, and three volumes so far of his ongoing autobiography. Born Julian Shapiro in New York City, Sanford was the boyhood friend of Nathanael West and, like West, changed his name after being advised to do so by William Carlos Williams. Sanford's screenwriting career involved working for Paramount and at MGM, where he obtained his single screen credit for *Honky Tonk*, starring Clark Gable and Lana Turner. Sanford, banned from screenwriting along with his wife, Marguerite Roberts, for refusing to name any names for the Committee, returned to the writing of books in order to make a living. In this endeavor our paths crossed a number of times, once when I asked him for some assistance when I was writing my first book, *Some Time in the Sun*. He corrected my portrait of Nathanael West as a left-wing screenwriter. Sanford wrote me, saying

You refer several times to West's liberal leanings and labor for liberal causes, as though you too accepted him as a leader on the Left. That's just bullshit. I was in Hollywood from 1936 to 1940, the last four years of his life, and I never once saw him at a liberal meeting, not even at a meeting of the Screen Writers Guild, which you seem to think he formed singlehandedly. The fact is, though he associated with some on the left, he almost always jeered at what they were doing, and when the men were separated from the boys in the House Committee days, no fink ever named him as belonging to anything, not even a tennis club. He was clean, Pep was, and they're myth-makers who say otherwise. (Letter 1975)

I've asked Sanford what he now thinks about the blacklisting period, and here is part of his answer:

You're right, though, in assuming that I'm still dead set vs the fuckers who acted as informers. They were shits then, and they'll be shits in their graves. Don't get bleary-eyed about complicated reasons for ratting. Every one of the blabbers did it for gain and don't be taken in by any pissy philosophy. (Letter 1986)

Mr. Sanford holds strong views about the informers and I'll be coming back to them, but now I want to discuss what happened in some parts of the publishing world in the 1950s. Shortly after I entered the paperback field in 1953, I suggested to my employers at Avon Books that they reprint Sanford's 1939 novel, *Seventy Times Seven*, a book I'd read that had made a lasting impression. In the process of negotiating for the rights which had reverted to the author from the original publisher, Alfred A. Knopf, I discovered that the hitherto obscure Sanford had that very week become the center of some controversy. After having been rejected by a dozen American publishers, presumably because of its author's refusal to name names before the House Committee, Sanford's fifth novel, *The Land That Touches Mine*, was about to be published here by Doubleday. The trade papers reported that Jonathan Cape, perhaps then the most adventuresome English publisher, had contracted to publish the book in England under the mistaken impression that it was a first novel that he thought rivalled Hemingway and Faulkner in its command of narrative technique and beauty of language. While on a buying trip in New York, Cape had dared the people at Doubleday to publish it here, a challenge they accepted and one very much to their credit in a fearsome era in publishing.

We were able to reprint *Seventy Times Seven* despite my editor-in-chief's worry about the salability of the title. Sanford obliged us by going immediately to his Bible and supplied us with a new one: *Make My Bed in Hell*, which is how we published his book. Our publication was accomplished while Avon was an independent publishing firm. A year later when the organization was acquired by the Hearst Corporation, things might well have been very different.

Another four years passed before Sanford's work again came to my attention. By that time I had become the executive editor of a new firm, Berkley Books, which was owned, surprisingly enough, by the actor John Wayne, perhaps the best known exponent of extreme right-wing positions in Hollywood. Wayne and his business associates, however, permitted his small and struggling reprint house virtually complete editorial freedom. We were not even required to publish a novelization of a terrible film, *Legend of the Lost,* written by Ben Hecht for Wayne's own production company which starred Wayne himself and Sophia Loren. (For the record, we did publish it and it failed as dismally as did the film.)

In 1957, I contracted with Sanford to publish the first book in his series of novels about Warrensberg, New York, *The Old Man's Place,* the book preceding *Seventy Times Seven.* Within a week or so of our signing the contract with Sanford, I was summoned for a "closed door" session about the book with my editor-in-chief, Mr. Byrne, who owned a very small part of the business. John Wayne's people did, in fact, keep up with what we were doing in New York—after all, they paid the bills. The name Sanford had caused strong repercussions in Hollywood and we were being begged not to publish him. It was made clear that we *couldn't* publish him. I explained that there was nothing remotely political about the book to make it controversial to Wayne or his friends. A bizarre if not surreal note to the situation lay hidden in the fact that the name of the only female character in the book, a victim of a brutal rape, was Wayne and that her father's first name was, predictably, John. This fact had no bearing on the case as I am sure that no one out there in California had actually *read* the book.

My observations about the non-political aspect of the novel were beside the point: it was simply the name Sanford that was unacceptable to them. I was informed that for Wayne to have his own publishing firm bring out a book by a man who had dared the lightning by defying the House Committee would invite him to considerable joshing if not open hostility from his friends on the Right. What to do? Mr. Byrne made it abundantly clear that we couldn't proceed even with a signed contract which made us legally responsible for the book's publication. After a pause, I asked him: "What if we can get somebody to take our place?" Byrne wanted to know how this could be done and I told him that I would let him know the following day.

Back in my office I called Marc Jaffe, then the Executive Editor of New American Library, at that time the leading American reprint firm. I knew what Jaffe admired in modern writing and asked him if he would be willing to read a book for me that we felt we couldn't publish ourselves. He not only agreed to read it but told me that if

I could get it over to him before five o'clock that night, he would have word for me the next morning. The next day the New American Library contracted with Sanford for the book, a feat that earned its author an advance one thousand dollars more than the one we'd agreed to pay. This would seem to be a happy-ending story for everyone concerned. But would that ending have been the same two years later? The answer is problematic: New American was completely independent in 1957, but by 1959 it had been acquired by the Times-Mirror Company of Los Angeles. Would they have as willingly have gone along with the publication of a book by John Sanford? Probably not.

A number of the banned writers who attempted to resume their literary careers with American publishers found the way closed to them. After publishing three highly successful novels with Little, Brown, Albert Maltz's next book was rejected by that house after the dismissal of its editor-in-chief, Angus Cameron, for his political affiliations. The manuscript was then rejected by another seventeen American houses, and it was not until 1957 that Maltz published another book and then only with a very small house with limited distribution. The same problem beset the work of John Wexley and George Sklar. Ring Lardner Jr.'s novel, *The Ecstasy of Owen Muir*, was eventually published in the United States by Cameron himself, who had gone on to start his own publishing firm so that these writers could get some sort of a hearing. Contrary to what Budd Schulberg claimed, the "unfriendly" writers had extraordinary difficulties in obtaining publication in their native land, a situation that did not prevail in Europe where many of these same writers were published without causing the social fabric to crumble. Sanford, for example, could not find a publisher for his novel *Every Island Fled Away* until 1964, by which time the tide of repressive hysteria had ebbed.

Some of the banned writers continued writing and selling film scripts under a variety of pseudonyms at greatly reduced prices on the literary "black market." Dalton Trumbo is the best-known of these writers, but Lardner, Abraham Polonsky, Michael Wilson, and Carl Foreman also wrote scripts at bargain-basement prices until the early 60s when the political climate thawed. All in all, somewhere between 100 and 150 writers were blacklisted, and at least half again that number were greylisted, a kind of purgatory in which the writer might or might not obtain work, sometimes the outcome depending on luck or a successful clearance from the professionals who took up this new line of work with a vengeance. Some writers, however, vanished from sight as writers and took up a variety of jobs: teaching, working in warehouses, and, in one case, employment as a lighting technician in a San Francisco night club. The blacklist and the corrosive fear that went with it destroyed many careers, friendships, and marriages; the effects of the moral devastation it caused have not gone away.

3

The screenwriter Daniel Fuchs, who wrote the script for *Love Me or Leave Me* and the Williamsburg Trilogy of novels, is not as harsh and outspoken about the inquisition years in Hollywood as John Sanford. In a 1986 letter to me, Fuchs observes

I knew some of the people involved—some who gave names; some who didn't and took the fifth amendment and were blacklisted; but, as I say, I knew only a few, and those in passing, as we do.

I'm sure some people acted out of conviction; some to get ahead in the business; some for social reasons—I have no way of knowing. Some I liked, what I knew of them; some not so.

I think Fuchs is correct when he ascribes a wide variety of motives for those who informed during the witchhunt in California. It was Arthur Miller who most astutely pointed out how this reign of terror came about when he said: "When irrational terror takes to itself the fiat of moral goodness somebody has to die" (Navasky 212). This quotation, taken from the pages of Victor Navasky's superb account of the blacklist, *Naming Names*, certainly goes far in explaining much but does not answer the question of why some individuals who knew better nevertheless betrayed their own friends. Again, Navasky furnishes some clues, prefaced by his observation that "lancing a boil means letting the pus out" (224). He quotes Abraham Polonsky's reference to Schulberg and his reasons for naming the names:

Why did he become an informer when they forced him to? And why didn't he become an informer *before* they forced him to? The reason was that before, he thought it wasn't a good thing to do. What made that change happen was a practical situation. The Nazis pointed a gun up against his head and said, "Look, give us some names," and he says, "Yeah I hate those guys anyway. You know I hate those guys." And they say, "Sure, that's why we're here. So give us their names." And he gave the names. The question to ask is, why then and not a week before?

If you wait till they put a gun up against your head, it's too late to claim that you're doing it for moral-political reasons. Time has passed. (Navasky 280)

In an attempt to reconcile those who talked with those who didn't, Dalton Trumbo made his famous (or infamous) speech in 1970 asserting that everyone connected with the blacklisting process, the persecutors *and* the persecuted, were, in a phrase that has taken on a life of its own, "only victims." He said that "it will do no good to search for villains or heroes or saints or devils because there were none; there were only victims." He concluded by saying that "none of us—right, left, or center—emerged from that long nightmare without sin" (Navasky 387-88). The speech produced an epistolary debate between Trumbo and Albert Maltz, in which Maltz insisted that there *were* villains, there *were* heroes, there *were* constitutional issues at stake. One of Trumbo's rejoinders to Maltz on this issue ran to forty-one pages, surely setting a record for justifying a moral issue. Again, it is Polansky who has come forth with what is perhaps the most powerful way of expressing what the banned writers—men and women sentenced to their literary death—felt about those who betrayed them:

I myself don't want to have anything to do with them. After all, I was on the ship and they got off and let us go down. In fact, the only way they could get off was by putting us down. That's the peculiar feeling: It wasn't only that they took the lifeboats from the *Titanic*, you know; they pulled the plugs. That leaves a disagreeable feeling about them—but no more than I have about other people who have done horrible things. There were fellas in the war who tried to kill me; they shot guns at me. I don't forgive them either. But I don't go to their country, now, and shoot them down, do I? (Navasky 404)

There are some who think that the black list in Hollywood is an aberration of the past, but it is surely still with us when the actress Vanessa Redgrave has shows cancelled or boycotted solely because of her views about the Palestinians. While the events of the 1950s in Hollywood are not to be compared to the Holocaust, the words of one camp survivor, speaking at the dedication of the Los Angeles Holocaust Center in 1986, contain what we might want most to recall about these years of terror:

"There is only one thing that could be worse than Auschwitz, and that is if the world forgets what happened there" (Weisel, "Tears at Groundbreaking" A 20).

Works Cited

Brecht, Bertolt. *The Threepenny Opera.* Libretto. Trans. Guy Stern. Columbia Odyssey, Y-232977, 1974.

Caute, David. *The Great Fear: The Anti-Communist Purge Under Truman and Eisenhower.* New York: Simon and Schuster, 1978.

Fuchs, Daniel. Letter to the author. 28 Nov. 1986.

Hellman, Lillian. *Scoundrel Time.* Boston: Little, Brown, 1976.

Navasky, Victor S. *Naming Names.* New York: Viking, 1980.

Sanford, John. Letters to the author. 15 Aug. 1975 and 29 Aug. 1986.

Weisel, Elie. "Tears at Groundbreaking for Holocaust Museum." 8 Dec. 1986: A20.

———. "Weisel's Speech at Nobel Ceremony." 11 Dec. 1986: A12.

"The Envy of Any Novelist":
Senator Joe McCarthy in American Fiction

Adam J. Sorkin

In an often-cited essay first published in *Commentary* as the Eisenhower years came to a close, Philip Roth criticized midcentury American fiction writing and lamented the novelist's difficulty "in trying to understand, and then describe, and then make *credible* much of the American reality. It stupefies, it sickens, it infuriates..." ("Writing" 144). Though not by a long shot the only contemporary attack on the cultural climate and sensibility of the affluent society of the fifties, Roth's blast is nonetheless a useful perspective on the nation's too easy acceptance of the conservative, cautious and patriotic official actuality, the confident "American high" (O'Neill) of material progress and seeming order and stability personified by the well-liked Ike who himself was to issue his valedictory warning about the military-industrial complex in the same year Roth's essay was published. In hindsight, the strength of this consensus is deceptive, for as Eisenhower's thoughtful warning suggests, the period was neither uniformly conformist nor smugly satisfied but a highly self-critical age at times painfully aware of its organization men and status seekers, its lonely crowds and ugly Americans.[1]

Yet even now, the notion of this world's incredible character is less readily apparent than a sense of its conventional ordinariness. This is especially true as compared to the extravagant, activist and irreverent ethos of what we know to be the period's traumatic aftermath, the sixties, a cultural freedom ride which was well under way by the time Eisenhower relinquished high office in 1961. To the future creator of such paradigm black-humor fables as *Portnoy's Complaint* and *Our Gang*, however, what captures the essence of the period is "the fixes, the scandals, the insanities, the treacheries, the idiocies, the lies, the pieties, the noise" which pervade newspaper, magazine and television accounts and in turn fill him with neither angry resistance nor political reformism, neither dull anxiety nor revolutionary or countercultural zeal, but the responses "of the spectator, or...reader": "wonder and awe...sickness and despair" ("Writing" 143, 145).

Behind Roth's sense of amazement, helplessness, cynical amusement, horror and disgust are thus aesthetic reactions, an aestheticism which derives from Roth's intelligence and sensitivity as analytic observer, skilled satirist and serious practicing novelist. His essay signals this authorial perspective in its title, "Writing American Fiction," and it opens with a summary of a long, sordid yellow-journalism saga that illustrates Roth's message. This is the amazing tale of the missing Grimes girls in Chicago and the ensuing celebrity of their murderer, Benny Bedwell, "no good," later extradited to Florida to face the accusation of having raped a twelve-year-old, who admitted that he and a fellow "degenerate" cohabited with the sisters for some weeks in various flea-bags before senselessly killing them. After confessing, and after his mother was brought together with the girls' mother for the benefit of news photographers, this "no good" reformed as if on cue and, though hitherto "a Skid Row bum,...a dishwasher, a prowler," was then asked to play his guitar and sing in a local nightclub while his story became the subject of a pop blues and the teenagers' deaths the basis of a newspaper contest. But this is not all. Roth's anecdote continues with the subsequent prosperity of the girls' mother, who wound up with the apparently ample consolations of donated money and a brand new kitchen, as well as a pair of parakeets touchingly named "Babs" and "Pattie" after the two dead teenagers—ravished but, it seems, perhaps not exactly "so rudely forc'd," to echo a line from *The Waste Land* (Eliot 43). Roth could not be unaware of the oblique iteration of the gruesome tale of Procne and Philomela, to which Eliot's passage is gesturing, but his tactic is not mythic reference or archetypal criticism, indeed not any kind of intellectual assimilation. Instead, in response, Roth can only marvel: "The actuality is continually outdoing our talents...." To the novelist, "the moral" of the parable of the two bobby-soxers' deaths is not, say, a prophet's excoriation appropriate to a world fallen from goodness, nor a fatalist's stoic or jaundiced acceptance of a cyclic world trapped in repetitiveness, nor an ascetic's philosophical disdain for the invincible vulgarity of a world which substitutes celebrity for beauty and truth, but rather, aesthetic dismay at one fallen from realness and as it were into competition with the writer's own faculties. Roth concludes with more or less the complaint that both daily life in America and its media and magazine counterpart (call it italicized *Life*, with a capital *L*—as in Luce) stand in extraordinary mockery of the writer of fiction, "finally...a kind of embarrassment to one's own meager imagination" ("Writing" 142-44).

Reality is thus at once all too real and all too incredible, "so weird and astonishing," Roth admits, "that I found myself beginning to wish I had invented it...that *someone* had invented it, and that it was not real and with us." The essay, however, stubbornly asks, "Who, for example, could have invented...?" and cites what amounts to a brief catalogue of representative curiosities: Charles Van Doren, member of the well-known literary family, handsome Columbia academician and corrupt quiz-show luminary; the peripatetic witch-hunting duo, arrogant, publicity-loving Roy Cohn and his best pal, the suave, pampered pretty face and Army private, G. David Schine; the President's most trusted adviser, poker-faced Sherman Adams, and his eleemosynary crony, Bernard Goldfine; and the national symbol of comfortingly middle-of-the-road Americanism, paternal, golf-playing Dwight David Eisenhower, and his eminently dislikable running mate, the shifty professional pol who ten years later in one of many literary avatars was to become Trick E. Dixon of *Our Gang* but in the *Commentary* essay of these more polite years was still merely "Mr. Nixon." The future President, even then discernibly "a little easy to pick on," is of note to Roth precisely "as someone to ridicule.... As a literary creation, as some novelist's image of a certain kind of human being, he might have seemed believable, but I myself found that on the TV screen, as a real public image, a political fact, my mind balked at taking him in." In the face of an "unreal" and "fantastic" reality that is acceptable to the perceiver's consciousness only paradoxically as a recognizable fictive distortion of itself, the writer is at a loss. Roth almost plaintively suggests, "the culture tosses up figures almost daily that are the envy of any novelist" ("Writing" 144-45).

Throughout the first half of the decade, one unbelievable but all too real figure who on an almost daily basis got himself tossed up in headline after sensational headline of American reality was Cohn and Schine's boss, Senator Joseph R. McCarthy. McCarthy, the Republican junior senator from Wisconsin, was first elected to his Senate seat in 1946 at the age of thirty-eight.[2] Although showing some of the traits and techniques that later gained him notoriety, he did not achieve prominence until he seized upon the already often tried and very effective domestic Communism issue, one both major parties tried to establish as their own. The Communism issue, it should be made clear, was a "backlash against the New Deal" and a Cold War phenomenon distinct from any demonstrated domestic Communism problem, as historian David Caute noted a decade ago; in words still true, Caute emphasized the point that *"There is no documentation in the public record of a direct connection...during the entire postwar period"* between what historians agree was, in any case, a pitifully weak post-Stalinist American Communist Party and any espionage, conspiracy or sabotage (54). But what the title of Caute's study calls the period's "great fear" was in part terror of precisely such covert treachery, which McCarthy exploited with a series of wild and inflammatory accusations beginning with his speech of February 9, 1952, to the Ohio County Women's Republican Club in Wheeling, West Virginia. McCarthy quickly became a one-issue politician, public enemy number one of Communists in government, the matinee idol of the great melodrama of the fifties inquisition. In his own professedly "rather...frank than coy" words, he became "the symbol of resistance to Communist subversion" (Matusow 98), a self-image expressed in a reckless Senate speech that sealed his fate in the December 1954 censure vote some nine months after his famous confrontation with Joseph Welch in what is known as the Army-McCarthy hearings. After 1954, McCarthy was a political has-been and nonentity, anathema to the mass media and personally in bad health, with chronic alcoholism hastening his arrival at an early grave. Thus his decline in power was, if anything, even more precipitous than his rise had seemed. Nonetheless, as Victor Navasky concludes in surveying the corrupting effects of the period's hysteria, "the vigilante spirit" and repressive "ism" that take their name from McCarthy continued to influence the decade, and, as "the institutionalization of misinformation," as a "distorted...a-bility to distinguish myth from fact" and as legislation, still compromise American politics and the health of society: "By conferring its prestige on the red hunt, the state...weakened American culture and it weakened itself" (333-34).

Although one of the effects of his, and other, committees was to put a chill on free speech and publication,[3] McCarthy also soon entered into American writing in a variety of guises and under a number of names. As a celebrity, with the "secular charisma" (Sennett 269), the "fabricated" "new kind of eminence" of modern times that Daniel Boorstin has defined as "the human pseudo-event," the big name " *known for...well-knownness*" (emphasis in original, 57-58),[4] McCarthy proved an all too tempting target for rage and ridicule. Thus during the Eisenhower years, he and his "ism" appear under various names and in various northern and southern locales in no fewer than eight novels, two of them, William Wister Haines's *The Hon. Rocky Slade* and Ernest Frankel's *Tongue of Fire,* full-scale chronicles of the career of vulgar, dangerous, cynical, opportunistic demagogues. However, like the public incarnations of two other tough guys of American lore, the sports aficionado and dashing war correspondent Papa Hemingway of the thirties and forties and the brawling, hard-drinking, self-advertised Norman Mailer of the fifties and sixties,[5] McCarthy's public creation of himself far surpasses any literary rendering. The decade sometimes blinked at its own extravagance which impelled Roth to assert that its public events and figures might be believable only as made-up satiric caricature—a denial echoed in the case of McCarthy, for instance, by *The Nation*'s anonymous reviewer's comment on another unmistakable McCarthy figure, William Shirer's "shifty" "mountebank" Senator O'Brien, and his "O'Brienism" (Shirer 13, 78, 196),[6] whom the disbelieving reviewer calls "outrageous," noting "Surely there could be no rogue like O'Brien" ("Education of an Repatriate" 548). But indeed, perhaps no novelistic imagination "could have invented" a literary character and human type as vivid and memorable as the flesh-and-blood Joseph Raymond McCarthy's creation of the scrappy, pugnacious, boisterous, hard-working, poker-playing, whiskey-drinking, bare-knuckled Commie-bashing war hero and regular guy, the real public image and political fact, Joe. Though unmentioned in Roth's rollcall of oddball notables and bigwigs,[7] McCarthy truly earned a central place among "the corruptions and vulgarities and treacheries of American public life" that the essay goes on to accuse most of the decade's storytellers, especially those in "bestsellerdom," of being finally unable "to imagine...any more profoundly than they can imagine human character—that is, the country's private life" ("Writing" 146).

I have emphasized Philip Roth and his essay in order to zero in on McCarthy not as, in his most familiar garb, a self-evident national evil (or, in the diehard minority view, a forsaken heroic martyr) but instead as a novelist's concern. To the creator of fiction, the representation of McCarthy, however the senator gets interpreted, is an artistic question, just like the representation of any other personage, invented or borrowed. Roth's writer's perspective on American fiction and American actuality sheds light on the precise dimensions of the dilemma the larger-than-life public persona of McCarthy presented to fifties writers. In Roth's terms, we can see McCarthy posed a potentially double artistic problem, or more precisely, one artistic challenge within another. The first difficulty was the traditional concern of realistic verisimilitude, the rendering the historical political fact of McCarthy giving full scope both to the atypical aberrations and excesses of the living individual and also to his meaningful typicality. This was indeed the predominant aim of most of the novelists who created McCarthy figures during the Eisenhower years. To these writers, the use of the senator in fiction predicated a strategy of making credible a recognizable version of the actual, inevitably as a consummate villain and reprobate, and in doing so, neither falsifying nor grotesquely stylizing his humanness. The literary character would have not only the impression of McCarthy's commanding, fascinating, even frequently engaging public persona but also, consistent with that, a psychologically plausible inward self—exactly the two categories, public and private life, that Roth in fact criticized most 1950s fiction writers of being unable to imagine and achieve.

The second, and more general, aesthetic consideration, mostly ignored by the novelists under consideration, was what Roth perceived as the fecund unreality, the fantastic essence, of American reality, the impression of its capacity to outdo the novelist's creativity and—I cite an oft-quoted, inadvertent witticism of McCarthy's upon the, to him, highly implausible occasion of his being ruled out of order—to body forth "the most unheard-of thing I ever heard of" (Oshinsky 479; Reeves

649). This is an abstract, absurdist response, akin to the characteristic sensibility of postmodernist fabulation. Based on an ironic sense of the duplicitous unreality of what the world calls reality, it is fundamentally inimical to traditional realistic vision—although, paradoxically, it might be said that an interpreter's sense of the inherent weirdness of ordinary life can be seen as symbolically suggested by such events as McCarthy's irresponsible actions and diatribes and equally by the widespread credence put in him and the inexplicable power he attained. What Irving Howe in discussing the "post-modern" as early as 1959 called "a certain obliqueness of approach" (137) soon became in many writers, to cite Roth again, fully "a spurning of life as it is lived in this world, in this reality" ("Writing" 150). In the later summary of Morris Dickstein, an aloof "abandonment of the public world" in an "atmosphere of withdrawal" to myth, psychology, solipsism, mysticism, fantasy, allegory, absurdism, camp, put on and macabre irony underlies much of the most serious and best fictional art of our period (38, 15). Whether it is part of shifting postwar literary and cultural sensibilities, in John Barth's classic formulation "the used-upness of certain forms or exhaustion of certain possibilities" ("Literature of Exhaustion" 267), or an avoidance of the embarrassing competition with American life that Roth suggests, is not an issue to decide here. But what is clear is that among writers who tried to confront the McCarthy phenomenon head-on, but not the implications of the existence in reality of such a marvelous, unexpected figure, in other words who tried, as Roth puts it, to look at "some topical controversy" but not at "a state of civilization...or a state of soul" ("Writing" 146), the result is a sterile, servile imitation of the immediate surface of historical actuality, with little inward interest—an imitation which indeed can at best be said to be, in Roth's terms, "a type of professional envy."

It is ultimately not surprising that in some ways the most satisfactory McCarthy-figures to arise from the pages of American fiction during the period therefore neither are realistic studies nor on the other hand feel to us much like exaggerations. Two such figures are Warren Miller's satiric butt, the Neanderthal Senator Mugonnigle in *The Sleep of Reason*, and Richard Condon's ugly, coarse, syntax-wrenching, politically ambitious senator, vice presidential nominee and (in his wife's sinister plotting) soon-to-be-president, Johnny Iselin in *The Manchurian Candidate*, neither one the central character of the novel. Warren Miller's Mugonnigle is given the physical characteristics of McCarthy the media heavy, the sick, alcoholic middle-aged man with stomach trouble and some crude personal habits who increasingly appears in McCarthy's career and, for instance, dominates Edward R. Murrow's March 9, 1954, attack on the Senator on *See It Now*, where, beyond browbeating witnesses and condescending to the President, the Senator is shown belching, giggling, picking his nose (Oshinsky 399). Mugonnigle is likewise a television crew's nightmare: "The make-up men referred to him as the Sweater. The sound men, having other preoccupations, called him the Belcher." (107). His low-comedy physical crudeness is outdone, however, by his know-nothing enormity, and despite his "hangman's affability" (109), Miller's Mugonnigle is a monster of unreason in the ironic triumph of ignorance, exactly what, in the Spanish proverb that serves as the book's epigraph, "the sleep of reason" breeds. Miller's "little gem," which the author notes in a foreword one publisher called the novel, albeit while timidly rejecting it (xi), was written during the 1954 Army-McCarthy hearings but was only put into print in London in 1956 and could not find an American publisher until 1960. Condon's Senator Iselin appears in a deceptively traditional looking 1959 novel which, in fact, accepts, exploits and investigates the fabulousness of the times with a Juvenalian fierceness.[8] In the plot gyrations of Condon's intricately convoluted, sensationalist, implausible yet gripping spy thriller, this McCarthy turns out to be the victim of the near perfection of McCarthy's own hyperbolic nemesis, an impossibly skillful international Communist conspiracy. Within the surprises, the wild nonsense, the shrewd poetic justice of the inversions and enough murders to populate a Mickey Spillane morgue, however, Condon's novel is implicitly about McCarthyite belief and Cold War paranoia, among other things such as manipulation, control, violence, aggression, ambition, absurdity and dignity. Condon's success in realizing McCarthy is directly the result of the fact that, in both the character's public and private life, the "fussin', fumin', fightin'," "lowd, lewd...belching, bawling, braying, blaspheming; snoring or shouting" Senator "Big John" Iselin and his "Iselinism" (103, 73-74, 81, 171) are taken seriously as comical and satirical extensions of a logically distorted actuality, not the envying imitation of some supposed real thing.

* * *

In contrast to Miller's and Condon's satirical works, two novels of the fifties chronicle the careers of characters who are—personally, politically and historically, as individuals and as types, as private citizens and as media images—intended to be critical, realistic versions of McCarthy. William Wister Haines's *The Hon. Rocky Slade* and Ernest Frankel's *Tongue of Fire*, both largely unknown minor works, are the only two books in American literary tradition which concentrate on offering a McCarthy as main character, dramatic focus, structural center and paramount thematic interest of a recognizable, historically specific American world.[9]

The Hon. Rocky Slade—the abbreviated adjective in the title is baldly ironic—concerns the early career of a neophyte McCarthy in the typical small midwestern city of Torrent in the generic northern midwestern state of Wiasota. Haines's novel was published in 1957, the year of McCarthy's death, and is obviously intended as a scathing and monitory portrait of unscrupulous, unprincipled demogaguery. Unfortunately, however, the political focus of the story of Rocky Slade's rise from poverty to power is more than somewhat blunted by the author's unfolding it within the context of not unusual small-town social interrelations and a formulaic love story between the narrator, Jim Denton, and the daughter of declining old money, Lucy Maynard, who, though for a time Rocky's girl, is not unexpectedly Jim's prize at the book's end. As retrospective narrator, Jim also serves as refracting intelligence and moral consciousness of the work. He is thus cut on the same literary pattern as Robert Penn Warren's hard-boiled newspaperman, Jack Burden, the voice of *All the King's Men,* though unlike Burden he is personally uninvolved in the thematic pattern of betrayals and rather less severely implicated by the action. At the same time, he is also less thoughtful and less incisively questioning; therefore he seems cut from far less rich a human fabric as well.[10] His greatest problem turns out to be not whether, but merely when, to propose to the woman he loves. Additionally, the old-fashioned and restrained narrator comes across as standoffish, his cool emotional tonality not unlike the aggressive and vain rationality of another literary lawyer whose words and, in his case, whose thwarted love story were put into print the previous year, Todd Andrews of John Barth's *The Floating Opera.*[11] The comparison reminds the reader that Jim is neither as extravagantly playful nor as sardonically controlled as Todd, to the detriment of stylistic interest and vitality of characterization. Similarly, though Lucy rejects Rocky because of his obdurate self-centered dishonesty, it is a foregone conclusion that she must, if for no other reason than the fact that he is socially so much beneath her. The heroine never becomes more than a pasteboard feisty rich girl while it remains unclear what she sees in the title character and protagonist, who is himself stiff and one-dimensional in his corrupt ambition. In short, Haines's work, as social novel, is shallowly imagined in the gray flannel run-of-the-middle-fifties private existence of its pallid, predictable characters.

Likewise, *The Hon. Rocky Slade* is less than convincing in its presentation of their public lives. Haines's central character and villain is a McCarthy-figure not in his emphasis on fighting Communism, a posture he explicitly rejects early in the book as not a compelling issue. This is perhaps historically short-sighted for 1947, when the action begins. But let us note that McCarthy himself did not particularly capitalize on the Commie issue until later—Nixon, for instance, " 'Nixie' the kind and the good" to the children of his close friend, influential professional anti-Red witness and fifties folk hero, Whittaker Chambers (Chambers 793), made his rep this way, well before "Tail-Gunner Joe" became "The Pepsi-Cola Kid" and darling of the sugar lobby, let alone the scourge of subversives. Haines's plot tactic likely represents an intrusion of the author's guess as to what the book-buying public would have tired of in 1957. The issue upon which Rocky Slade arbitrarily seizes in order to win popular attention is inconsequential, the building of a local freeway, and his opportunism might be said to be based on an interest in civil engineering shared with the unlikely fellow travelers of the author of another novel published in the same year, Jack Kerouac, and the President of the United States, whose administration's fondest domestic achievement was the Interstate Highway System. In any event, despite immediate differences, Rocky very specifically brings to mind the man who to many was the archfiend of early 1950s politics by the author's repetitive echoing of details and situations from McCarthy's career. Thus Roscoe Slade's going by his nickname like Joe, and thus also his athletic background, his family poverty, his unheroic war record, his initial rise in county government, his ties to local businessmen, his support from the state party boss, his indefatigable politicking and his skill at speechifying,[12] his money troubles over his campaign and his relationship to the local bank president, his unsavory reputation as eligible bachelor and womanizer, the suspect idealism at the service of his ambition, his smearing others to gain advantage, his opposition's charges of financial chicanery. Likewise, his effective homely rhetoric—for instance, "I've had to get down...and fight" in the "slime" (264), which reminds the reader of McCarthy's typical reference to alleged Communists as "slimy creatures" and a favorite anecdote of his about hunting skunks on the farm, which he used as a parable about digging out Reds, "not a pleasant job and sometimes we did not smell too good when the job was finished. But the skunks were dead and the chickens were alive" (Oshinsky 212, 207).[13] All these suggest the former chicken farmer and savior of the flock, Senator Joe McCarthy, is perched above the novel. Most crucially to Haines, Rocky is a danger by dint not just of his McCarthy-like ambition but also his lack of honor. In the phrase repeated by Army counsel Joseph Welch in what even the McCarthy committee's chief counsel, Roy Cohn, called "the emotional climax" of "the big show," the "incredible theater" and "extravaganza" of the famed hearings, Haines's Rocky has "no sense of decency" (Cohn 137, 197). As one character says to the novel's narrator, "You cannot corrupt a politician, Jim; the words are a contradiction. The best you can do is control him" (248). But the outcome of this effort "to fight that kind of fire with fire" (248) is that Rocky is not controllable as he heads for Washington, which is where Haines leaves him off-stage in a closing chapter, more like an epilogue set several years after the main action, with the average voter getting "a kick out of seeing him push 'em around in the senate" (310) on the novel's final page, while Jim and Lucy retreat to marriage, children and sedate apolitical hometown life.

Ernest Frankel's *Tongue of Fire*, written 1954-55, was originally scheduled for publication by Putnam's, but it was suddenly postponed just three weeks before the publication date, then canceled (Frankel, Letter)—as in the case of Miller's publication troubles, a clear sign of how McCarthy's reign of accusation effectively censored American free speech.[14] Finally released by Dial in 1960, three years after *The Hon. Rocky Slade* and McCarthy's death, *Tongue of Fire* is even more straightforwardly than Haines's novel a fictionalized chronological account of the career of McCarthy, not only his rise but also his fall, to the author a necessary and unavoidable demise as the title suggests in internal allusion to the words spoken by "Lincolnesque" senior Congressman Shepherd Reade. Reade first supports but later defies the novel's demagogue, Kane O'Connor, who vengefully turns on him and engineers his defeat in his home state of Alabama, just as McCarthy triumphed over Millard Tydings in 1950 in a highly tainted Maryland campaign. Unmistakably the kind and courtly Reade represents superior insight and superior humanity, and the author therefore makes this good shepherd his mouthpiece for reading out the work's overt moral: "The lying tongue is like a fire that consumes everything around it and then, in the end, must consume itself" (299). And so Frankel's O'Connor dutifully self-destructs, albeit not from the weight of evil or dementia in the spontaneous combustion of the literary gothic—I am thinking of Charles Brockden Brown's *Wieland, or The Transformation*, in which paranoia about the Illuminati, an anxiety about "a pestilence of the mind" (Caute 18) that during America's first episode of "the great fear" led to the Alien and Sedition Acts of 1798, figures heavily. O'Connor's holocaust, instead, takes place according to equally crass modern means. Rejecting and rejected by his various women, one his hometown sweetheart from Manton, North Carolina, another his doting and proud Washington golden girl, the third a New York professional who, alas, is "booked" (474) on his pathetic last evening, in the slang sense Kane burns himself out, with bourbon, desperation and a wild drive performing the consuming fire's work. The reader supposes he is to react with awe, though not much woe, at this tragic decline, the inevitable fall in fortune of a self-made, if ingloriously crude, prince, like a high Renaissance grandee fearsome in his ambition, grandiose in his egomania, magnificent in his ruthless opportunism, and cruel and callous in his disregard for those close to him.

Frankel's Kane O'Connor is, however, too mechanically base, his crass Machiavellianism more lucky than regal, his fate too narrowly personal and too pettily deserved. His novelistic milieu is likewise too self-consciously rendered as mildly shocking in the somewhat sensational style of popular documentary naturalism. Moreover, the progress of O'Connor's career from local backrooms to the halls of power in Washington is also diminished almost beneath political significance in that his lust for power gets reduced to flare-ups of sexuality and joyrides in fast cars. His ambition is thus made more Freudian than Faustian or frightful. As in the case of Haines's novel, the myth of the public McCarthy, the self-creation in a myriad of speaking engagements and news stories, is too heavy for Frankel's fictional imitation to bear. It is likewise too literally borne, the novelistic re-creation becoming a dancing doll not unlike the degrading paper Sambo the princely Tod Clifton hawks on the street in despairing and painful mockery of human dignity (*sub specie* Black dignity) near the end of Ralph Ellison's 1952 classic, *Invisible Man*. Though disguised as a Democratic representative from North Carolina, Frankel's O'Connor is, *mutatis mutandis*, a newsprint puppet of immediately recognizable features straight out of the informational media. With likable Irish Catholic charm, instinctive political shrewdness and noisy acceptance of any political advantage, O'Connor mouths in black and white printer's ink the spiel of the historical Wisconsin Republican, glibly distorting truth, relishing innuendo and assassinating the character of high and low. His biography mirrors flashy details of McCarthy's life, as he accepts money from a manufacturer for writing a pamphlet, loosely smears supposed security risks and subversives in the State Department, speculates with both personal and donated money, guides his special subcommittee of the Committee on Governmental Administration in nationally televised hearings (McCarthy's official forum was the Permanent Subcommittee on Investigations of the Senate Committee on Government Operations), personally creates a fanatical staff of reactionaries, privately raises cain almost to the threshold of public scandal,[15] investigates the National Experimental Center (McCarthy similarly subjected the Army Signal Corps to his scrutiny), gets attacked by a TV documentary patterned after Murrow's *See It Now,* and finds himself investigated by his congressional colleagues. Like McCarthy, he responds by hardening his position and becoming more desperate in his defense, by counterattacking and by drinking, with his requiem mass in Washington's St. Matthew's Cathedral well attended. In the end, however, as a living literary character, he is buried in advance by reality.

Perhaps because both writers are so intent upon rendering the notorious public political figure who time after time would outdo the worst even his enemies could imagine of him, nowhere in either novel is there the contrary human richness of the McCarthy the period knew, for instance his puppydog chumminess to those whose honor he had just publicly violated and whose livelihood he destroyed, his off-the-record dime-store personal gallantry and explosive, tense edginess, his ingratiating earthiness, and lacking from this politico-Sambo on a string is any sense of the personal aftermath, what must have been McCarthy's despair, pain and intense confusion after his downfall. The failure of American novelists directly to capture in full-length portraiture this legendary figure of political evil, in many ways a definitive icon of his age, is, as Roth suggests in "Writing American Fiction" about midcentury reality in general, "Not that these writers aren't sufficiently horrified... — quite the contrary" ("Writing" 146). Nor is it their horror, itself, or their individual political stance. In *Invisible Man*, the last part of which is a more graphically vicious and, in many ways, historically more accurate attack on domestic Communism, McCarthy's nemesis, than any McCarthy himself made, Ellison's nameless title character and narrator is moved to reflect back on the renegade Tod Clifton's words and wonder if "he had chosen...to fall outside of *history*... To plunge" (424). What a cruel trick American literature has played on McCarthy in the only two works in which he is protagonist. In Haines's and Frankel's novels, he is deprived of the very vitality which went into his public persona, his crude hyperbolic glitter and (the other side to this self-coinage) his fascination as an abomination, and at the same time he is denuded of a individualized psychological self, a credible psyche. Instead, *The Hon. Rocky Slade* and *Tongue of Fire* wind up plunging the figure outside the hospitable, if fabulous, stupefying, sickening, infuriating, embarrassingly weird, fantastic, unreal, astonishing, and prolific dimensions of historical fact and into a conceptually narrow, too plausible and, hence, wooden fictive world. As Roth's terms suggest, however, this all too realistic world is itself denuded of life by being denied actuality's self-caricaturing absurdity and phantasmagoria. Finally, American fiction writing failed McCarthy who, in a last sense, thus won an ironic hollow victory by himself creating "the envy of any novelist," a better, and more compelling, more real character.

Notes

[1]"Ugly Americans" as the term is (and was) popularly misunderstood to suggest that Americans abroad are materialistic, greedy, boorish, stuck up, thus ugly in character, not as referring to the title character, the homely, good-hearted engineering whiz Homer Atkins who practices effective grass-roots foreign aid in the very popular 1958 novel by William J. Lederer and Eugene Burdick.

[2]The thorough, scholarly modern biographies by Oshinsky and Reeves supersede previous ones. All details about the life and activities of McCarthy are taken from these two works.

[3]In the areas of American high and mass culture alone, Navasky notes other "emblems of the terror," beyond the infamous blacklist in the fields of stage, screen, radio and television. For instance, Little, Brown's editor-in-chief had to resign because of his left-wing politics (Navasky doesn't identify the editor by name, but this is Angus Cameron); a prize-winning 1938 Albert Maltz short story, reprinted seventy-six times previously, was not republished between 1950 (when Maltz went to prison as one of the Hollywood Ten) and 1963; and some obviously very cautious liberal publications such as the *New Republic* and *New York Post* would not run ads for just the transcript of the Rosenberg trial (334). Similarly, Caute cites absurdities like the banning from school libraries of Howard Fast's biography of the author and American hero who himself was indicted for libel and sedition for his *Rights of Man*, Thomas Paine (18). Additional instances can easily be enumerated (as the essays in this book by Tom Dardis and Ruth Prigozy attest).

[4]Boorstin is critical of the "lack of qualities" of the celebrity (57), and Sennett even more severe about mass society's "narcotic charisma" which "has ceased to be a civilized force" (271, 269), but James Monaco's essay, "Celebration," takes a much more positive attitude about the phenomenon of the replacement of "heroes"—who "have *done* things, acted..."—by celebrities, "passive objects of the media" whose "function isn't to act—just to be" (5-6). Thus Monaco concludes, "celebrity permits a public voice.... And...the public life is the only one recorded. The media are history...." (14).

[5]Mailer and his work, particularly his late fifties cultural criticism, can serve as a touchstone for these decades. In "Writing American Fiction," in fact, Roth cites Mailer's "magnificent disgust" and "despair" in *Advertisements for Myself* and "sympathizes with the impulse that leads [Mailer] to be...a critic, a reporter, a sociologist, a journalist, a figure, or even Mayor of New York" (147-48). Dickstein, in a characteristic view of Mailer as a "fifties moralist" and political radical who "gradually...shifted from a Marxian to a Freudian terrain" (51-52), uses Mailer's classic "The White Negro," written in 1957 and collected in *Advertisements*, as a sign of a shift to sixties sensibility. To my mind, however—not to deny Mailer's stress throughout the essay, as its opening section puts it, on "the *psychic* havoc of the concentration camps and the atom bomb upon the *unconscious* mind" (emphasis mine) and the "individual...isolated courage of isolated people"—Mailer's diatribe retains a strong political slant that sounds like a not very submerged, indeed a quite direct response to the 50s. Take, for instance, this familiar, much cited passage early in the essay before Mailer gets to his hero, the existential rebel, hipster or white Negro: "these have been the years of conformity and depression. A stench of fear has come out of every pore of American life, and we suffer from a collective failure of nerve" (311-12). It is worth adding that Roth, with his emphasis on art, art that speaks not so much to (journalistically, topically), but of, and for, the age, goes on to criticize Mailer's substitution of becoming "an actor in the cultural drama" for his being a creator of fiction: "For what is particularly tough about the times," insists Roth, "is writing about them, as a serious novelist or storyteller" (147-48).

[6]Shirer's O'Brien is not treated here, because Shirer's novel is less a portrait of the McCarthy figure (which Haines's and Frankel's are) than a story focused from the perspective of his victims, in particular on how McCarthyism affected broadcasting. For a similar reason, I also do not treat Howard Fast's *Silas Timberman*. Other

McCarthy figures appear in Ruth Chatterton's *The Betrayers* and Allen Drury's *Advise and Consent*.

[7]In *The Great American Novel*, however, McCarthy *is* mentioned (394), and his logic of conspiracy, and some of his traits and phrases, as well as anti-Red paranoia, all appear.

[8]In his study of popular works of the 1950s, William Darby, in an otherwise perceptive discussion of Condon's novel, suggests that "Condon errs by eschewing facts for satire" and substituting "prejudice" and "tone" for representative detail (87). But the world of the book is satirical, precisely in Darby's sense, to begin with. For Darby to assert that the novelist "takes certain popular fears and pushes them to extremes" (81) is thus to miss the given of the book's universe: the "facts" are inherently ironic and significant—*because*, if you will, extreme and "satirical." Darby is right in his way, however, in calling the novel both "a thriller and a symbolic nightmare" (81), although not as discrete, alternating modes. Joseph Blotner, whose *The Modern American Political Novel* is the most comprehensive survey of the subject still, notes that the McCarthy figure in Condon is "ancillary" but "nonetheless a mainspring of the novel's wild plot" and observes that by the time of Condon's work (1959), McCarthy has become a type, a "stock character" (299-300). Blotner, I should add, also treats Miller's novel, describing it as "witty and urbane" as well as effectively satiric and expressive of thematic seriousness (303-05).

[9]Neither Haines's nor Frankel's novel is mentioned in the only article on the subject, "Senator Joseph McCarthy in Fiction" by John O. Lyons. This sensible and suggestive study mainly looks at Shirer, Fast and Miller. Lyons aptly notes that Shirer's "thinly disguised" work is replete with "shrill indignation" but lacking "the macabre comedy" of the original figure, judges Fast's "programmatic morality tale" as more effective, and praises "the wild lunacy" that infuses Miller's comic farce. Lyons goes on to ask why "no novelist effectively exorcised the ogre" of McCarthy, and his answer (which underscores my own contention that no writer could outdo McCarthy's creation of himself) has to do with the "sheer audaciousness" it takes "to reinvent a Joseph McCarthy" in a *roman à clef* and with the "moral relativism" of modern times making it hard to render a judgment with, say, Swiftian certitude (8-12). Blotner's survey does consider both Haines's and Frankel's straightforward, noncomical McCarthy novels, defining the former as a *roman à clef* with a moral to the story and finding that its real-life topical detail "blunts the story rather than sharpening it" (297), but placing the latter in the context of fictional versions of the political boss, perhaps because the scholar was unaware of the extent of the many parallels between Rocky Slade's and McCarthy's careers.

[10]It also did not help novelists of the fifties that a primary model according to which to assimilate McCarthy, other than to tall-tale notions of hyperbole and satire, was the flamboyant demagogue and barefoot-boy-with-cheek already fully and memorably achieved in fiction in the Willie Stark/Huey Long of *All the King's Men*. Warren's novel is a naturalistic work of social realism and historical concern and of strongly dramatized ethical and moral cogency; in his introduction to the Modern Library edition of the early 1950s, the author calls the protagonist a thematic example of "the kind of doom democracy may invite upon itself" and speaks of his central focus on an "idealistic...but...corrupted" politician whose "means defile his ends" (vi. i). Haines's echoing of the novel's narrative strategy is no accident. Published in 1946 and winner of the 1947 Pulitzer Prize for fiction, Warren's work was a dominant force in postwar political fiction. Thus to the writer trying to render McCarthy as a recognizable aspect of American actuality and also as representative

of political, historical and ethical interpretations of that actuality, there was the superadded immediate difficulty that any McCarthy-figure was not just a mimetic version of reality but a dual imitation: also inescapably a derivative, too easily a mere version, of a prior fictional imitation of accepted reality (as it were, a metacreation)—let alone the rendering of an aspect of reality that itself seemed more incredible than real, as Roth suggests.

[11]The book is usually seen as a philosophical (or anti-rational) novel (or inchoate anti-novel) that rejects (or makes a game of) the social-realistic universe; as Barth has quipped, "If you are a novelist of a certain type of temperament, then what you really want to do is re-invent the world. God wasn't too bad a novelist, except he was a Realist" (qtd. in Scholes 106). *The Floating Opera* is therefore usually read as a precursor to this fabulator's parodic, labyrinthine, allegorical, self-referential later works. I merely wish to note the novel's mid-fifties political topicality that is comically related to—I apply a phrase Robert Scholes uses about a later Barth work—its "excremental gaiety" (80). E.g., in one strand of the plot, Harrison Mack, who is termed in court "a blue blood with a Red heart," loses a three million dollar inheritance (a defeat later to be reversed on appeal because of the destruction of jars of bodily wastes, a discovery made by the narrator after the olfactory hint from a decorous secretary's fart). Harrison's claim to the money, however, is earlier denied, in the judge's interpretation of the will, because of Harrison's left-wing political contributions and sympathies dating from the 1930s. With impeccable McCarthyite logic, Harrison's discarded values become reinterpreted as conspiratorial and subversive, a "surreptitious Bolshevism" (Barth, *Floating* 91-92).

[12]Among Rocky's speeches, Blotner obliquely notes that the one Rocky gives in an episode that saves his career is based on the widely discussed 1952 crisis in Nixon's career and the Republican vice-presidential candidate's infamous "Checkers speech" on nationwide nationwide TV (90-91). O'Neill offers a brisk overview of the events that led up to the speech and of its aftermath, aptly describing Nixon's skillful manipulation during the address of "everything in the lexicon of political kitsch" (186-90).

[13]As one would expect of all public orators, McCarthy repeated what was effective. For another, more odoriferous, version of this political fable, which Oshinsky reports McCarthy used on hundreds of occasions, see Matusow (52). Here, too, the purpose the fable serves is to dramatize McCarthy's own self-sacrificing and heroic, if plebeian, role.

[14]Two other novels which had severe publication troubles are works by the blacklisted Hollywood Ten writer, Ring Lardner Jr. (*The Ecstasy of Owen Muir*, not directly about McCarthy), and the very popular Howard Fast (*Silas Timberman*, in which Senator Brannigan is a highly critical version of McCarthy). Lardner could not find a commercial American publisher for his work, and it first appeared in England, then in the U.S. under the limited distribution of the left-wing publishing firm headed by Angus Cameron, the fired Little, Brown editor (for a cursory account of these problems, see Lardner 344-45). Fast was an outspoken Communist who founded his own Blue Heron Press because he could not get published, and he issued *Silas Timberman* himself. A brief overview of Fast's career and his 1950s publishing troubles can be found in Manousas.

[15]The name Kane is likewise a pun in the sense that politically he "murders" his brother congressman, Reade. That Reade is almost a father figure only makes this Cain's fratricide double as patricide.

Works Cited

Barth, John. *The Floating Opera*. Rev. ed. 1967. New York: Bantam, 1978.

———. "The Literature of Exhaustion." Klein 267-79.

Blotner, Joseph. *The Modern American Political Novel, 1900-1960*. Austin: U of Texas P, 1966.

Boorstin, Daniel J. *The Image, or What Happened to the American Dream*. New York: Atheneum, 1972.

Caute, David. *The Great Fear: The Anti-Communist Purge Under Truman and Eisenhower*. New York: Simon and Schuster, 1978.

Chambers, Whittaker. *Witness*. New York: Random, 1952.

Chatterton, Ruth. *The Betrayers*. Boston: Houghton Mifflin, 1953.

Cohn, Roy. *McCarthy* New York: New American Library, 1968.

Condon, Richard. *The Manchurian Candidate*. 1959. New York: Signet-NAL, 1960.

Darby, William. *Necessary American Fictions: Popular Literature of the 1950s*. Bowling Green: Bowing Green SU Popular Press, 1987.

Dickstein, Morris. *Gates of Eden: American Culture in the Sixties*. New York: Basic Books, 1977.

Drury, Allen. *Advise and Consent*. Garden City: Doubleday, 1959.

———. "Education of a Repatriate," *Nation* 26 June 1954: 548.

Eliot, T.S. *The Waste Land. The Complete Poems and Plays, 1909-1950*. New York: Harcourt, Brace, 1962. 37-55.

Ellison, Ralph. *Invisible Man*. 1952. New York: Vintage-Random House, 1972.

Frankel, Ernest. Letter to Judith Serebnick. 21 April 1958. *Library Journal* First Novelist Collection. Penn State U Libraries—Pattee Library, University Park.

———. *Tongue of Fire*. New York: Dial, 1960.

Haines, William Wister. *The Hon. Rocky Slade*. Boston: Little, Brown, 1957.

Howe, Irving. "Mass Society and Post-Modern Fiction." Klein 124-41.

Klein, Marcus, ed. *The American Novel since World War II*. Greenwich: Premier-Fawcett, 1969.

Lardner, Ring, Jr. *The Lardners: My Family Remembered*. New York: Harper, 1976.

Lederer, William J., and Eugene Burdick. *The Ugly American*. New York: Norton, 1958.

Lyons, John O. "Senator Joseph McCarthy in Fiction." *American Examiner* 3.3 (1975): 6-13.

Mailer, Norman. "The White Negro: Superficial Reflections on the Hipster." *Advertisements for Myself*. 1959. New York: Berkley Medallion-Putnam, 1966. 311-31.

Manousas, Anthony. "Howard Fast." *Dictionary of Literary Biography*. Vol. 9, *American Novelists, 1910-1945*. Ed. James J. Martine. Detroit: Gale Research, 1981. Part 1, 277-81.

Matusow, Allen J., ed. *Joseph R. McCarthy*. Englewood Cliffs: Prentice-Hall, 1970.

Monaco, James. "Celebration." *Celebrity: The Media as Image Makers*. Ed. Monaco. New York: Delta-Dell, 1978. 3-14.

Miller, Warren. *The Sleep of Reason*. Boston: Little, Brown, 1960.

Navasky, Victor S. *Naming Names*. New York: Viking, 1980.

O'Neill, William L. *American High: The Years of Confidence, 1945-1960*. New York: Free Press, 1986.

Oshinsky, David M. *A Conspiracy So Immense: The World of Joe McCarthy.* New York: Free Press, 1983.

Reeves, Thomas. *The Life and Times of Joe McCarthy: A Biography.* New York: Stein and Day, 1982.

Roth, Philip. *The Great American Novel.* New York: Holt, Rinehart, 1973.

———. "Writing American Fiction." Klein 142-58.

Scholes, Robert. *The Fabulators.* New York: Oxford UP, 1967.

Sennett, Richard. *The Fall of Public Man.* New York: Vintage-Random House, 1978.

Shirer, William L. *Stranger Come Home.* Boston: Little, Brown, 1954.

Warren, Robert Penn. *All the King's Men.* Introduction by Warren. 1946. New York: Modern Library-Random House, 1953.

I wish to thank the Penn State Institute for the Arts and Humanistic Studies and the College of Liberal Arts for their support of my research.

Waiting for Odets:
A Playwright Takes the Stand

George L. Groman

The House on Un-American Activities Committee (HUAC) has been a major political force in this century—influencing and even shaping American attitudes and actions.[1] Congressman Martin Dies took charge of the newly authorized Committee in 1938, and subsequently such well-known chairmen as John Rankin and J. Parnell Thomas guided its work, which involved or embroiled political parties, political factions, and individuals in some of the fiercest battles of this century. It was the Committee's stated purpose to investigate subversion in the United States, which initially included Nazi as well as Communist organizations. However, the Committee soon decided to focus its attention on the Communist menace and to create a climate favorable to legislation dealing with the dangers which Communism and Communists posed. Committee members, other officials in government, and a large segment of the American public came to believe that as there had been a "fifth column" in World War II, there was in the post-World War II era a new threat from the left—a threat that was genuine, pervasive, and growing. The Committee did not mince words: unless the government moved quickly and vigorously, all that was best in American life would inevitably be undermined and perhaps even destroyed.

The Communist Party was at the center of subversive activities. In addition, there were Communist-Front organizations in the process of being investigated by the Attorney General as well as countless individuals in government, education, the sciences, the media, and the arts to be investigated and exposed. Some were foreigners, some first or second-generation Americans, and still others had deep roots in American soil, but whatever their background, HUAC would reveal their identities and, where appropriate, make them pay for what they had said and done.

The Committee's treatment of witnesses was usually, although not always, predictable. Friendly witnesses who had had no association with the Communist Party or Front organizations but provided useful information could be assured of courteous treatment and even the collective thanks of the Committee. Other friendly, usually more important, witnesses were those who had had Communist associations of one kind or another but were now ready to offer the Committee their cooperation. Such witnesses went through a ritual, one which was endlessly repeated. They expressed regret for their mistakes, sometimes profusely. They provided a detailed explanation, first in executive session and then in public, of their connections with the Communist Party and Front groups and of the causes they had supported which were also supported by these groups. Then, in what was often the climactic part of the testimony, the witnesses named names. They named those with whom they had been involved either in Communist or allegedly Communist-related activities. This form of confession was the most difficult for those named because it often led to their loss of reputation and ability to make a living. Some were even jailed. It did not matter that such confessions soon disrupted or ended professional associations or personal friendships; they demonstrated to HUAC and to the American public that witnesses were or had become patriots. Victor Navasky has put it succinctly: "The naming of names was not a quest for evidence; it was a test of character. The naming of names had shifted from a means to an end" (ix). With the interrogation completed, witnesses who had named names were excused and usually able to continue their own lives free of harassment and loss of employment.

It is instructive to look back at some representative examples of testimony before the Committee. Young Ronald Reagan, testifying in October 1947, was a well-known actor and also at the time President of the Screen Actors' Guild. In his appearance before the Committee, Reagan claimed that the Communists had not "ever at any time been able to use the motion picture industry as a sounding board for their philosophy or 'ideology' " (Bentley 146-47). However, he did claim that a "small clique" had been "*suspected* of more or less following the tactics that we associate with the Communist Party" (italics mine; Bentley 144). Somewhat more ambiguously, Mr. Reagan indicated his opposition to outlawing political parties unless it could be proved that they were agents of a foreign power. Chairman J. Parnell Thomas, who was soon to be tried, convicted, and jailed for improper use of government funds, warmly thanked Mr. Reagan for his cooperation. He noted that the American people needed and would get the facts, and would do the job that needed doing. As a result, America would be "just as pure as we can possibly make it" (Bentley 147).

Another kind of witness, University of Chicago Professor Daniel Boorstin (formerly a student and teacher at Harvard and later to become the Librarian of Congress), testified in 1953 about his early days in the 1930s as a Rhodes scholar at Oxford where he and other American Rhodes scholars (there was some confusion about the number) attended Marxist study sessions. He now justified such activity, basing it on his hatred of fascism, to some extent the result of his Jewish origins. Although Dr. Boorstin balked at giving the Committee his unqualified support, he did identify associates who had had Communist connections and also suggested restrictions for the hiring of teachers. As Dr. Boorstin put it, "my feeling is that no one should be employed to teach in a university who was not free intellectually, and, in my opinion, membership in the Communist Party would be virtually conclusive evidence that a person was not intellectually free" (Bentley 610).

In the arts and entertainment communities, responses varied widely. Some witnesses cooperated fully, some offered limited opposition, and others risked their careers and personal liberty in defense of their principles. Playwright-director-actor-novelist Elia Kazan, former Group Theatre member and associate of Clifford Odets, cooperated fully with the Committee in 1952, going so far as to take out a full-page advertisement in the New York *Times* explaining his position. John Howard Lawson, another Group Theatre playwright and also a loyal Party member, refused to cooperate and denounced the Committee. He was cited for Contempt of Congress in 1947 and imprisoned for a year. Playwright Lillian Hellman in 1952 indicated her readiness to testify about herself but not others. However, under the law, if she testified about herself, she would be obligated to reveal what she knew about her associates. As a result, she used the Fifth Amendment and thereby avoided legal difficulties although, as she stated, she herself had nothing to hide. Miss Hellman put it this way: "I cannot and will not cut my conscience to fit this year's fashions, even though I long ago came to the conclusion that I was not a political person and could have no comfortable place in any political group" (Bentley 537). Playwright Arthur Miller was eloquent in his own defense. He denied any Communist Party affiliations and argued that any individual in the United States should have the freedom to make political choices. He suggested further that "the then prevalent, rather ceaseless investigating of artists was creating a pall of apprehension and fear among all kinds of people" (Bentley 802). Like Miss Hellman, he refused to testify about others although he did not use the Fifth Amendment. Miller was excused by the Committee but, in the more relaxed atmosphere of 1956, faced only token penalties.

The case of playwright Clifford Odets was both typical and unusual. Odets had joined the Communist Party in 1934, quitting in 1935 or shortly thereafter. Nevertheless, he continued as an active supporter of liberal and sometimes radical causes until 1952, when, as a reluctant witness, he provided HUAC with information about himself and others. In the early 1930s, Odets had been a minor actor with the experimental

Group Theatre in New York, but he achieved instant recognition in 1935 with his play *Waiting for Lefty*, which described events leading to a strike of New York taxi drivers. Although, as many critics have pointed out, some of the characters were middle class, the basic thrust of this "agit-prop" play was working class, and the stirring call of "Strike! Strike! Strike!" at the end of the performance moved audiences time and again. Odets' major biographer, Margaret Brenman-Gibson, has noted that *Waiting for Lefty* became the most widely produced and widely banned play in all of theatre history (316). After the phenomenal success of this effort, the Group Theatre went on to produce such Odets plays as *Awake and Sing!* (1935), the story of an American Jewish family in the Bronx, *Paradise Lost* (1935), the tale of another depression-era family, and *Golden Boy* (1937), the story of a violinist turned boxer.

Although known primarily as a political writer, Odets moved on to themes generally removed from the political arena. His play *Rocket to the Moon* (1938) dealt with the personal problems of a middle-aged dentist in depression-era America, and *Night Music* (1940) portrayed the search of a young couple for values in the seemingly rootless urban wilderness. *The Big Knife* (1949), focused on Hollywood,[2] and *The Country Girl* (1950), focused on Broadway, both described the uncertain world of producers, directors, and actors, and their continuing search for personal satisfactions and public approval. In his last play, *The Flowering Peach* (1954), Odets retold the biblical story of Noah and his ark, and sought to connect in both serious and comic ways the world of the Old Testament with the American-Jewish milieu which had played such a large part in his early life.

From the mid-thirties until his death in 1963, Odets spent a large part of his time in Hollywood, primarily as a screenwriter and director. His own *Golden Boy* appeared as a film (this time with a happy ending) in 1939, starring Barbara Stanwyck and a young William Holden, and in 1955 Hollywood produced an undistinguished film version of *The Big Knife*. Odets was also active, most notably, as a screenwriter for *The General Dies at Dawn* (1936), a story of wartorn China starring Madeleine Carroll and Gary Cooper, as a director for *None but the Lonely Heart* (1944), a story of personal disappointments and renewal of faith which featured Cary Grant, and again as a screenwriter for the satiric film *Sweet Smell of Success* (1957) which starred Burt Lancaster as a newspaper columnist who controls or significantly affects the lives of those around him. As legend has it, Odets went into a decline because he was cut off from the environment and stimulus that had initially nourished his imagination (Rabkin 191). It is not my purpose here to argue for or against the merits of Odets' later work as a playwright and screenwriter. It is important, however, to note that Odets himself commented on his move to Hollywood. Sometimes he justified it in terms of his economic needs or his belief that he could contribute artistically in another medium. At other times, he seems to have recognized that he could no longer deal directly with political themes as he had in his earlier plays.

In his appearance before HUAC in May of 1952, Odets sought to play down his early political commitment, testifying that in the 1930s he had been politically naive, and, as a result, he had sometimes become a dupe of Communist Party officials. His brief membership in the party, his widely publicized trip to Cuba in 1935 as chairman of a committee to investigate political conditions, his support of Communist Front organizations, and many of his political statements, he now claimed, were at least partially the result of misplaced idealism. In retrospect, much of what he had done, he said, was the result of ignorance and bad judgment.

Yet even a cursory review of the early plays provides a somewhat different picture. If Odets was uninformed about dialectic materialism and Party policy and practice, he did understand very well indeed both the possibilities for and the consequences of radical political activity. In *Waiting for Lefty*, Lefty Costello, the rebel labor organizer, never appears in the play because, as his fellow workers on the strike committee learn, he has been murdered for his efforts. In the same play, a lab assistant is given the opportunity to become a spy and informer, but refuses although he is offered promotional opportunities and a large increase in salary. Instead, he strikes the "industrialist" who has made him the offer, and can look forward in the Depression year of 1935 to the loss of his job, poverty, and even starvation.

In another strike play called *The Silent Partner*, which Odets worked on in the late 1930s (1936-39) but which was never produced because, as he said during the hearings, it was "imperfectly written" (Bentley 500), a strike leader named Lovelace is killed. Like Lefty Costello, he pays the price for activism. In contrast, a second strike leader, Barney Diamond, describes the dilemma of those who want to fight *and* to survive. He says, "It's sensible in a world of crooks and grafters to take what they give you and keep your mouth shut! and right now it's sensible I should keep my mouth closed because I'm full of gall, and with what I feel in my heart I could wake up even the dead" (Lincoln Center Archives I-i-5). In Odets' *Till the Day I Die*, an anti-Nazi play of 1935, Ernst Tausig, a Communist organizer, is caught by the authorities. He is tortured and then forced to appear in public with his captors, and it seems to his former associates that he has betrayed them. As Gerald Rabkin notes, Tausig is "blacklisted by his former friends..." (176). Ironically, the playwright through his use of the blacklist was anticipating, if in modified form, a method used in the 1940s and 1950s to punish those who refused to cooperate with the HUAC investigations.

Odets in his early plays also described vividly the consequences for those who *fail* to take political action. Grandfather Jacob in *Awake and Sing!* is a devout Marxist, but he lives quietly on the generosity of his children and, as he put it, is willing to settle for "a glass tea" (*Six Plays* 778). His salvation is personal rather than political and comes when he commits suicide and leaves the insurance money to his grandson Ralph, who represents the hope of the future. Again, in the short dramatic monologue *I Can't Sleep* (1936), Sam Blitzstein, a New York factory worker, has played it safe and in so doing has betrayed his deepest instincts and sense of commitment. Blitzstein puts it this way to a stranger:

Last week I watched the May Day. Don't look!
I hid in the crowd. I watched how the comrades marched with red flags and music. You see where I bit my hand? I went down in the subway I shouldn't hear the music. Listen, I looked in your face before. I saw the truth. I talk to myself. The blood of the mother and brother is breaking open my head. I hear them cry, "You forgot, you forgot!" They don't let me sleep. All night I hear the music of the comrades. Hungry men I hear. All night the broken-hearted children. Look at me—no place to hide, no place to run away. Look in my face, comrade. Look at me, look, look, look!!! (Filler 217)

The dilemma for Odets was clear enough. He could present it in strong dramatic terms but not resolve it satisfactorily in his own life.

Odets' writing and political involvements inevitably led to surveillance, first by the FBI and then HUAC investigators. Although HUAC files on Odets are currently unavailable, FBI files may be obtained under the Freedom of Information Act. Of the 131 cross-referenced documents on the playwright (334 pages in all), I was able to obtain 88 pages—though with classified or formerly classified documents heavily excised. The stringent review (energetically enforced under the current Washington administration) was intended to eliminate materials in a variety of sensitive areas: those which affect national security or foreign policy, compromise the methods used by the Bureau, provide information on seemingly unrelated matters or people, or reveal the names either of informants or those being investigated in connection with Odets. Nevertheless, a more flexible policy some twenty-five years after the writer's death would, without greatly endangering the future of the republic, shed greater light on the story of Odets and his associates and would project a clearer picture of this FBI investigation during an important period in America history.[3]

Despite obvious limitations, available documents do provide at least some useful information. There are some reports on Odets himself by unnamed agents, usually based in New York or Los Angeles, and items provided by unnamed informants cooperating with the Bureau. In the material the Bureau provided me, there is also heavy reliance on published reports in newspapers, magazines, and books. There are accounts of plays in rehearsal, plays being performed, and plays reviewed. There is some description of special educational institutions where Odets' work was discussed or where he himself taught. There are accounts of political events and petitions sponsored by organizations on the Attorney General's list which included Odets' active participation or sponsorship as well as a collection of political speeches by Odets and others associated with him. Finally, there are extensive published reports on and analyses of Odets' appearance before HUAC in 1952. Available files begin in 1931, some four years before Odets rose to prominence, and, with a few unimportant exceptions, end at the time of the hearings, after which the playwright appears abruptly to have ceased all political activity.

One of the educational institutions singled out for observation by the FBI was the New Yorkers School at East 12th Street in New York City. According to a memorandum originally marked confidential, the curriculum was based on the writings of Marx, Engels, and Lenin. The "informant advised that throughout this course [Marxism-Leninism] and others, it is stated many times that the only way conditions for the workers can be improved is by the complete change from the capitalistic (democratic) form of government to Communism. Overthrow of the present form of government was implied, it was said, not stated outright." Selected students were also given a course in the Science of Military Art. In addition, students might select a course entitled "Literature of the World We live in," which included the work of such writers as Steinbeck, Sholokov, Richard Wright, Hemingway, and Odets (FBI files, 11/4-15/43, 1/10/44).

In 1950, when Odets himself accepted an invitation to teach at the famed Actors Studio in New York, the news was duly recorded by *Show Business* and became part of the growing FBI file, this time under a heading entitled "Communist Infiltration of Intellectual and Entertainment Groups." Again in 1951, when Odets' 1940 play *Night Music* went into rehearsal at the Jefferson School of Social Science, designated as subversive by the Attorney General, the information was included by the FBI in its records.

In another FBI file marked "URGENT...PERJURY," there was discussion about asking Odets for the current Communist party status of someone he knew (the name is blacked out). Although the request to interview the playwright was granted by someone in authority (after Elia Kazan's disclosure in HUAC testimony that Odets had left the party), doubts persisted. The Bureau memorandum indicates the following:

Bureau files fail to disclose that Odets has been the subject of investigation by the Bureau; however, references to Odets indicate in the past he has been associated with front groups in the capacity of sponsor, committee or board member, signer or contributor. Prior to contacting Odets, the New York office should check their files for recent information of a derogatory nature which would indicate the inadvisability of such a contact at this time. (FBI files, 1/14/52)

It is noted here that according to the files, the FBI did interview Odets about an associate of his on June 3, 1957, some five years after his HUAC hearing, and he appears to have cooperated at that time.

As indicated, the Bureau kept a record of Odets' involvement with or support of political organizations, and one of the most influential of these was the National Council for the Arts, Sciences, and Professions. This group, which supported Henry Wallace for President in 1948, was later described by the California Committee on Un-American Activities[4] as "one of the most important Communist Front organizations in the country" (FBI files, March/1952). The Council supported a variety of efforts aimed at ending the Cold War, one of the most widely publicized being the Conference for World Peace, which was held at the Waldorf Astoria in New York from March 25th to March 27th in 1949. As the Bureau informant put it, "International guests included delegates from Russia and Communist dominated countries and many speakers directed criticism to U.S. policy while holding Russia blameless for the present world crisis" (FBI files, 4/22/49).

It is important to note that the Waldorf Conference took place at the same time that American Communist Party leaders were being tried for conspiracy in the courthouse at New York City's Foley Square, and this concurrence of events should account, at least in part, both for the anti-Communist fervor and the anguished response of Conference participants (Caute 187ff). One of the important panels reflecting such tensions was chaired by playwright Arthur Miller and included the Russian composer Dmitri Shostakovich, Odets, and others. Odets' remarks, duly recorded by the FBI, are of interest here not only because they suggest his belief in the need for dialogue among the superpowers but also because they emphasize his own fear of government and the dangers inherent in opposing government policy. The playwright expresses his uneasiness this way:

Imagine! we, who are here today in the name of peace—we, who are here to talk of the happy future of the peoples of the world—we are forced to meet here in an air of conspiracy and crime! Already the press and some high government officials have pre-judged us; already they have marked us down, each of us, as inconvenient, dangerous and subversive! (FBI files, 4/22/49)

In October of the same year, Odets appeared at a rally titled "In Defense of Dignity" at the St. Nicholas arena in Manhattan to protest the jailing of the Communist Party officials, who had by now been convicted at Foley Square under the Smith Act, not of any *overt* action, but of *conspiring to advocate* the overthrow of the government. Odets' speech is quoted in its entirety in the Bureau file and also reported in *The Daily Worker* (11/2/49) according to Bureau record. Here the playwright praises party members who persist in opposing the power structure, but again, in a somewhat plaintive tone, notes the danger of doing so. Odets, the son of Central and East European immigrants, also argues that the words and actions of the convicted men are truly American.[5] He describes his anger and frustration this way:

I must be coldly indifferent to the hysterical stories in the press that these men have turned upside down a sane court, that they have worn a good judge to a frazzle. Apparently, it is expected that men who are clubbed, ganged-up upon, decried, imprisoned unjustly, hounded even in the small streets of the city—it is expected that these men are to observe order and decorum. No, they are not to wince. They are not to cry out and protest. Instead they are asked to remain humble, to pass remarks on the condition of the weather and the judge's good taste in pin-stripe suits. Let them, say the papers, be well-bred, let them, like us, observe good taste and decorum and truth! Let them walk in silent repose by the sides of their well-bred executioners! And let them, again like us, not disturb the deep, expectant hush which lies so sinisterly upon our land today!

Well, for better or worse, whether the court or the tender gentry of the press like it or not, these tasteless men have like real Americans asserted their rights to exist as a minority party. They have insisted upon their rights not only to live but to denounce and expose fraud as they see it, and to work with steady unrewarded patience for their beliefs!

All my reading, all my life and all my heart tell me that what they have done, in and out of court, is good old solid American practice! That I believe!!! (FBI file, undated)

Some two and a half years after this impassioned plea for political justice, in May of 1952, Odets was finally called to testify before the House on Un-American Activities Committee. And like many other HUAC witnesses, he now faced hard and bitter choices. He could, like the "Hollywood Ten," defy the Committee and maintain his reputation as a supporter of leftist causes—though at a considerable personal cost.[6] He could, like his Group Theatre associate Elia Kazan and many others, confess his error publicly and thereby win not only the thanks but the blessings of the Committee. Finally, he could grudgingly satisfy the demands of the Committee by naming names and, like James Wechsler of the New York *Post*, maintain a posture critical of the Committee, thereby *attempting* to save his conscience in the bargain. That he took this last route may seem puzzling to some, but is consistent with Odets' continuing vacillation, his espousal of leftist causes *and* his oft-expressed fear of the personal cost of such commitment. The writer Benjamin Appel, an alumnus of Odets' playwriting class at Actors Studio, does in fact support this last view of Odets' position during his testimony:

I followed the hearings in the press and later read the full record issued by the Government Printing Office. It seemed to me that *two different men* [italics mine] had testified before the Committee. A defiant Odets who eloquently upheld the constitution and the bill of rights. And a confused, worried Odets who eventually revealed the names of friends and associates who had once been communists as Odets had been himself. He had "named names" and yet I heard on the grapevine he didn't regard himself as an informer or "friendly witness." Hadn't all the names been named by previous witnesses? It was true. They had all been named and Odets felt, it seemed, that he had divulged nothing new or incriminating. (Appel 475)

As noted, Odets met Committee demands. He admitted membership in the Communist Party, he expressed at least some regret for his political activities, and he named names. However, Odets also insisted on defining his own position as a political person and, in doing so, antagonized the Committee. He was *not* accorded the usual "Thank you" at the end of the sessions.

Counsel, Frank Tavenner, pursued the facts. Odets admitted attending Party meetings from 1934 to 1935 and to reading Party literature, though without comprehending much of it. He named J. Edward Bromberg as the man who recruited him (he had offered a tribute at Bromberg's funeral some months previously), along with such Group Theatre associates as Art Smith, Phoebe Brand, and Elia Kazan (who at a previous session with the Committee had named Odets as well as Bromberg, who died soon after testifying against doctor's orders).

Here the playwright sought to justify his decision to join the Party. He put it this way:

There were perhaps fifteen or sixteen million unemployed people in the United States, and I myself was living on ten cents a day. Therefore, I was interested in any idea which might suggest how I could function as a working actor who could make a living at a craft he had chosen for his life work. These were the early days of the New Deal, and I don't think one has to describe them. They were horrendous days that none of us would like to go through again. On this basis, there was a great deal of talk about amelioration of conditions, about how one should live, what values one should work for, and in line with this there was a great deal of talk about Marxist values. One read literature. There were a lot of penny and two-cent and five-cent pamphlets. I read them, along with a lot of other people, and finally joined the Communist Party, in the honest and real belief that this was some way out of the dilemma in which we found ourselves. (Bentley 501)

However, Odets, like many other writers of the period, soon became disillusioned, he said, first, because he came to believe that he was being manipulated by a professional cadre of Party officials, and second, because his writing was viewed primarily as an ideological tool rather than a personal means of artistic expression. Odets' trip to Cuba in 1935 as Chairman of a Committee to investigate political conditions under a dictatorial regime was a case in point. He had gone, he told the Committee, because there had been "oppressive measures taken against thousands of intellectuals and college students. They were thrown into jail under the previous Machado regime, which was a horrible regime. I was glad to go down. If nothing else did happen, we would dramatize what the issues were down there" (Bentley 510). However, the trip had been widely reported in advance, and when the group arrived in Cuba, they were promptly jailed overnight and then sent back to the United States on the first available ship.

The real leader of the expedition, Odets said, was one Conrad Komorowski. As the playwright, who apparently did not like to be upstaged, put it:

I was only nominally the chairman of the committee. When I got on the boat and the committee started for Cuba, I discovered—should I say, to my disgust—that this man actually was the expert and I was the idealist, so to speak. I was the idealist who had some kind of publicity value and he was the expert on Latin-American affairs. He spoke with such authority and such knowledge that I simply supposed, if there were other Communist Party delegates on this commission, that he was the top one. (Bentley 507)

To add insult to injury, Odets learned that a veteran Communist named Mother Bloor rather than he himself had been the party's original choice for chairperson. However, she had been passed over because of her age and because the trip was a dangerous one. Odets noted that there had been "dozens of secret police there [in Cuba] with machine guns, some of them dressed as dock workers in overalls. I said it was a very dangerous matter.... He [Komorowski] might have at least told me this, and given me the chance to decide whether I wanted to face machine guns" (Bentley 509). Luckily, for Odets and his companions, this adventure—with its comic opera overtones—came to a safe conclusion.

The Committee's major interest in Odets was, of course, in his role as a writer of the radical Left. The Committee wanted to know what use the Party had made of his plays and film scripts, how he had been used as a member of the Party's "Cultural Front," and how he had responded to Party demands. There was much discussion of *Waiting for Lefty*, with Odets remarking, curiously, that although the play had been produced all over the world in many languages, it had not netted him even a thousand dollars. The Committee had done its homework and came up with favorable criticism of *Lefty* and other plays taken from radical publications. Now Odets, who was never one to forget or forgive a bad review, resolutely produced poor notices from the same or similar sources. Eventually, Committee Counsel Tavenner and Odets began to look at individual reviews, with Tavenner pointing to favorable sections and Odets citing unfavorable ones (Bentley 518). Although critics like James T. Farrell had written "horrifying reviews," others, like Michael Blankfort, had offered both praise and blame. The playwright suggested that this carrot-stick approach was really the Party's attempt to keep writers within the fold and focused on ideological concerns. Odets said that he was a writer of changing interests, and he refused to be so bound:

I knew that, as fumbling as my beginnings were, I could only write out of my own experience. I couldn't be given a theme and handle it. It was not my business. It meant to me, if I may say it this way, a loss of integrity. And so I persisted in going along my own line and writing what did come out of my true center. And whenever this happened, I got this violent opposition in the press, and I became further disgusted and estranged. (Bentley 517)

When Tavenner asked whether Odets had not *continued* to write on "Communist themes," Odets replied with what must have been a deeply felt statement of belief:

I have always tried to write, not out of any themes to one side of myself, but to themes that were central and germane to my own life. I do remember stating at our last meeting that if I were moved by certain situations of poverty, this would be because my mother worked in a stocking factory in Philadelphia at the age of eleven and died a broken woman— at the age of forty-eight. When I wrote, sir, it was out of central, personal things. I did not learn my hatred of poverty, sir, out of Communism. (Bentley 520)

In the concluding part of the hearings, the Committee sought to assess Odets' and the Party's influence in Hollywood, but the writer firmly denied that Leftist influence could or would be a part of the Hollywood scene. And in his own final statement, Odets vigorously defended his political beliefs, pointing to the need for political action:

the lines of leftism, liberalism, in all of their shades and degrees, are constantly crossing like a jangled chord on a piano. It is almost impossible to pick out which note is which note. I have spoken out on what I thought were certain moral issues of the day, and I found myself frequently on platforms with Communists that I did not know about then but evidently are now known Communists. Many of these people have some very good tunes. They have picked up some of our most solemn and sacred American tunes and they sing them. If I as an American liberal must sometimes speak out the same tune, I must sometimes find myself on platforms, so to speak, with strange bedfellows. I have never wittingly, since these early days, joined or spoken on an exclusively Communist program or platform. I see that one must do one or two things: One must pick one's way very carefully through the maze of liberalism and leftism today or one must remain silent. Of the two, I must tell you frankly I would try to pick the first way, because the little I have to say, the little that I have to contribute to the betterment or welfare of the American people could not permit me to remain silent. (Bentley 531)

After the hearings were over, Odets sadly discovered that he had been politically discredited everywhere. He was to write of his frustration and anger to Benjamin Appel, his former student: "For the most part the judgments...of what I did and said have been disgustingly mechanical, based on a few lines printed in newspapers, right or left, when actually there were three hundred pages of transcript. Personally, I find this a disturbingly immoral time and this immorality exists as much on the left as on the right" (Appel 475). Another of Odets' protégés also recorded the writer's frustration and anger at the treatment he had received after the hearings were over:

Leslie Weiner, who took a playwriting course with Clifford Odets, recalls visiting Odets in California after his belligerent appearance before the Un-American Activities Committee, when he simultaneously named names but gave the Committee a hard and boisterous time. "He had all the testimony in a bound book and he told me he tried to get Charlie Chaplin to read the whole thing but he wouldn't do it. That hurt him a lot. People were reacting to the headlines and not listening to what he said and he resented that and was frustrated by it. He wanted to be thought of as a resister, not a namer." (Navasky 376).

Odets' lonely eloquence makes good reading now, but it failed to impress those who had risked and lost so much. That eloquence would also fail to impress HUAC members and staffers who had waited for Odets for so long, pending lengthy investigations and testimony in closed sessions, and then found him so lacking in contrition when he appeared before the Committee in public. Nevertheless, Odets would now continue his career free of political threats or reprisals. He was to work hard and display his typical energy in commercial, but non-political efforts, writing the screenplay for *Sweet Smell of Success* (1957), writing and directing the film *The Story on Page One* (1959), writing a screenplay for *Wild in the Country* (1960), experimenting in 1963 with scripts for NBC's early television ventures ("The Affair," "Big Mitch," and "The Mafia Man"), and planning with playwright William Gibson in the early 1960s for a musical version of *Golden Boy*. Odets' last play, *The Flowering Peach* (1954), was also far removed from the political world to which he had devoted so much time and effort. Indeed, Odets had now cut himself off from a political past which had done so much to nourish his imagination and from a political future which would nurture new and different voices and visions.

Notes

[1]During the early 1930s, Congressmen with such varied backgrounds as Samuel Dickstein of New York and Martin Dies of Texas argued for the establishment of a Congressional committee to investigate subversive groups in the United States. Dickstein, whose constituency was New York City's lower East Side with its heavily Jewish immigrant population, focused on the American Nazi Party and related organizations, while Dies, whose Texas constituency was heavily dominated by native-born Americans of Anglo-Saxon background, sought to investigate the American Communist Party and groups of similar background subject to suspicious foreign influences (Goodman 3-24).

[2]*The Big Knife*, although not directly concerned with politics, does seem to reflect the uncertainties, anxieties, and pessimism of the late 1940s. In the play, Charlie Castle, a successful film star, must decide whether or not to sign a new contract with his studio. Although his wife Marion reminds him of his early ambitions and enthusiasm for a career in the theatre, he eventually does sign because of blackmail as well as the obvious inducements—money and continuing fame. He remarks ruefully that the theatre is "a bleeding stump. Even stars have to wait years for a decent play" (22). Now in the movie business, he can't afford "acute attacks of integrity" (15). Charlie is at best "the warrior minstrel of the forlorn hope" (81). Hank Teagle, a family friend, puts it another way: "Half-idealism is the peritonitis of the soul. America is full of it" (110).

[3]FBI Special Agent Paul F. Keppler explained the heavy deletions in the Odets files as follows, in a letter to the author dated January 15, 1987:

Enclosed is one copy of 88 pages which contain information responsive to your request. Excisions have been made on this material, and an addition 146 pages are being withheld in their entirety, in order to protect information which is exempt from disclosure pursuant to the following subsections of Title 5, United States Code, Section 552:

(b) (1) information which is currently and properly classified pursuant to Executive Order 12356 in the interest of the national defense or foreign policy.

(b) (2) materials related solely to the internal rules and practices of the FBI.

(b) (7) records or information compiled for law enforcement purposes, the disclosure of which could reasonably be expected to:

   (C) constitute an unwarranted invasion of the personal privacy of another person;

   (D) reveal the identity of a confidential source or reveal confidential information furnished only by the confidential source.

[4]About this California Committee, historian David Caute writes:

"Foremost among the state 'un-American' legislative committees whose inquisitorial methods so closely resembled those of HCUA and the SISS was California's Fact-Finding Committee on Un-American Activities, an agency of misery almost universally known as the Tenney Committee, in honor of its forceful chairman from 1941 to 1949, Jack B. Tenney. Like his friend Mayor Samuel W. Yorty of Los Angeles, Tenney had once belonged to the pro-Communist wing of the Democratic Party and had been named as a subversive before the Dies Committee in Washington. It was after a bitter factional fight within Local 47 of the American Federation of Musicians, culminating in Tenney's failure to win reelection as president, that he turned to red-baiting on a grand scale" (77).

[5]Caute notes that excluded from the indictment was "the board's one woman member, Elizabeth Gurley Flynn. (Her turn came later)" (187). See Caute's history of the period's anti-Communism for a summary account of Judge Medina's harsh treatment of the Communist defendants (including jail sentences for contempt) and his prejudicial charge to the jury in their case (192-93), which were part of what Odets was reacting to in his speech.

[6]For an interesting account by one of the "Hollywood Ten" who defied the Committee, see Alvah Bessie, *Inquisition in Eden.*

Works Cited

Appel, Benjamin. "Odets University." *The Literary Review* (Summer 1976): 470-75.

Bentley, Eric. *Thirty Years of Treason.* New York: Viking Press, 1971.

Bessie, Alvah. *Inquisition in Eden.* New York: Macmillan, 1965.

Brenman-Gibson, Margaret. *Clifford Odets: American Playwright.* New York: Atheneum, 1981.

Caute, David. *The Great Fear: The Anti-Communist Purge Under Truman and Eisenhower.* New York: Simon and Schuster, 1978.

Federal Bureau of Investigation files on Clifford Odets. 88 pages, no pagination.

Goodman, Walter. *The Committee.* New York: Farrar, Straus, and Giroux, 1968.

Keppler, Paul F. (FBI Special Agent). Letter to the author, January 15, 1987.

Navasky, Victor. *Naming Names.* New York: Viking Press, 1980.

Odets, Clifford. *I Can't Sleep. The Anxious Years: America in the 1930s.* Ed. Louis Filler. New York: Capricorn Books, 1964. 214-17.

——. *The Big Knife.* New York: Random House, 1949.

——. *The Silent Partner.* Unpublished manuscript in the New York Public Library's Lincoln Center Division.

——. *Six Plays of Clifford Odets.* New York: Modern Library, 1939; rpt. New York: Grove Press, 1982.

Rabkin, David. *Drama and Commitment.* Bloomington: Indiana UP, 1964.

A Small Trumpet of Defiance:
Politics and the Buried Life in
Norman Mailer's Early Fiction

Gabriel Miller

In one of the *Presidential Papers* Mailer wrote, "Our history has moved on two rivers, one visible, the other underground; there has been the history of politics which is concrete, practical, and unbelievably dull...and there is the subterranean river of untapped, ferocious, lonely and romantic desires, that concentration of ecstasy and violence which is the dream life of the nation" (46). Much of Mailer's writing, like much of the American writing from which he consciously borrows, is concerned with such dualities. As he declared in "The White Negro," Mailer finds the twentieth century, for all its horror, an exciting time to live because of "its tendency to reduce all of life to its ultimate alternatives" (33). This fascination with dynamic polarities is reflected in Mailer's style as well, as he has struggled in his modeling of language and form to fuse the real, political/social world with the world of dream and myth. In reading his novels chronologically, one can trace Mailer's process of borrowing and merging different styles, then discarding them, and experimenting with others in quest of a voice that will be most compatible with his own recurrent themes and emerging vision. Mailer's central subject is the relationship between the individual will and a world that attempts to overwhelm and extinguish it. Intimately connected with this spiritual warfare is the subject of power, particularly political power, and the individual's need to resist the encroaching forces of totalitarianism. Mailer's early fiction clearly warns that modern man is in danger of losing his dignity, his freedom, and his sense of self before the enormous power of politics and society.

These concerns are already apparent in his first novel, *The Naked and the Dead* (1948), which despite its brilliant, evocative scenes of men at war, is ultimately a political novel. Mailer describes his attitude about the Second World War in "The White Negro":

The Second World War presented a mirror to the human condition which blinded anyone who looked into it...one was then obliged also to see that no matter how crippled and perverted an image of man was the society he had created, it was nonetheless his creation, his collective creation...and if society was so murderous, then who could ignore the most hideous of questions about his own nature? (312)

The Naked and the Dead elaborates this harrowing perception of the individual who exemplifies and perpetuates what is wrong with the society he inhabits. In this first novel Mailer equates the army with society and thereby explores the fragmented nature of that society, which has militated against social development, revolutionary or otherwise. In so doing, Mailer demonstrates his own loss of faith in the individual's ability to impose himself creatively, perhaps redemptively, on the oppressive condition of the post-war world.

The novel exhibits a hodgepodge of styles and influences: the works of James Farrell, John Steinbeck, and John Dos Passos inform its structure and form. Herein the thirties novel, with its emphasis on social engagement and reform, collides with a pessimistic, even despairing world view, as Mailer blends naturalism with symbolism, realistic reportage with nightmare images and hallucinatory dream landscapes, documentary portraits with political allegory. The dramatic thrust of the novel, however, springs from Mailer's fascination with his three central figures: General Cummings, Sergeant Croft, and Lieutenant Hearn.

Cummings is presented as a despotic fascist, wholly preoccupied with the power he wields over the island which his troops occupy. When Hearn accuses him of being reactionary he dismisses the charge, claiming that the war is not being fought for ideals but for "power concentration" (140). His plan to send a patrol to the rear of the Japanese position to determine the validity of a new strategic theory is prompted by raw opportunism, and it results in the death of three men. Croft, on the other hand, is a brave but illiterate soldier who embraces the war cause to satisfy his lust for killing and conquest. He is Cummings' collaborator, carrying out the general's orders without question. It is Croft who leads the men through jungles and swamps to pit them and himself against Mt. Anaka, even after the Japanese have surrendered (though the patrol does not know it), to further his own ambitions.

Hearn is the character who bridges the gap between the soldiers and command. Although he represents the liberal voice in the novel and so seems ideally positioned to embody the moral center in this desperate society, he emerges as a rather vague and empty character, even less sympathetic than most in Mailer's vast array of characters. This surprising deficiency in Hearn is surely intentional, as Mailer introduces an intelligent and sometimes outspoken man only to emphasize how ineffective he is. Resented both by the commanders and by the soldiers, he is eventually killed for no purpose; such is the fate of liberalism in Mailer's universe.

The political argument develops primarily in dialogues between Cummings and Hearn, whom Cummings is trying to convert to his autocratic views. This overt confrontation of ideologies, a staple of the political novel and a device Mailer would repeat less successfully in his next novel, provides an abstract gloss on the narrative, while the use of the "Time Machine" episodes to delineate the lives of the men more subtly equates the structure of society with the army. America is thus portrayed as a place of social privilege and racial discrimination, as exploitive and destructive as the military organization that represents it. Mailer presents the individual as either submitting to these repressive forces or attempting to maintain some spiritual independence. The fates of Hearn and, to some degree, Red Valsen, a Steinbeckian hobo and laborer who struggles to preserve his private vision, indicate that defiance is fruitless. Both men are destroyed, while Cummings and Croft, in their ruthless drive to power, prevail and triumph.

However, this schematic simplification does not reflect the complexity of Mailer's view, conveyed in some aspects of the novel that undercut the apparent political formula, most notably his narrative style. Mailer recounts his tale in a tone of complete objectivity, his authorial voice remaining detached and disinterested. Considering the moral dimensions of his story, this lack of anger or indignation is disorienting, and the effect is strengthened by Mailer's unsympathetic treatment of Hearn and the vibrant images of Cummings and Croft, who seem to fascinate him. Clearly Cummings' egoism repels Mailer, but it also attracts him, for in this island tyrant he perceives also the individualistic impulse to reshape and recreate an environment and in so doing, to form a new reality.[1] Cummings thus possesses a kind of romantic aura as a dream-like projection—which Mailer will recast in different forms in his subsequent fiction—of the active response to life which Mailer advocates in principle, if not on Cummings' specific terms. Croft, too, seeks a channel in which to funnel his powerful drives. Both men see evil as a vital force and their apprehension of it (not only in people, but in nature as well) provides them an energy and a decisive manner that the weaker, idealistic characters lack.

Still, at this point in his career Mailer did not want to exalt Cummings and Croft at the expense of Hearn. Therefore, in his climb up Mt. Anaka, Croft is left finally with feelings of despair: "Croft kept looking at the mountain. He had lost it, had missed some tantalizing revelation of himself. Of himself and much more, of life. Everything" (552). At another point Mailer sums up Croft thus: "He hated weakness and he loved practically nothing. There was a crude unformed vision in his soul but he was rarely conscious of it" (124). This man has energy but no form. Mailer the novelist is himself searching for the kind of form necessary to shape his vision. The liberal philosophy of a Hearn is rejected as insufficient to the challenges of modern history. It lacks the energy and daring of Croft and Cummings, but they still frighten Mailer, and he refuses to align himself with their authoritarian methods. Concluding the novel with Major Dalleson, a mediocre bureaucrat, enjoying the monotony of office details, Mailer instead pulls back from taking a definite position on the struggle he has chronicled. As Richard Poirier points out, he "has not yet imagined a hero with whose violence he can unabashedly identify himself" (26).

After completing *The Naked and the Dead*, Mailer went to Paris, where he met Jean Malaquais, an anti-Stalinist Marxist philosopher and novelist. They spent countless hours discussing politics and philosophy, during which Malaquais laid the groundwork for Mailer's broader understanding and thinking about politics. By the time Mailer returned to America he had come to believe in collective political action and the necessity of the artist's direct engagement in the political sphere. He put this new creed into practice by working vigorously in the 1948 presidential campaign of Henry Wallace, who was running on the Progressive Party ticket against the incumbent Harry Truman and Republican Thomas Dewey. Wallace's campaign was marked by much controversy and dissent, as many leftist intellectuals felt that Wallace was deceived by the Communists and so refused to vote for him. Mailer, however, remained loyal to Wallace, whose candidacy was effectively repudiated by the electorate, with only 2.37 percent of the vote. This overwhelming defeat ended Mailer's involvement in collective political action; in bitter disillusionment he later dismissed the whole affair, commenting, "The Progressive Party, as an organization, was almost as stupid as the army" (qtd. in Mills 111).[2]

Mailer's political orientation is presented in a very direct way in his second novel, *Barbary Shore* (1951). Making plain his disenchantment with Stalinism, he also reasserts his view that liberalism is dead, the proletariat in despair, and the right in control. Not only is the liberal dream dead, but so is the the Marxist vision, which the novel maintains was mankind's last hope, now blasted by the Stalinist subversion of socialist ideals. Russian communism and American capitalism are both seen as reactionary and repressive; privilege and oppression are now ascendant.

In his second novel Mailer is attempting to cut himself off from the past and forge his own personal vision, and although he will not succeed here, *Barbary Shore* nevertheless heralds a bold departure. In structuring this work Mailer abandons the omniscient narrative technique of *The Naked and the Dead*, adopting in its place the first-person narrator, a device to be retained in his subsequent fiction. Mickey Lovett is an amnesiac, a psychic casualty of war who becomes part of a nightmarish present. He has no real past—though he manages to recollect bits and pieces as the novel progresses—and so must make a commitment to the present. The novel's action takes place in a rooming house in Brooklyn Heights, where Lovett's relationships with its various inhabitants form the story, which is told partly in realistic and partly in symbolic/ allegorical terms.

This narrator's amnesia opens the way for a significant stylistic ambivalence, as Lovett's probing of self and memory infuses his story with numerous surreal, dreamlike moments. It is clearly implied in the book's first half that the world cannot be fully understood by rational means; the "subterranean river" is always winding its way through consciousness, undercutting any reliance on reason alone. In these sections Mailer achieves his best writing, for his obsessions with individual psychology and motivation seems to interest him more than the political novel he obviously wants to write. When the action switches from Lovett's relationships to the confrontation between Hollingsworth, a government agent, and McLeod, a former revolutionary Socialist, the novel becomes didactic, much of it devoted to arguments about politics and history. Ultimately *Barbary Shore* becomes more a polemic than a novel as Mailer loses his grip on his fictional voice and his book's design.

As a novelist Mailer does not fully break free from the past, for this book owes much to Hawthorne's *The Blithedale Romance*, which is also concerned with a failed attempt to create a new and better world.[3] Mailer's skepticism about the viability of social progress and the allegorical structure of his work parallel Hawthorne's, as does his choice of the name Hollingsworth for his villain. In *Blithedale*, Hollingsworth, a reformer of criminals, is revealed to be an egoist who is blind to the complexity of human nature and incapable of real love. Mailer's Hollingsworth is a government undercover agent who is in the building to investigate McLeod and to recover from him a mysterious "little object" which disappeared from the State Department some years ago. This Hollingsworth also likes to present himself as a humanitarian, but he is exposed as a fascist, equally incapable of love. Another strong echo is provided in Mailer's use of the symbolically and ironically named Guinevere, a temptress who draws Hollingsworth, McLeod and Lovett into her orbit, much like Hawthorne's Zenobia.

Furthermore, Mailer's narrative method recalls Coverdale, the narrator of *Blithedale* (which is Hawthorne's only novel narrated in the first person). Hawthorne has Coverdale fashion his material, as

Hawthorne writes in the preface, like a play, "where the creatures of his brain may play their phantasmagorical antics, without exposing them to too close a comparison with the actual events of real lives" (27). Lovett/ Mailer attempts to organize and shape his material in a similar way. In *Barbary Shore* Mailer has deliberately narrowed his canvas from the expanse of his first novel to a small cast whose actions are situated almost exclusively in the small boardinghouse. Here they are carefully manipulated as they come and go, performing their allegorical and political functions as they act out their various parts in the story. It is also a convenient device for Lovett, who has lost his past, to try to structure and so control his present as he structures the novel he is writing.

The novel's political expression centers around McLeod, whose career represents in microcosm the recent history of Russian socialism. Affiliated with the Russian Communist Party for nineteen years, he embodies the altruistic ideal of Trotskyism now degenerated into Stalinism and incriminated in the Nazi-Soviet pact, the purges, and the labor camps. McLeod, who had come to be known as the "hangman of the Left Opposition" (130), abandoned the Party and came to America where he worked for the State Department. His leftist sympathies causing him to leave that job, he has assumed a new identity and married Guinevere, and he is now hiding out in the Brooklyn boardinghouse, where he spends time studying history and striving to understand through rigorous Marxist analysis why the revolution went wrong.

Guinevere, unlike her husband, remains ignorant of politics. Sexually vital and self-indulgent, she attracts all the men in the novel. In the novel's allegorical scheme her union with McLeod emphasizes the degeneration of the intellectual Marxist ideal as it merges either with materialism or, more broadly, with the lack of social engagement that she represents.

McLeod's antagonist is Leroy—Mailer puns ironically on the French word for king—Hollingsworth, a reactionary who seems more sinister than General Cummings because he disguises his fascist views behind a friendly manner. Like Hawthorne's Hollingsworth, however, he is a cold, vapid, robot-like functionary whose power Mailer sees as signalling the approach of Barbary. McLeod connects Hollingsworth with an advancing "state capitalism" which conjoins "state profit and state surveillance" and in which "the aim of society is no longer to keep its members alive, but quite the contrary,...how to dispose of them" (200), and indeed, Mailer's Hollingsworth displays no moral comprehension nor intellectual depth. Greedy and sadistic, he merely serves the system that empowers him, and his elopement with Guinevere at the novel's end constitutes the author's ultimate comment on the fate of America, merging the fascist with the materialist.

The other central player in Lovett's vision is Lannie Madison, a young woman spiritually formed by the ideals of the Russian Revolution. A Trotskyite, she has been decimated psychologically by the war and its aftermath, and she is now a pathological remnant of her former self. Like Guinevere, she casts a spell over Lovett, reminding him of his own radical days, when he, too, was fired by a vision of human progress and betterment. Now bitterly reproaching herself for being foolish enough to hope for a better world, Lannie views the post-war society as a larger version of the concentration camps, similarly dedicated to the eradication of individualism and emotion. She blames McLeod for the betrayal of the ideals of the revolution.

Lovett, too, is a former Trotskyite, and he describes his early devotion in terms at once realistic and dreamlike:

I was young then, and no dedication could match mine. The revolution was tomorrow, and the inevitable crises of capitalism ticked away in my mind with the certainty of a time bomb, and even then could never begin to match the ticking of my pulse...For a winter and a spring I lived more intensely in the past than I could ever in the present, until the sight of a policeman on his mount became the Petrograd proletariat crawling to fame between the legs of a Cossack's horse.... There was never a revolution to equal it, and never a city more glorious than Petrograd....(91)

The passage is haunting and suggestive, like the feeling it describes, because it vividly characterizes the spiritual fervor of the youthful idealist, while its images convey the elusive intensity of the ideal itself. This Petrograd is an eternal city, a symbol of human perfectibility, yet beyond human reach. Lovett's amnesia, the novel suggests, results not only from the war but also from the death of his ideals and his devotion to an ennobling cause, which has cut him off both from his sense of self and from his past.

Barbary Shore concludes with McLeod's suicide, as Hollingsworth and Guinevere run off together and Lannie is arrested by the police. McLeod has, however, willed the "little object," the subject of Hollingsworth's search and the emblem of his own endangered Marxist ideals, to Lovett. Thus it is left to Lovett to keep the socialist dream alive while awaiting the apocalyptic war to come. The novel ends on a note of pessimism as Mailer echoes Fitzgerald:

But for the present the storm approaches its thunderhead, and it is apparent that the boat drifts ever closer to shore. So the blind will lead the blind, and the deaf about warnings to one another until their voices are lost. (223)

The final line also concludes Chapter One, and the resulting suggestion of cyclical movement underscores Mailer's cynical view of human possibilities.

That pessimistic perspective is most prevalent in the dream-like sequences which evoke the narrator's personal sense of loss, but it is also supported by the political collapse narrated in realistic, historical terms. Again, Mailer portrays the human race as spiritually bankrupt, unable to grow or evolve beyond the state of Barbary. The spiritual malaise of the modern world colors much of the novel's prose, ultimately picturing a dark and barren landscape where no dreams may take root. In the face of this enveloping gloom, McLeod's legacy to Lovett seems weak and ultimately, as Mailer never specifically defines it, merely symbolic. Probably Mailer's belief in politics is only symbolic as well: at this point in his career he surely seems to be saying that political solutions have no practical value. If McLeod leaves anything to Lovett, it is a renewal of feeling, a rejuvenation of the psyche, but the effect of this endowment on Lovett's troubled spirit remains unexplored. In Mailer's later work, on the other hand, the individual's spiritual/psychological vitality will become paramount, and it will be linked not to political urges but to existential ones.

Like *Barbary Shore* Mailer's next novel, *The Deer Park* (1955), is a first-person narrative by a spiritually dislocated would-be novelist. Serguis O'Shaugnessy is both an orphan and a victim of historical disaster: a wartime bomber pilot, he became sickened by the recognition of his role as a killer. Revolting against the horror of this "real world" (47), he suffered a nervous breakdown and then retreated to the fictitious community of Desert D'Or, a Palm Springs-like enclave situated near the cinema capital of Southern California and on the edge of the western desert. There Sergius drifts in search of some meaning to compensate for the emptiness of his world. Creatively and sexually impotent—Mailer's emphasis on sex in this novel signals an important shift in his thematic concerns—Sergius finds a perfect haven in Desert D'Or, which is full of aimless people like himself. Most prominent among these lost souls are Charles Francis Eitel, once a powerful Hollywood director, and Marion Faye, a drug dealer and pimp.

Eitel occupies the political center of the novel. Once recognized as a gifted artist who made socially responsible films in the thirties and as a committed radical who fought for democracy in Spain, he refused to cooperate with the House Committee on Un-American Activities in its Hollywood witch-hunts in the 1940s and 50s. There-upon blacklisted by the industry, he forfeited his power and his identity, and when Sergius meets him, he is hiding out in Desert D'Or, ignored by its more prosperous citizens. Eitel's loss of artistic and sexual potency represents for Sergius the betrayal of past values, which he feels he has lost as well, and so Eitel's future becomes a matter of personal significance to him.

The destructive power of the congressional committee makes it an obvious example of the totalitarian nature of American life, but the energy of evil permeates the novel's setting in another way, for Desert D'Or is a place of extraordinary sexual license. The title of the novel refers to Louis XV's infamous Deer Park, a description of which is used as an epigraph which reads in part: "Apart from the evil which this dreadful place did to the morals of the people, it is horrible to calculate the immense sums of money it cost the state." The carnal atmosphere of the isolated desert community is not for Mailer representative of America, a sexually repressed society; instead he implies that the libertine life enjoyed by the inhabitants of Desert D'Or is their reward for supplying the American public with movie myths about its democratic ideals. Charles Eitel once measured himself in rebellion against such a world.

In his exile Eitel is given a chance to recover his sense of self through his relationship with Elena Esposito, a failed dancer and actress who remains, nonetheless, a natural and courageous woman. With her his sexual potency is restored, and he begins work on an ambitious script which he hopes will reclaim his integrity as an artist. However, this burst of personal and artistic fortune does not last, as Eitel, becoming fearful of the risks his renewed vitality exposes him to, finally capitulates to the pressure of Hollywood. He confesses before the committee, recanting his youthful ideals, and is allowed to make a watered-down version of his original script. This apostasy blights his relationship with Elena, and she leaves him for a time.

Interestingly, the autocrat-figures in *The Deer Park*, the studio heads and producers, while formidable in power and prestige, are represented in a generally comic fashion. Their despotic control of the creative community seems neither frightening nor appalling, as was the grim dedication of Hollingsworth. Eitel well knows how to handle Herman Teppis (a studio head) and Collie Munshin (a producer and Teppis' son-in-law), although he fails to challenge their authority in any meaningful way. By undercutting the Hollywood power structure with such deliberate ridicule, Mailer seems to be opening the door for a character to defeat the oppressive system, but Eitel is a broken man, no longer possessed of the stamina needed for sustained rebellion. His capitulation before the committee signals an end to Mailer's preoccupation with politics as a solution.

Mailer's prescribed alternative to Eitel is Marion Faye. As Richard Poirier perceptively point out, "Faye is the secret center of *The Deer Park*.... The truth was simply that perversity and power interested [Mailer] far more than those efforts at health which led to limpness

or defeat'' (30). This partiality for vigor in preference to virtue, apparent
in the subtexts of Mailer's first two novels but suppressed because it
discomfited him, here rises to the surface for the first time: Eitel is defeated
because he has lost his passion and his courage. Of little worth now
are his refining powers of intelligence, a certain amount of compassion,
and a large residue of guilt; according to Faye, these "vices" (159) only
weaken men and turn them into "slobs" (147). In a deceptive world
of compromise and illusion, more forceful modes seem called for, and
Marion Faye believes in pushing himself to the limits of experience,
seeking the "experience beyond experience" (332) that will empower him
to overcome all obstacles to his existential freedom. He cultivates this
mystical bravado by leaving his doors unlocked, thus exposing himself
to the metaphoric threads of the desert and the very real threats of his
local enemies; in fact, he hopes to open a door to some authentic
experience at the precipice of reality. He enjoys driving at great speed
to a mountain top where he looks out over the desert, the gambling
city, and the atomic testing grounds. This last sight fills him with loathing
for the military and the political leaders who justify its destructive power.
At the same time, Faye yearns for the cataclysm it promises, for he
recognizes in Desert D'Or a prime locus of the rationalized immorality
of modern society, and he dreams of its violent destruction. Anticipating
the perverse attitude Mailer would formulate two years later in "The
White Negro," Faye is, in fact, a deliberate psychopath, regarding
irrational violence as a means to exercise some control under repressive
conditions. Perceiving that a violent act committed without regret or
regard for social restraints can give him unlimited power and authority,
he replaces the guilt that infuses Eitel's life with a numbing apathy.
Faye, however, is too wholly a nihilist, repudiating all feeling, to represent
an acceptable alternative to the defeated idealism of Eitel.

The central intelligence who strives to make sense of these psycho-
socio-political phenomena is, again, the narrator, Sergius O'Shaugnessy.
Like Mailer, Sergius views the world as a divided landscape:

I had the idea that there were two worlds. There was a real world as I called it,...and
this real world was a world where orphans burned orphans. It was better not even to
think of this. I liked the other world in which almost everybody lived. The imaginary
world. (47)

The escapist, "imaginary" world of Desert D'Or teaches him, however,
that this, too, can be a painful and destructive place. At the end of the
novel Sergius imagines Eitel sending him a message to confess that he
has lost his artistic drive, his belief that the created world is "more real

to us, more real to others, than the mummery of what happens, passes and is gone." He then urges Sergius,

So...try for that other world, the real world, where orphans burn orphans and nothing is more difficult to discover than a simple fact. And with the pride of an artist, you must blow against the walls of every power that exists, the small trumpet of your defiance. (374)

From the voice of an exhausted generation of idealists, the young man thus receives the charge to persevere in the artist's quest for individual truth and validity against the oppressive forces of delusion and distortion.

After much tribulation, Sergius finally leaves Desert D'Or, to travel in Mexico and then settle in New York. At last he has cut himself off from politics—"I was still an anarchist, and an anarchist I would always be" (355)—and devotes himself instead to sex. Concluding with the injunction, "Rather think of Sex as Time, and Time as the connection of new circuits" (375), he (and Mailer) have clearly rejected engagement in the fortunes of a larger society in favor of the pursuit of personal relationships. In this novel Mailer seems to be moving in new directions, seeking to refocus his attention to the individual rebellion against repression rather than the society-wide political activism that has yielded him no solutions in the past. Unfortunately, the central voices here remain weak, perhaps because he is still struggling for definition and real commitment to his new ideas. Faye, while provocative, is too extreme a character to command sympathy, and even Sergius is not a very compelling personality. Passive and unresponsive, he projects no convincing sense of the emotional consequences of his experience.

In examining Mailer's early fiction it is important to consider his masterful short story, "The Man Who Studied Yoga" (1952), written after the disillusionment expressed in *Barbary Shore* but before *The Deer Park*. Here Mailer writes for the only time about "normal" middle-class characters, Sam and Eleanor Slovoda, who are presented as a mature, well-adjusted couple. Sam is an ex-radical and aspiring novelist who makes his living writing continuities for the comics; Eleanor thinks of herself as a painter, but is also a housewife and mother. The story's central event occurs when they host a dinner for some friends, one of whom brings along a pornographic film, which they all watch and discuss. After the guests leave, the Slovodas run the film again and make love as they watch it. Then, his wife having fallen asleep, Sam thinks about his unrealized life as a writer and as a man. The film has reminded him of longings which are never to be satisfied, of the frustrations which underlie his comfortable life. In contrast to the sedate existence of these characters is one guest's tale of Cassius O'Shaugnessy, the man who studied yoga. A world-traveler who has spent his life testing himself against a variety of experiences, he occupies the moral center of the story. His example of self-realization highlights by comparison Sam's own inability to express or extend himself or to relieve his anxieties. Apparently he is doomed to live out his life in conformity to social convention and to be forever secretly despairing and frustrated.

Sam is clearly a more prosaic middle-class model for Eitel, and the story of Cassius a preparation for the extremist alternative of Marion Faye. However, Mailer would specifically elaborate on the response to life he was working toward in his early fiction in his famous essay, "The White Negro" (1957). Therein he declares that it is the fate of modern man to live with death, which is the heritage of the Second World War. The only response to such a situation is "to accept the terms of death, to live with death as immediate danger, to divorce oneself from society, to exist without roots, to set out on that unchartered journey with the rebellious imperatives of the self" (313). The exemplar of this condition of instinctual consciousness is the urban American Negro: by replacing the imperatives of society with the more vital and life-affirming imperatives of the self, the Negro makes it impossible for social institutions to account for him in their own terms. This form of rebellion is for Mailer the essence of "hip:

So there was a new breed of adventurers, urban adventurers who drifted out at night looking for action with a black man's code to fit their facts. The hipster had absorbed the existentialist synapses of the Negro, and for practical purposes could be considered a white Negro. (315)

The hipster, then, defies "the collective murders of the State" (328) by becoming a psychopath. The strength of the psychopath is that he knows what is good or bad for him and knows that he can change "a negative and empty fear with an outward action" (320). He is an existentialist in that his values are determined by his inner psychological needs. His energy derives from the orgasm: "Orgasm is his therapy— he knows at the seed of his being that good orgasm opens his possibilities and bad orgasm imprisons him" (321). Thus Mailer finds sources for energy and being in the self, and so he turns away from society towards an inner world which contains the seeds of his well-being. Poirier explains: "The 'Negro' is the child in all of us, but the child after Freud, and the essay is a call to us to become 'children' not that we might escape from time but that we might re-engage ourselves with it" (79).

Mailer's first attempt to explore this inner, subconscious world in his fiction was *An American Dream* (1965), an extraordinary tour de force in which his language and style attain a new level of poetic suggestiveness, bridging the two worlds of external and internal reality. It is, again, a first-person narrative, told by Stephen Richards Rojack, a war hero, former congressman and professor of psychology, who recounts a thirty-two-hour psychic journey in which his old self is destroyed as he struggles toward spiritual and psychological rebirth. His odyssey begins with the murder of his estranged wife, Deborah, who represents for him an anti-life force. To be reborn involves immersing oneself in the destructive element, so Rojack must court death and so gain a heightened awareness of life. In order to free himself of the shackles of societal conformity, he must push himself to the limits of experience. Symbolically Rojack realizes this self-liberation when he visits his father-in-law, Barney Kelly, high atop the Waldorf Towers, where Kelly has summoned him to discuss his daughter's death. In order to free himself of Kelly, a man of enormous wealth and power, Rojack realizes that he must go to the terrace and walk the parapet: the performance of this act symbolizes his self-renewal.

Rojack thus makes of himself the kind of primitive being who is in contact with his non-rational self, and Mailer apparently envisions him as a prototype of the heroic new individualist who will emerge in modern America to assault the repressive state. The subconscious being a state outside time and civilization, Rojack arrives there in classic American literary fashion when he "lights out" for the prehistoric jungles of the Yucatan and Guatemala at the end of the novel.

Since *An American Dream* Mailer has written only three novels— *Why Are We in Vietnam?* (1967), *Ancient Evenings* (1983), and *Tough Guys Don't Dance* (1984)—reaffirming in each case his devotion to individual consciousness as the rightful sphere of aesthetic concern. In his early work the social world retained sufficient importance that Mailer felt obligated to serve the demands of mimesis even while moving away from it; in the later fiction that ambiguity is resolved in favor of a subjectivity that supersedes realism. It seems clear that the Norman Mailer of the past twenty years is more comfortable in the realm of non-fiction, where the demands of social and political reality force him to keep a tighter rein on the extravagant energies of his imagination. In works such as *The Armies of the Night* (1968), *Of a Fire on the Moon* (1971), and *The Executioner's Song* (1979), Mailer's narrative talents and his prodigious capacities as an observer of American social and political life merge into a fluent and compelling whole. Perhaps he realizes that the "big book" about America that he has longed to write will have to unite the two voices, the realistic and the romantic, in a coherent and sustained vision. So far the ability to do so seems to have eluded him.

Notes

[1]Mailer's attraction to Cummings and Croft is also discussed by Norman Podhoretz in "Norman Mailer: The Embattled Vision."

[2]Another excellent source for biographical information is Peter Manso, *Mailer: His Life and Times.*

[3]The relationship between *Barbary Shore* and *Blithedale Romance* is discussed by Laura Adams, *Existential Battles: The Growth of Norman Mailer* (41-42), and John Stark, *"Barbary Shore:* The Basis of Mailer's Best Work."

Works Cited

Adams, Laura. *Existential Battles: The Growth of Norman Mailer.* Athens: Ohio University Press, 1976.

Hawthorne, Nathaniel. *The Blithedale Romance.* New York: Norton, 1958.

Mailer, Norman. *An American Dream.* New York: Dell, 1971.

_____ *Barbary Shore.* New York: Signet, 1953.

_____ *The Deer Park.* New York: G.P. Putnam's Sons, 1955.

_____ "The Man Who Studied Yoga." *Advertisements for Myself.* New York: Berkeley, 1966. 145-173.

_____ *The Naked and the Dead.* New York: Signet, 1951.

_____ *The Presidential Papers.* New York: Berkeley, 1976.

_____ "The White Negro." *Advertisements for Myself.* New York: Berkeley, 1966. 311-331.

Manso, Peter. *Mailer: His Life and Times.* New York: Simon and Schuster, 1985.

Mills, Hilary. *Mailer: A Biography.* New York: Empire Books, 1982.

Podhoretz, Norman. "Norman Mailer: The Embattled Vision." *Partisan Review* 26 (1959): 371-391.

Poirier, Richard. *Norman Mailer.* New York: Viking, 1972.

Stark, John. *"Barbary Shore:* The Basis of Mailer's Best Work." *Modern Fiction Studies* 17 (1971): 403-408.

Innocence Regained:
The Career of Leslie Fiedler

James Seaton

For most readers, there are two Leslie Fiedlers.[1] There is the Leslie Fiedler who is the author of *Love and Death in the American Novel.* This Fiedler helped shape the present critical consensus on 19th-century American fiction. If the American novels of that century are no longer seen as stages on the road to the "triumph of realism," Fiedler's work is surely one of the reasons. But if many readers first encounter Leslie Fiedler on the reading list for Ph.D. exams in 19th-century American literature, Fiedler is also an important author for those who would wish to revise such lists completely or do away with them altogether. He is one of the founding fathers of the popular culture movement, and his latest book *What Was Literature?* forcefully articulates the views of those who see popular culture studies not merely as another academic specialty but as a fundamental challenge to some of the basic assumptions of traditional academic categories. it is a striking example of the—often unacknowledged—influence of Fiedler that he is on the one hand one of the creators of the modern orthodoxy and also one of the sources for the rebellion against it.

But there is yet another Fiedler whose work is the focus of this essay. Few of those required to read *Love and Death in the American Novel* and even fewer of those influenced by Fiedler the cultural radical realize that Fiedler once was best known as a spokesman for liberal anti-communism, a view defended in controversial essays on the Hiss case, on the trial and execution of Ethel and Julius Rosenberg, and on Joseph McCarthy. When these essays are mentioned, it is usually to dismiss them as particularly egregious examples of cold-war rhetoric. In his 1987 work *The New York Intellectuals*, Alan Wald, for example characterizes them as "virulent anticommunist essays...full of dubious psychologizing and calls for atonement by the entire left..." (279). Ten years earlier, Morris Dickstein had asserted that "It would be hard to find more vicious examples of serious political writing than the first three essays in Leslie Fiedler's *An End to Innocence....*" (41).[2]

In my view, however, these essays, and particularly the essays on "Hiss, Chambers and the Age of Innocence" and "Afterthoughts on the Rosenbergs," present examples of cultural-political criticism far superior to anything Fiedler wrote later, and especially superior to his later radical writings, such as *Being Busted* and *What Was Literature?* I wish to argue that the significance of these essays is not limited by the validity of their political position of liberal anti-communism. In fact, it is the thesis of this paper that the cultural criticism which they exemplify has much more to offer contemporary political radicals than do Fiedler's books written from an anti-establishment position.

But how can one judge cultural criticism? For Theodor Adorno the very words "cultural criticism" have "an offensive ring" since the cultural critic "speaks as if he represented either unadulterated nature or a higher historical stage. Yet he is necessarily of the same essence as that to which he fancies himself superior" (19). The same objection would apply to those, like myself, who would attempt to judge cultural criticism. What standards are relevant when the very issue of "standards" is itself one of the topics to be debated? If the question cannot be resolved in this paper, at least the outline of a possible response can be sketched. If critique of one's own culture is not to be mere sermonizing on the basis of one's implied superiority, then, I would argue, it must be self-criticism, either implicit or explicit, since the critic is indeed "of the same essence"— part of the same culture—as that which he or she criticizes. How then is one to judge the validity of self-criticism? Freudian theory suggests that true self-knowledge leads to an integration of reason and emotion within the individual. If cultural criticism is judged by analogous standards, its achievement may be gauged by its ability to point to hidden connections between divergent aspects of society, between best-sellers and masterpieces, between culture and politics, and ultimately by its ability to contribute to the integration of reason and emotion in the larger world. Such, at least, is the viewpoint which informs this discussion.[3]

In *What Was literature?* (1982) Fiedler offers his own interpretation of the movement of his career. Repeatedly, Fiedler insists that the movement of his thought can be seen as a turn from hypocrisy to honesty, from shame-faced moralizing to open expression of his inmost feelings. Whereas "sentimentality" was once the key curse-word of his criticism, now "hypocrisy" seems virtually the only sin that is really sinful—against which "sado-masochistic voyeurism," for example, seems downright healthy (*What* 49). Over and over again, *What Was Literature* tells us how its author's onetime commitment to elitist standards forced him to deny his own literary experience and his own emotions. Now, however, he has come out of the closet, not only admitting but reveling in his willingness to be moved by schlock movies like *Beyond the Valley of the Dolls* (*What* 21) and, conversely, his boredom with much high culture.

In an introduction to *Inadvertent Epic*, a 1979 work incorporated into *What Was Literature?*, Barrie Hayne sums up Fiedler's work with the assertion that "the whole direction of his career is towards affirmation" and asserts that "health and self-understanding lie in the direction Fiedler is pointing" (*Epic* xi). I would agree that "affirmation" is indeed the dominant mood of Fiedler's later work, but I would question whether the personal and cultural affirmations of *What Was Literature?* lead to self-understanding, either for an individual or for society.

My own criticism of the later Fiedler—roughly, that work including and after *Being Busted*—parallels the critique of political and cultural innocence which Fiedler articulated especially in *An End to Innocence* and in *Love and Death in the American Novel*. I will argue that Fiedler himself has not so much moved to an advocacy of cultural and political radicalism from an earlier anti-communist liberalism and cultural elitism, which I gather would be his own interpretation, so much as he has moved toward a refusal of complicity or responsibility for the culture and, especially, for the politics of his time—and thus to an implicit assertion of innocence. I will argue that the writings of the later Fiedler, despite their putative radicalism, are much less useful for critical political thought than the essays he wrote during his most conservative, most strongly anti-communist phase.

A consideration of the essays in Fiedler's collection from the fifties, *An End to Innocence*, reveals an author quite different from the portrayal in *What Was Literature?* of a snobbish elitist, secure in his insider position within the bastions of high culture and academic respectability. Instead, one sees an author engaging in the most difficult form of analysis, criticism from within, criticism of political and cultural tendencies with which one shares the most. Fiedler's essays collected in 1955 as *An End to Innocence* criticize intellectuals, especially liberal intellectuals, and, even more specifically, liberal intellectuals of his own generation. Not that Fiedler is interested in presenting himself as one somehow beyond such labels; instead he asserts proudly

I have, as a matter of fact, been pleased to discover how often I have managed to tell what still seems to me the truth about my world and myself as a liberal, intellectual, writer, American, and Jew. I do not mind, as some people apparently do, thinking of myself in such categorical terms; being representative of a class, a generation, a certain temper seems to me not at all a threat to my individuality. (*End* xiii)

For this discussion the most important essays in *An End to Innocence* are those dealing with the Hiss case and with the Rosenbergs.[4] Although Hiss was convicted of perjury rather than espionage, his trial convinced many that liberal intellectuals, even those who appeared most respectable, were capable of treason and were inclined to lie about it when caught. The trial and execution of the Rosenbergs smeared left-wing Jewish intellectuals in particular with the charge of treasonous disloyalty. Both cases remain controversial today, more than thirty-five years later. Fiedler's essays assume the guilt of both Hiss and the Rosenbergs, and at this point the evidence seems to bear him out (see fn. 2). But the essays do not depend for their significance on whatever the facts of the cases finally turn out to be. Fiedler is primarily concerned to analyze the political-cultural significance of the trials for American liberals, especially those, like himself, who had moved to liberalism from an earlier communism or sympathy with communism.

Fiedler argues that the willingness of many liberals to defend both Hiss and the Rosenbergs was not based on a reasoned analysis of the evidence in either case. Instead, he argues that the liberal defenders of both held to a sentimental belief that people of good will—meaning people on the left like themselves—could not possibly commit the crimes of which they were accused. More desperately, some believed that even if Hiss or the Rosenbergs were factually guilty, such guilt was merely a kind of technical detail. Perhaps they had made errors, but their hearts were in the right place, and their accusers were evil men whose accidental factual justification mattered little in the light of their vicious right-wing ideology.

For Fiedler, on the other hand, the guilt of Hiss and the Rosenbergs is an ugly but unavoidable reality. Fiedler notes that Hiss was tried for perjury rather than treason, since the statute of limitations prevented prosecution for his possibly treasonous actions in 1936-7. Why, then, did Hiss not tell the truth and thus avoid indictment for perjury? For Fiedler, Hiss' unwillingness to admit and take responsibility for his past actions exemplifies the moral failure of his own generation of liberal intellectuals, a generation which had refused to grow up, since "the qualifying act of moral adulthood is precisely this admission of responsibility for the past and its consequences, however undesired or unforeseen" (*End* 4).

Fiedler finds the statement of Henry Julian Wadleigh, a minor figure in the Hiss case, symptomatic of the era; Wadleigh's "confession" was really "a disguise for self-congratulation, a device for clinging to the dream of innocence. He cannot, even in the dock, believe that a man of liberal persuasion is capable of wrong" (*End* 8).

It is the perpetuation of this myth of innocence which, Fiedler argues, connects American liberalism with Hiss and Wadleigh, and it is the collapse of this myth which is one of the inadvertent, even illogical, but nonetheless most important results of the Hiss trial:

It was this belief that was the implicit dogma of American liberalism during the past decades, piling up a terrible burden of self-righteousness and self-deceit to be paid for on the day when it would become impossible any longer to believe that the man of good will is identical with the righteous man, and that the liberal is *per se* the hero. That day came at different times to different people....for a good many...it came on August 17, 1948, when Hiss and Chambers were brought face to face before the House Committee on Un-American Activities. (*End* 8)

What makes Fiedler's analysis still exemplary, I would argue, is that he includes himself in the criticism he offers against his own generation and—equally important—he refuses to use the case and his critique as a basis for rejecting politics or disowning liberalism itself. His indictment is, indeed, sweeping:

Certainly, a generation was on trial with Hiss—on trial, not, it must be noticed, for having struggled toward a better world, but for having substituted sentimentality for intelligence in that struggle, for having failed to understand the moral conditions that must determine its outcome. (*End* 21)

The character witnesses for Hiss included many respected liberal figures whose trust in Hiss proved them to be, according to Fiedler, "in some sense, fools" (*End* 20). But for Fiedler this judgment is not a charge but "an admission":

It is not an easy admission, certainly not for them, but not even for those (among whom I include myself) who have admired in them a vision of national life that still appears worth striving for. (*End* 21)

Thus Fiedler does not use the Hiss case to make a simple about-face to the right or to withdraw from politics, saying "a plague on both your houses." The hard-won knowledge that "there is no magic in the words 'left' or 'progressive' or 'socialist' that can prevent deceit and the abuse of power" (*End* 24) would mean little if the political aspirations summed up in those words were simply abandoned. Rejection of politics, after all, would mean merely the attempt to protest one's innocence by renouncing complicity. Instead, Fiedler issues a call to "move forward from a liberalism of innocence to a liberalism of responsibility" (*End* 24). Out of context, the phrases seem typical political slogans. As the conclusion to "Hiss, Chambers, and the Age of Innocence," they take on meaning, since they reveal Fiedler's refusal to distance himself from the political tradition which he has criticized so harshly.

It is this refusal, I believe, which infuses the essay with real moral weight and makes it relevant to radicals thirty-five years later, even those who might quarrel with its factual assumptions. Disillusionment is a political experience which affects every generation and which is likely to be more wrenching for the left than for the right. A characteristic American response is simply to give up politics altogether. It is Fiedler's refusal simply to renounce liberalism which, in my opinion, makes this essay exemplary today, especially for those on the left, even though the politics advocated in the essay are the most conservative of Fiedler's career, those of conventional Cold War liberalism.

"Afterthoughts on the Rosenbergs," first published a little over two years later in 1953, raises some of the same issues as the Hiss essay. However, the emotional intensity of "Afterthoughts" is even greater, because Julius and Ethel Rosenberg were tried for espionage rather than perjury, because they were not merely imprisoned but executed, and because they were linked to Fiedler not only as leftists but as Jews. As in the Hiss essay, Fiedler takes issue with those leftists who affirmed the innocence of the accused in order to assert their own innocence. In contrast to the Hiss essay, however, Fiedler here does not criticize liberals alone. Instead, he finds that both political officials of unquestioned patriotism and ordinary citizens have betrayed a "lack of moral imagination" which has left them with "a certain incapacity to really believe in communists as people" (*End* 34). The editorial "we" implies that Fiedler himself has shared this "lack." Both leftists and rightists, argues Fiedler, have been eager to see the Rosenbergs merely as symbols, to see the case as a mythical confrontation between good and evil.

Although Fiedler believes that the Rosenbergs' "legal guilt...was clearly established at their trial" (*End* 37), he argues against their execution on two grounds. One involves a humane use of political symbolism:

The world had turned to us...for a symbolic demonstration that somewhere a government existed willing to risk the loss of political face for the sake of establishing an unequivocal moral position. (*End* 34)

But Fiedler's more important point is that the case against the execution of the Rosenbergs rests ultimately on a realization that they themselves, Julius and Ethel Rosenberg, are not simply mythic figures but actual human beings, a point Fiedler himself italicizes:

Under their legendary role, there were, after all, *real* Rosenbergs, unattractive and vindictive but human; fond of each other and of their two children; concerned with operations for tonsillitis and family wrangles; isolated from each other during three years of not-quite-hope and deferred despair; at the end, prepared scientifically for the electrocution; Julius' moustache shaved off and the patch of hair from Ethel's dowdy head...finally capable of dying.... This we had forgotten...thinking of the Rosenbergs as merely typical.... (*End* 32-33)

The passage seems tasteless—who is Fiedler to call the Rosenbergs "unattractive and vindictive" or to talk about "Ethel's dowdy head"?— but its recognition of the limits of myth, of the importance of an unpleasant, grubby reality, from a writer who seems to find myth everywhere seems to me impressive. Here Fiedler attempts not simply to inflate what he later called the "*mythic* resonance" (*No!* 152) but to explore the relation between myth and reality and the moral consequences of that relation. Ronald Radosh and Joyce Milton later concluded their important study of the evidence by making much the same point: "But if the Rosenberg case has an ultimate moral, it is precisely to point up the dangers of adhering to an unexamined political myth" (453).

No! in Thunder and Love and Death in the American Novel, both published in 1960, are transitional works. Their criticism of self and society is blunted by an attempt to find a position beyond criticism— a position of innocence. A study of the introduction to *No! in Thunder* and of the discussion of Twain's *Adventures of Huckleberry Finn* in *Love and Death in the American Novel* reveals the ambiguities of Fiedler's new stance.

Although *No! in Thunder* is not concerned with politics, the introduction stresses Fiedler's continued unwillingness to look at literature as a mere academic subject. If politics may be momentarily ignored, moral principles cannot. For Fiedler, "the practice of any art at any time is essentially a moral activity.... I do not know how to begin a book or talk about one without moral commitment" (*No!* 1).

And Fiedler defines the moral greatness of literature in terms which correspond to the kind of self-criticism he had undertaken in his essays on Hiss and the Rosenbergs:

When the writer says of precisely the cause that is dearest to him what is always and everywhere the truth about all causes—that it has been imperfectly conceived and inadequately represented, and that it is bound to be betrayed, consciously or unconsciously, by its leading spokesmen—we know that he is approaching an art of real seriousness if not of actual greatness. The thrill we all sense but hesitate to define for ourselves— the thrill of confronting a commitment to truth which transcends all partial allegiances— comes when Dante turns on Florence, Molière on the moderate man, de Sade on reason,

Shaw on the socialists, Tolstoy on the reformers, Joyce on Ireland, Faulkner on the South, Graham Greene on the Catholics, Pasternak on the Russians and Abraham Cahan or Nathanael West on the Jews. (*No* 7)

Yet in the same introduction in which Fiedler makes this eloquent statement, he seems to disengage himself from that tradition. He himself says "No! in Thunder" to "the last widely held *Weltanschauung* of the West: the progressive and optimistic, rational and kindly dogma of liberal humanism" (*No!* 10). However, Fiedler does not here identify himself in any way with the liberal view of the world, as in *An End to Innocence* he did identify himself with liberal politics even while critiquing liberal attitudes. Now his formulation of the "liberal view of man" contains no acknowledgement of shared assumptions:

This view sees man as the product of a perhaps unplanned but rationally ordered and rationally explicable universe, a product which science can explain, even as it can explain the world which conditions him. (*No!* 11)

Since elsewhere in the introduction Fiedler identifies himself not with liberalism but rather with "the truly contemporary writer" for whom the world is "not only absurd but also chaotic and fragmentary" (*No!* 17), apparently his critique of the "liberal view of man" now costs him nothing.

Fiedler asserts that the "No! in Thunder"—with which he does identify himself—"is never partisan; it infuriates Our Side as well as Theirs, reveals that all Sides are one, insofar as they are all yea-sayers and hence all liars" (*No* 7). Thus Fiedler, as a spokesman for the "No! in Thunder," seems to take a position which avowedly transcends all "partisan" wrangling and therefore remains himself above the battle, innocent of partisan or political involvement. Fiedler's presentation of the "No in Thunder!" seems essentially vacuous for the very reasons presented in his evocation of the "commitment to truth" in great literature—which comes when a writer judges not merely others but himself or herself as well.

Fiedler's most famous, most ambitious, and longest book, *Love and Death in the American Novel*, reveals similar ambiguities. To most readers, the book lives as a celebration of the peculiarly American romance between two males of different races, both escaping the chains of society as personified in women. And it is true that Fiedler finds in such romances the "No! in thunder!" which is now for him the mark of great literature. The difference between Tom Sawyer and Huckleberry Finn lies in the depth of their respective renunciations:

Huck ends with a total renunciation, not only of Aunt Sally but implicitly of Tom, too; for he learns at last that the world of boys sustains the world of mothers, privileged make-believe understraps "sivilization"... He rejects not only the claims which sanctify slavery (that was easy enough in 1884), but also those which sanctify work, duty, home, cleanliness, marriage, chivalry—even motherhood! (*Love and Death* 587)

However, it is worth remembering that Fiedler throughout his study argues that the evocation of male comradeship, whether in Cooper, Melville, or Twain, begins with an imaginative failure to grow up, a failure to accomplish the "qualifying act of moral adulthood," the acknowledgement of one's involvement in society's ills, the same failure for which Fiedler had earlier criticised both Alger Hiss and his own generation of liberal intellectuals. Likewise, Fiedler's eagerness to reveal the "dirty," hidden significance of books apparently dealing with asexual innocence is comparable to his earlier attempt to criticize the political versions of the myth of innocence. Fiedler's emphasis on the "duplicity" of the classic American novel points to his own concern for the truth and his belief that it is his task as critic to reveal the hidden, sometimes unpleasant or unsavory truths of his own tradition. His references to Marxism and psychoanalysis suggest that his treatment of the mythology of American literature is critical, an unmasking of the "duplicity" of myth in the name of truth and reason.

Yet the overall mood of the book is one of celebration. After all, the "total renunciation" which Huck achieves is, in Fiedler's reading, not without its rewards for him and for us. It makes possible the affirmation of innocence offered by the black victim to the white offender. In Fiedler's words,

Certainly, our classic writers assure us that when we have been cut off or have cut ourselves off from the sources of life, he ("our dark-skinned beloved") will receive us without rancor or the insult of forgiveness. (*Love and Death* 368)

This is too good to be true—" 'It's too good for true, honey,' Jim says to Huck. 'It's too good for true' " (*Love and Death* 369)—and thus it is sentimental, but it is also too good to reject either in the name of reason or heterosexual maturity. Instead, Fiedler rejects the critical task of analysis. He refuses to make use of either Marxism or psychoanalysis in a systematic way—a refusal made more damaging because of his own idiosyncratic handling of each—thereby making it impossible for him to analyze the "archetypes" he discovers. Instead, he simply celebrates their raw emotional power.

If in *Love and Death* Fiedler had trouble making up his mind as to whether he wished to finally celebrate innocence or the achievement of maturity, the events of the sixties helped him decide that innocence, particularly political innocence, would be the more attractive stance. Perhaps if Fiedler had not been "busted" on a charge of "maintaining a premise" (*Busted* 139, 159) where marijuana was consumed, he might have viewed his life differently; perhaps he would have written an autobiographical work dealing with the ambiguities of middle age. However, Fiedler was busted and his autobiographical statement, *Being Busted* (1969), presents his life as a series of struggles between himself and one or another establishment.

Fiedler had once expressed the wish that Alger Hiss and Julius Rosenberg not proclaim their innocence but proudly admit their deeds and announce their adherence to a higher law than that of the United States legal system. How much more satisfying, he had mused, to hear in court the clear expression of conflicting principles rather than grubby debates over minute factual details. But Fiedler himself, suddenly put in the position that Alger Hiss and the Rosenbergs claimed for themselves—a defendant framed by the establishment for political reasons—does not rise to the occasion. One might argue that such a comparison is not fair, since in fact Fiedler was really innocent of the legal charges against him while Hiss and the Rosenbergs were really guilty. However, Fiedler himself admits that his account has been tailored to fit the difficulties of his legal situation—the truth has had to come second to what is expedient:

And, indeed, though what I wrote is nothing but the truth, it is not quite the whole truth—not even in the approximate sense in which that phrase is used in courtrooms. It is, however, as much of the truth as I could then and can now tell without endangering other people whose lives and fates are inextricably bound up with my own. I might have said a little more without my lawyer looking over my shoulder; but I am not finally unhappy that the account I give is incomplete and must remain so forever. (*Busted* 128)

If one were to indulge in the same kind of analysis that Fiedler does in his essays on Hiss and the Rosenbergs, one might argue that this passage constitutes a kind of "code" statement implying without explicitly admitting legal guilt. After all, if Fiedler can't tell all the truth because to do so would cause him to endanger "other people whose lives and fates are inextricably bound up with my own," isn't it reasonable to assume that what he is saying is that he can't tell the reader that members of his own family used illegal substances, because to do so would "endanger them"? And, of course, it would endanger Fiedler himself as well. He was charged, after all, not with personal consumption of marijuana, but simply with "maintaining a premise" where it was used by others, a charge which he explicitly denies throughout *Being Busted*. So was he after all guilty as charged? Here is the seemingly unqualified "judgment" which Fiedler asserts he and his wife have made of themselves:

> That judgment was and remains "innocent": collectively and individually innocent, not only of the absurd police charges (about which there was never any real doubt), but also of having in any essential way failed our own personal codes.
>
> To make this clear to everyone, my wife and I intend to keep insisting not just that we are "not guilty," which is a legal formula only, but that we are "innocent," in the full sense of the word. We will make this assertion in conversation, bugged or not bugged, in writing public and private, as well as before any judge and jury we may eventually have to face. . . . (*Busted* 249)

But such protestations of total innocence were exactly what troubled Fiedler most about Hiss and the Rosenbergs—and moreover, Hiss and the Rosenbergs both continued to insist on their innocence in exactly the way Fiedler describes his own conduct above. The issue here is not whether anybody at Fiedler's house ever smoked grass. The issue is to what extent Fiedler regained the pose of innocence which in *An End to Innocence* he had ascribed to his own generation. I would argue that Fiedler in *Being Busted* and in later works assumes a pose of political innocence, of one unimplicated in the complexities of political life, the pose of a permanent outsider. In the preface to *Being Busted*, Fiedler describes the "true subject" of the book as "the endless war, sometimes cold, sometimes hot, between the dissenter and his imperfect society" (*Busted* 7). The qualifying adjective for "society" and the lack of one for "dissenter" implies the pose of innocence to which I allude. The Fiedler of *Being Busted* tells us that he has achieved the moral purity of a stance beyond politics:

> I am, in fact, adverse to politics itself as ordinarily defined. . . only saying with Bartleby the Scrivener, "I would prefer not to," which is good unmelodramatic American for the satanic Latin of "Non serviam." (*Busted* 234),

The stance of *Being Busted* is twofold: on the one hand, Fiedler is perceived as and generally accepts the role of a cultural rebel, a "spokesman for an adversary culture more progressive, more revolutionary" (*Busted* 234) than the traditional high culture. On the other hand, he rejects the political involvements which led him first to radical Marxism, then to Trotskyism, then to anti-communist liberalism. In cultural matters he is willing to take a stand, even though it involves misunderstanding, even though his "new identity" as a cultural rebel "robs me of a dimension" (*Busted* 230). But he will no longer commit himself to a specific political program, to any political identity more specific than that of "dissenter."

What Was Literature? reveals the consequences of this split between culture and politics. The essays which make up *What Was Literature?* argue for a divorce between emotion and reason in order to liberate the passions. The implicit stance is that of the "outsider," the self-marginalized individual, the clown, whose ideas, whatever their apparent audacity, can never be cause for guilt because they are not meant to be taken seriously, are not meant to be put into practice. The voice of the dissenter is the voice of the innocent, whatever the personal idiosyncracies of the dissident. And because Fiedler is a political innocent, he is free to confess to bad taste or bad manners without really risking anything, without accepting responsibility.

In the foreword to *No! in Thunder* Fiedler insisted that

I am not, let it be clear, for all my occasional hamminess, an entertainer.... My aim is to create not the shallow joy felt in the presence of virtuosity but the difficult pleasure possible only to one recognizing a truth which involves a personal humiliation or the surrender of values long held. (*No!* x)

In *What Was Literature?* such scruples have been forgotten. Fiedler is now "bugged" to realize that most readers of *Love and Death in the American Novel* "are likely to encounter it on assignment and in a classroom," when after all he is not an intellectual engaged in the search for truth but an entertainer "paid to allay boredom" (*What* 34). If earlier he had argued that "the practice of art at any time is essentially a moral activity" and that writer and critic shared a common commitment to truth, now he argues that the critic, like the artist, should seek not truth but ecstasy:

The only critical works which long survive...are those which attempt not to prove or disprove, construct or deconstruct anything, but to compel an assent scarcely distinguishable from wonder, like the songs or stories which are their immediate occasion. (*What* 131)

Although Fiedler insists that "I am not suggesting that the search for standards be abandoned completely and that evaluation be confined to noises of admiration or distaste..." (*What* 126), he specifically rejects the traditional belief that literary myth criticism of the sort that he himself has practised "represents an attempt to speak logically, rationally, objectively about the *mythoi* which lie at the heart of all works which please many and please long" (*What* 37).

If criticism should eschew logic and reason, it is not surprising that the primary task of literature itself seems to be to induce the momentary triumph of passion over reason in the reader:

It is indeed an essential function of literature to release in us unnatural impulses—including the need from time to time to go out of our heads—which we otherwise repress or sublimate for the sake of law and order, civilization, sweet reason itself. (*What* 136)

Art moves us "viscerally rather than cerebrally" (*What* 133), and "the most honest name for what we seek in mythic art" is "privileged insanity" (*What* 137).

The critical position at which Fiedler has arrived is at odds with his stance in *An End to Innocence* in many ways, of which the least important is his new interest in popular culture. In *An End to Innocence* he criticized the disjunction between feeling and reason which vitiated liberalism's view of the world. Liberals, he argued, were all too ready to reject reasoned analysis which conflicted with cherished emotions. Both *An End to Innocence* and *No! in Thunder* argued that a commitment to truth, especially unpleasant truths, was the most important requirement for meaningful literary and cultural criticism. And especially in *An End to Innocence*, Fiedler insisted that he remained part of the political tradition which he was criticizing, so that his cultural criticism was essentially self-criticism. In *What was Literature?* all these values have been reversed. A disjunction between reason and emotion is held to be proper and necessary, and it is the function of literature and literary criticism to further this disjunction. Truth, whether unpleasant or otherwise, is no longer an important issue for either literature or criticism. And Fiedler himself, despite his self-dramatizing confessions—quite different from the reflective activity of self-criticism—presents himself as entirely on the side of the angels. He is a radical who takes on the establishment, and the very extremism of his views insures that he will remain "innocent"—without complicity, not responsible, for whatever happens in our society in either culture or politics.

In my closing comments, I will argue that Fiedler's new position is far from "innocent," either in its cultural or its political implications. For Fiedler, elitism in culture and authoritarianism in politics are now the great sins. He sees himself as an anti-elitist in culture, one whose program calls for "Opening up the Canon," as Part Two of *What Was Literature?* is entitled. Politically he is anti-establishment, libertarian, but also democratic and populist (*What* 129, 140). But the implications of his positions are not necessarily as unambiguous as he now believes.

Fiedler intends his emphasis on the mythic power of art to widen the realm of what is considered true art. But if one takes seriously his declaration that the sign of real art is its ability to induce us "to go out of our heads," then his definition becomes enormously restrictive. It seems to rule out some of the most popular classics, such as the works of Jane Austen or Anthony Trollope, or, in popular culture, the songs of Cole Porter or the Gershwins. If "privileged insanity" is the state of mind which true mythic art arouses, then not much true art is around— unless "privileged insanity" means nothing more than the traditional academic formula of "suspension of disbelief." In the name of "Opening up the Canon," Fiedler has formulated a criterion for "literature" which is much more restrictive than those embodied in the canon which he rejects.

Likewise, although Fiedler presents the movement "From Ethics and Aesthetics to Ecstatics" (*What* Chapter 13) as an aspect of his conversion to an anti-elitist, radically democratic, populist stance, his cultural position has no necessary connection with such anti-establishment rhetoric. Indeed, the closest analogue to Fiedler's position is to be found in the writings of a highbrow of the highbrows—Thomas Mann, during Mann's most reactionary, most anti-democratic phase. In *Reflections of a Nonpolitical Man*, written during World War I as a defense of Germany on the basis of the superiority of its authoritarian, hierarchical culture. Mann stresses as strongly as does the later Fiedler the necessarily amoral, irrational, even primitive quality of authentic art. However, while Fiedler makes his argument in the name of a populist justification of popular and mass culture, Mann offers the same theory on behalf of a German high *Kultur* which he opposes to the shallow, "enlightenment" literature of democratic France and England. And if the cultural implications of Mann's argument are precisely the opposite of Fiedler's, the political implications of the thesis point in the opposite direction as well. Furthermore, Mann's political position seems to flow much more directly from his aesthetics than does Fiedler's.

A few quotations suffice to indicate the similarity—and suggest the danger for those who, like Fiedler, attempt to link a renunciation of reason to an anti-establishment position:

It [art] will speak of passion and unreason; it will present, cultivate and celebrate passion and unreason, hold primordial thoughts and instincts in honor, keep them *awake* or reawaken them with great force, the thought and instinct of war, for example. (291)

Art will never be moral in the political sense, never virtuous....It has a basically undependable, treacherous tendency; its joy in scandalous anti reason, its tendency to beauty-creating "barbarism," cannot be rooted out, yes, even if one calls this tendency hysterical, anti-intellectual, and immoral to the point of being a danger to the world....(289)

In short, then: war, heroism of a reactionary type, all the mischief of unreason, will be thinkable and therefore possible so long as art exists.... (291)

For Mann the glorification of war is an important, inevitable aspect of his aesthetics. War, he declares "has nothing at all to do with brutalization, it would signify much more an elevation, intensification, and ennoblement of human life" (339)—at least it would so signify once the viewpoint of mere "civilization," with its privileging of reason, is replaced by the perspective of German high culture, with its emphasis on passion. And, for the Mann of this book, that is what World War I is all about and why a German victory is essential.

I have spent so much time quoting the Mann of the World War I years because it seems to me that his writing reveals the inner significance of the positions at which Fiedler has finally arrived—and how far their implications are from the innocence of the simple "dissenter." But there is a difference between Mann and Fiedler that is also relevant to this essay. After World War I, Mann rethought the ideas that he had worked out with such intensity during the war. If *Reflections of a Nonpolitical Man* in retrospect seems to have at least the seeds of a cultural Nazism embedded in it, Mann's later works, such as *The Magic Mountain* and especially *Doctor Faustus,* embody an impressive and thorough critique of those aspects of German high culture which had some affinity with Nazism. Mann moved from the irresponsibility of the "non-political man" to an acceptance of the burden of political responsibility unique among the modern masters—a burden in which self-criticism was the central task.

Fiedler, on the other hand, has moved from requiring both himself and his generation to accept responsibility for their cultural and political past through self-critical analysis to the celebration of emotion for its own sake, detached from reason and immune to self-criticism. Fiedler himself sees his career as a movement from intellectual elitism to cultural populism, from hypocrisy to honesty. Those who oppose elitism and admire honesty need to study that career closely rather than accept Fiedler's description at face value. In doing so, I believe that we will come to honor the early Fiedler even while rejecting the creed of the later.

The early Fiedler rejected the pose of innocence, particularly political innocence. The later Fiedler has regained his lost innocence by refusing to adopt a specific political position. Instead, he has assumed the pose of the outsider, the clown, the anti-establishment radical. The very fact of having been "busted" becomes, paradoxically, a certification of "innocence," since it certifies his position as an anti-establishment figure. And the more "confessions" he makes about his "pop" tastes, the more his stance as an anti-elitist is guaranteed.

But a meaningful critique of modern culture and politics cannot be based on a vision which rejects political analysis and commitment in order to achieve political innocence. Even cultural analysis will be vitiated when politics is ignored; the attempt to connect culture to politics is an inescapable aspect of the more general attempt to reconcile reason and emotion, which I take to be the fundamental task of the cultural critic. Leslie Fiedler remains one of the few critics who continues to raise large questions without retreating into a special jargon. My critique of his career is premised on a recognition of the importance and significance of the task which he has taken up, the work of cultural criticism. But I would argue, with Theodor Adorno and with the early Leslie Fiedler, that the first insight of the cultural critic must be his or her own complicity with the culture which is criticized.

Notes

[1] I wish to thank my colleague at Michigan State University, Barry Gross, for a reasoned yet passionate response to an earlier version of this paper. I would also like to thank my editor, Adam Sorkin, for his comments and questions and for his generosity in opening his anthology to an essay whose central thesis is so much at odds with his own reading of the same material (see fn. 2).

[2] In contrast, a number of other recent books on both the Rosenbergs and the Hiss case have done much to strengthen the case for Fiedler's fifties' essays. *Perjury* by Allan Weinstein concludes that Fiedler's assumption of Hiss' guilt was correct. Likewise, Weinstein's comment that

For anti-Communists of the liberal left, accepting Hiss' guilt implied renouncing one's own earlier hopes concerning the Soviet Union, the American Communist Party, and the benefits that Communism supposedly held out for American society (515)

bears out Fiedler's view of the cultural significance of what might seem to be a simple question of fact. Incidentally, Weinstein's undocumented statement that Fiedler later "recanted" (551) his position on Hiss is not borne out by Fiedler's 1971 introduction to a new edition of *An End to Innocence*.

The Rosenberg File, by Ronald Radosh and Joyce Milton, argues convincingly that the Rosenbergs were indeed guilty of espionage but that the death sentence was unjustified— precisely Fiedler's point of view in his 1953 essay on the case. *The Rosenberg File*, in its analysis of the use of myth by both sides and in the examples it offers of the kind of "doublethink" by which the Rosenberg's guilt was transmuted into innocence by some (xii-xiii, 329, 340)—points stressed by Fiedler—suggests that a full historical analysis only increases one's respect for Fiedler's essay. Radosh and Milton examine Dickstein's arguments against both Fiedler's essay and a similar analysis by Robert Warshow ("The 'Idealism' of Julius and Ethel Rosenberg" in *The Immediate Experience*) and conclude that "Dickstein's comments do not speak to the critique offered by both Fiedler and Warshow" (55).

Although Harold Rosenberg excoriates Fiedler's point of view as a "vision of wrestling stereotypes, Right and Left wing" in "Couch Liberalism and the Guilty Past" in *The Tradition of the New* (228), the strategy of his essay is to distinguish liberals and independent radicals from communists or fellow travelers by himself stereotyping all communists or communist sympathizers as "fakers, fools and position seekers" (232), "scoundrels" (236), "middle-class careerists, closed both to argument and evidence, impatient with thought, psychopaths of 'radical' conformity" (236), a "sodden group of Philistines" (237). Apparently, only by such name-calling can he make a case against Fiedler's argument that there was indeed a problematic relation between many liberals and communism.

Adam Sorkin's "Politics, Privatism and the Fifties," *Journal of American Culture*, criticizes Fiedler for implying that "The necessities of history deny idealism and call for informing! Adult responsibility requires confessing!" (70). There is no doubt that many readers have found exactly this message in Fiedler's essays on Hiss and the Rosenbergs. But I would argue that Fiedler rejected sentimentality rather than idealism and called on liberals not to confess—presumably few had actually committed either perjury or espionage—but to reexamine their belief in the intrinsic goodness of anybody who was on the left.

[3]Freud's famous declaration that "Where id was, there shall ego be" appears in lecture XXXI, entitled "The Dissection of the Psychical Personality," *New Introductory Lectures on Psychoanalysis* (71). However, my conception of the relation between Freudian analysis and cultural criticism, as well as my stress on self-criticism as a mode of analysis, is most directly indebted to Jurgen Habermas, *Knowledge and Human Interests*, especially chapters 10-12.

[4]Fiedler also commented on the Rosenberg case in a 1952 essay, "The Rosenbergs: A Dialogue," which did not appear for some two decades until the *Collected Essays*.

Works Cited

Adorno, Theodor. "Cultural Criticism and Society." *Prisms*. Trans. Samuel and Shierry Weber. Cambridge: MIT P, 1981. 19-34.

Dickstein, Morris. *Gates of Eden: American Culture in the Sixties*. New York: Basic Books, 1977.

Fiedler, Leslie. *An End to Innocence*. 2nd ed. New York: Stein and Day, 1972.

——— *Being Busted*. New York: Stein and Day, 1969.

——— *Inadvertent Epic*. Introduction by Barrie Hayne. New York: Simon and Schuster, 1979.

——— *Love and Death in the American Novel*. New York: Criterion, 1960.

——— *No! in Thunder*. Boston: Beacon P, 1960.

——— "The Rosenbergs: A Dialogue." *Collected Essays*. 2 vols. New York: Stein and Day, 1971. 2: 199-209.

——— *What Was Literature? Class Culture and Mass Society*. New York: Simon and Schuster, 1982.

Freud, Sigmund. "Lecture XXXI: The Dissection of the Psychical Personality." *New Introductory Lectures on Psychoanalysis*. Trans. and ed. James Strachey. New York: Norton, 1965. 51-71.

Habermas, Jurgen. *Knowledge and Human Interests*. Trans. Jeremy J. Shapiro. Boston: Beacon P, 1971.

Mann, Thomas. *Reflections of a Nonpolitical Man*. Trans. Walter D. Morris. New York: Ungar, 1983.

Radosh, Ronald and Joyce Milton. *The Rosenberg File*. New York: Holt, 1983.

Rosenberg, Harold. "Couch Liberalism and the Guilty Past." *The Tradition of the New*. New York: McGraw-Hill, 1965. 221-40.

Sorkin, Adam J. "Politics, Privatism and the Fifties: Ring Lardner Jr.'s *The Ecstasy of Owen Muir*" *Journal of American Culture* 8. 3 (1985): 59-73.

Wald, Alan. *The New York Intellectuals: The Rise and Decline of the Anti-Stalinist Left from the 1930s to the 1980s.* Chapel Hill: U of North Carolina P, 1987.

Warshow, Robert. "The 'Idealism' of Julius and Ethel Rosenberg." *The Immediate Experience: Movies, Comics, Theatre & Other Aspects of Popular Culture.* Garden City: Doubleday, 1962. 69-81.

Weinstein, Allen. *Perjury: The Hiss-Chambers Case.* New York: Knopf, 1978.

A Fiction of Politically Fantastic "Facts": Robert Coover's *The Public Burning*

Paul A. Orlov

In an oft-quoted harsh review of Robert Coover's *The Public Burning* (1977)—a literary rendition of the historical events surrounding the Rosenberg case—Norman Podhoretz condemns the author for "the freedom [he] grants himself from respect for the evidence, respect for the known facts, by which any historian is bound, no matter how politically tendentious he may be." Ultimately, in fact, Podhoretz charges the book as a whole with being "a lie. And because it hides behind the immunities of artistic freedom to protect itself from being held to the normal standards of truthful discourse, it should not only be called a lie, it should also be called a cowardly lie" (27, 34). But Podhoretz's review is instructively misguided. For not only does the reviewer let his own political bias blind him to the need for aesthetic criteria in evaluation of a novel (as he implicitly imposes a historian's precise task upon a novelist's creative enterprise), but also he fails to see Coover's concern in the work with *questions* of truth and falsehood in the controversial historical episode that is his subject.

It is quite ironic that a reviewer should accuse Coover of not respecting "known facts" and his book of being "a lie," since Coover's fictional treatment of the trial and execution of the Rosenbergs blends the historical and the surreal, recorded "truth" and absurd fantasy, to convey the essentially equivocal reality he finds in the drama. His vision in *The Public Burning* suggests the actually fantastic nature of the political characters and events of the infamous A-bomb spy case and of the political climate prevailing in that era in America when the case unfolded (the time of the Red Scare culminating in the early 1950s). And in the process, Coover's artistic representation of the case's political "facts" powerfully implies that they involved fictions making the meaning of history itself a kind of "lie."

That a novel by Coover about the Rosenbergs would essentially see them as victims of legal deceit bred of political hysteria might have been foretold when, four years before its publication, the novelist turned reviewer himself to comment on a renowned jurist's study of the case, *The Implosion Conspiracy* by Louis Nizer. In a review expressing hostility toward both the book and (in *ad hominem* terms) its author, Coover attacks the work as a simplistic, complacent endorsement of the conviction of the "spies," reflective of Nizer's reactionary, anti-Communist attitude. After conveying these ideas and raising new questions about the nature of the "evidence" the prosecution claimed to have, yet never produced in court for supposed security reasons, Coover concludes:

> Without the famous missing evidence, one can only guess that the F.B.I. was fumbling in the dark, had a hunch they were right or nearly right, and took a chance that by putting maximum pressure on the Rosenbergs they would crack into the spy ring they believed must be operating in the country. And in so doing, and with the cooperation of all parties except perhaps the defense, produced a satire on Anglo-Saxon juris-prudence, Louis Nizer's comforting banalities notwithstanding. (Rev. of *Implosion*, 5)

As if inspired by his own final words in this review, Coover uses *The Public Burning* to satirize savagely the American political psyche of the early '50s—and the legal system it shaped—that determined the Rosenbergs' fate through communal fantasies which distorted all perceptions of fact. For Coover, even if the Rosenbergs were not innocent of all charges against them, they were victims of injustice because their society needed them as scapegoats to support its patriotic myths. And as Kathryn Hume has pointed out in an important essay, the victimization of the Rosenbergs is the consummate example of a pattern prevailing throughout all of Coover's novels: human beings respond to their fundamental sense of vulnerability by creating myths in which they seek protection and meaningfulness; these myths, which include religious and political ideologies, often lead to the scapegoating of individuals sacrificed for what society considers its common good (133, 138-40).

Thus in *The Public Burning*, Coover envisions this pattern resulting from American society's intense need for victims whose ritualized execution shall offer catharsis and reassurance for followers of the political religion of U.S. Democracy's Divine Destiny, at a historical moment when the menace of Communism—dramatized by Soviet acquisition of the A-bomb, the Korean War, and McCarthyism—has unleashed pure panic in every red-white-and-blue heart. The novel projects this national vision of hysteria as a political Manichaeanism in which Uncle Sam, the very embodiment of Good (that is, light and the American Way), opposes in holy global conflict the force of the Phantom, personifying the Evil and darkness of all Communists. In representing the events of such a time, as a nation nurtured by this myth seeks to purge itself of fear of dangerous enemies, Coover envisions the extraordinary sacrificial rite which gives the book its title: since they supposedly conspired to give the Phantom the secret of "the Bomb," exposing Americans to the possibility of a "public burning" by atomic attack by Russia, the Rosenbergs are to be publicly burned—in the electric chair—in New York's Times Square. Culminating in this imagined public burning, originally scheduled for June 18, 1953 (the victims' fourteenth wedding anniversary) but delayed by one night when Supreme Court Justice William Douglas issued a stay of execution that was then revoked, the novel is structured in a manner meant best to reveal the worldview which demanded their deaths.

So the narrative unfolds in chapters alternating between the point-of-view of Uncle Sam (the national temper made tangible), and that of His future Incarnation, then Vice-President and champion Commie-fighter, Richard Nixon. And a key element of the mythic vision expressed in this structure, also anticipated by his earlier review comment on Nizer's book, is Coover's sense that the entire case, like the execution ceremonies he depicts, was elaborately *staged*, making "history" out of a play based more on artifice than on facts. Writing about Nizer, Coover had stated this indictment related to such a theme:

As a man excited by the dramaturgy of the courtroom and who believes that right judgments flow, not from the testimony so much, but from the styles of the players, he might at least have asked how fair play is possible when the prosecution has so much more rehearsal time and knows what the script is going to be, while the defense has to play it as improvisation theater, not even sure what props are going to be used or where they are coming from. (Rev. of *Implosion* 4-5)

Similarly, in his fictionalized treatment of the times and the sensational "atom spy case" so expressive of them, Coover portrays the historical events as facets of a drama in which the Rosenbergs play roles they do not understand, cast in them by the stagecraft of the State. From the novel's epigraphs through its narrative language and chapter forms (including "Intermezzos") to its final spectacle in Times Square, the work insists upon the "true" story's theatricality.

More specifically, Coover characterizes the Rosenbergs as the doomed antagonists in a politicized *morality* play. In one of his chapters in the story, narrator Nixon makes this clear in his overview of the "fantastically smooth performance" by which presiding Judge Kaufman and prosecutor Saypol manipulated the trial toward its triumphant conviction of the defendants.

Applause, director, actors, script: yes, it was like—and this thought hit me now like a revelation—*it was like a little morality play for our generation!* During the Hiss case, I had felt like a brash kid among seasoned professionals; now my own generation was coming into its own—and this was...our initiation drama, our gateway into History!

Or part of it anyway, for the plot was still unfolding. In the larger drama, of which the Rosenberg episode was a single act, I was a principal actor—if not, before the play is ended, *the* principal actor—but within this scene alone, I was more like a kind of stage manager, an assistant director or producer, a presence more felt than seen. This was true even of the trial itself: I felt somehow the author of it—not of the words so much, for these were, in a sense, improvisations, but rather of the *style* of the performances....(119-20)

Both the rationale for these claims by Nixon and a sly judgment by Coover of the Vice-President's part in creating the climate of the times, are made clear elsewhere in the narrative when Nixon boasts that he has "made Communism a real issue...changed the very course of America and the Free World, and ultimately...made these electrocutions possible." Thus he concludes, "To hell with your goddamned 'McCarthy Era'! *I'm* the one!" (80). But despite the relentlessly self-romanticized way Nixon sees himself as a current influence on and future hope for the nation, he also shows a cynical pragmatism about the place of truth in politics and law when the anti-Communist crusade is at stake. First admitting that the ends justify any means as he thinks of the dirty, Red-baiting tactics he had used to gain election to Congress—"If I hadn't played it that way I wouldn't be where I was now, America's history and that of the entire world would have run a different course, the Phantom might well have had his way with us, maybe none of us would even be here now" (49)—Nixon later implies the same outlook in reflecting on the crucial spy case: "Thus, the Rosenbergs and their lawyers were the only ones not rehearsed, and were in effect having to attempt amateur improvisation theater in the midst of a carefully rehearsed professional drama. Naturally they looked clumsy and unsure of themselves...and so, a bit like uneasy liars" (121). And so the Rosenbergs are condemned not by truth but by a staged manipulation of appearances mandated by patriotic fervor. Indeed, in the America determined to burn the "atom spies," Nixon knows "not merely that convictions depend upon dramatic entertainment, but that justice *is* entertainment" (121).

Underlying the American mythic vision of the time that justifies the scapegoating of the Rosenbergs on these or any terms, is a paranoid perspective that may usefully be understood through an analogy to Yeats's "The Second Coming." Although *The Public Burning* has several epigraphs and is an enormously allusive novel, it never makes any reference to Yeats. Yet his famous poem on an era in which "Things fall apart; the center cannot hold; Mere anarchy is loosed upon the world" and in which a nightmare of the Apocalypse unfolds in the approach of a demonic force, a dark Antichrist "come round at last" (184-5), is strikingly suggestive of the frightened outlook Uncle Sam's loyal servants have on *their* world. As if adapting Yeats's Apocalyptic view to the special circumstances of early 1950s America, Coover depicts their dread of the dark force called the Phantom that seems to threaten them with Atomic annihilation; in their view, the rise of Communism and the Korean War indicate the advent of chaos, subverting that divine order manifested in the American Way. And the novel shows that these sacred assumptions call forth the frenzied reactions in which the nation's sense of "facts"—in all political realities of the time pertinent to their paranoia—becomes quite distorted by their shared nightmarish fantasies.

The novel's Prologue immediately indicates these communal notions of mounting anarchy and resultant danger from the Red enemy without and within. Looking back less than ten years to the end of World War II, Americans see a shifting in the balance of power and a shaking of the foundations of what they deem world order:

How did it happen? The score in the middle of the [1940s] is 1,625,000,000 people for Uncle Sam, only 180,000,000 for the Phantom, and most of them in declining health, thanks to Overlord, German tanks, and the A-bomb.... And yet, suddenly, by the end of the decade, the Phantom has a score of 800,000,000 to Uncle Sam's 540,000,000 and the rest—about 600,000,000 so-called neutrals—are adrift. What went wrong? Who's responsible? People wonder if this is what the astronomers are talking about when they speak of the "red shift": God drifting away and losing touch. The Phantom's dark gospel has spread throughout the world, he has acquired dozens of new disguises and devices, Uncle Sam's most private councils have been infiltrated. (13-14)

While the people of light wonder how the game thus began going against them, Uncle Sam's divine lieutenant, the Reverend Billy Graham, speaks on television to stress the theological implications of the vast political struggle and the Apocalyptic nature of the stakes: " 'Communism is a fanatical religion,' he declares, 'a great sinister anti-Christian movement masterminded by Satan, that has declared war upon the Christian God! Only as millions of Americans turn to Jesus Christ can the nation be spared the onslaught of a demon-possessed Communism!' " (11-12).

Soon Russia explodes her first A-bomb, cries of "treason" ring out throughout America, and the assumption of an espionage ring responsible for the theft of our atomic secrets—called by FBI Director and Chief Crimebuster J. Edgar Hoover "the Crime of the Century" (17)—leads to the arrest, trial, and conviction of the Rosenbergs. These convicted "spies" are presumed to be at the center of the dark force making "things fall apart," and Hoover, Graham, and others find confirmation of their guilt in the fact that the couple renounced their Judaic faith, never refer to a Supreme Being, and talk always about "Peace, bread, and roses...their materialist dream" of Marxist doctrine (104-05). So both the form and the scene of these public enemies' punishment are carefully chosen to help save the spirit of the theocratic Democracy and to stem

the sinister tide of the un-American (and *thus* unholy) forces threatening
to engulf the nation:

It is thought that such an event might provoke open confessions: the Rosenbergs, until
now tight-lipped and unrepentant, might at last, once on stage and the lights up, perceive
their national role and fulfill it, freeing themselves before their deaths from the Phantom's
dark mysterious power, unburdening themselves for the people, and might thereby bring
others as well—to the altar, as it were—to cleanse their souls of the Phantom's taint.
Many believe, moreover, that such a communal pageant is just what the troubled nation
needs right now to renew its sinking spirit. Something archetypal, tragic, exemplary. (3-
4)

And the site chosen is crucial to the cause as well. Not only is Times
Square the major gathering place in America's greatest city, and thus
supremely suited for the Rosenberg drama's didactic conclusion meant
to both educate and entertain "the people." More meaningfully, it is
also "an American holy place long associated with festivals of rebirth,"
a fitting connection for the close of the so-called "Easter trial" of those
evil exemplars whose deaths will symbolize a "fierce public exorcism"
needed to restore strength and life to the Chosen People's body politic.
(3-4) Finally, these reasons, as well as its link to the newspaper "naming"
it and reporting the sense of the nation's experiences, make Times Square,
which "is not a square at all, of course" (5), a vital *center*—a center
of American consciousness emblematic of that mythic "center" which
(in Yeatsian terms) a triumph over darkness should again allow to "hold."
   As America awaits this great ceremony of salvation, Coover's novel
indicates the spurious nature of the political drama being played out,
through the news issuing from that center, through the thoughts of Nixon,
and through the lessons of Uncle Sam on stage-and state-craft. Emanating
from the "holy place" is the daily disclosure of what the people take
as received truth, from a sacred source:

The Friday-morning commuters into the center gather, as is their ancient custom, before
their great civic monument, *The New York Times*, there to commune with the latest
transactions of the Spirit of History as made manifest in all the words and deeds of living
and dying men fit to print. On great slabs of stone, lead, and zinc, words and pictures
appear and disappear, different ones every day, different yet somehow reassuringly familiar.
(188)

That the *Times*'s ongoing record of the times is "reassuringly familiar"
because it simplifies and thus falsifies the complex truths of reality, is
expressed by Julius Rosenberg's perceptions of the paper:

He used to think that if he could just find his way onto these tablets everything would be all right, but now he knows this is impossible: nothing living ever appears here at all, only presumptions, newly fleshed out from day to day, keeping intact that vast, intricate, yet static tableau—*The New York Times*'s finest creation—within which a reasonable and orderly picture of life can unfold. No matter how crazy it is...it dismays him to see cruelty politely concealed in data, madness taken for granted and even honored, truth buried away and rotting in all that ex cathedra trivia—my God! something terrible is about to happen, and they have time to editorialize on mustaches, advertise pink cigarettes for weddings, and report on a lost parakeet! Ah, sometimes he just wants to destroy all this so-called history so that history can start again. (192-93)

Amidst such a time in which pseudo-history is made from "presumptions, newly fleshed out from day to day," the individual can readily be cast in a role demanded by the play of unfolding events as society perceives them. Thus the authorial voice reflects, "In the old days, before *The New York Times*, if you wished to destroy a man, you inscribed his name on a pot and smashed it. Or stuck a clay image with a pin. Now you attach his name to a sin and print it. Such an act is beyond mere insult or information, it is a magical disturbance of History. It is a holy act and an act of defilement at the same time" (194-95).

Under the influence of the falsified "truths" and complacent myths of the historical moment it reads in these pages, the nation responds hysterically to a temporary delay in the executing of those "spies" it has cast as official scapegoats:

And as the fatal midnight hour, when all evil things have power, closes down on them, the children of Uncle Sam, slipping uneasily into their beds, are beset with nightmare visions of Soviet tanks in Berlin, dead brothers lying across the cold wastes of Korea, spreading pornography and creeping socialism, Phantomized black and yellow people rising up in Africa and Asia in numbers not even Lothrop Stoddard could have foreseen, and the Rosenbergs, grown monstrous, octopuslike as Irving Saypol depicted them, breaking out of their cells, smashing down the walls of Sing Sing with their tentacles, and descending upon the city like the Beast from 20,000 Fathoms....(107)

We are easily reminded that the novelist's vision of these nightmarish fantasies is no more fantastic than the facts of the time he is caricaturing, by a source like historian David Caute's authoritative study *The Great Fear*. After quoting Judge Kaufman's comments on the Rosenbergs' "diabolical conspiracy to destroy a God-fearing nation" and guilt in causing the "Communist aggression in Korea," Caute offers a sarcastic summation: "Yes, Julius Rosenberg, seventy-ninth in his class of eighty-five at City College, his wife, who had left school at the age of fifteen, and her brother, David Greenglass, a simple and by all reports rather incompetent machinist, had among them contrived to give Russia the bomb 'years before our best scientists predicted Russia would perfect the bomb.' Even allowing for the temper of the time, one can only marvel at the judge's ignorance" (67). Moreover, even the recent study *The Rosenberg File*, which offers a much more conservative view of the case and its protagonists' actions than does critic/novelist Coover, concedes that expert scientific testimony has established David Greenglass' incapacity to transmit the knowledge needed for "the secret" of the bomb (Radosh and Milton 433). This volume's authors, Ronald Radosh and Joyce Milton, end their chapter on the "scientific evidence" in the case by quoting a long-suppressed startling admission by General Leslie Groves, military chief of the Manhattan Project that developed the atomic bomb. Groves, "the man who had done the most to promote the myth of an 'atomic secret,' " after U.S. nuclear monopoly was lost, admitted secretly to the AEC: "I think that the data that went out in the case of the Rosenbergs was of minor value. I would never say that publicly. Again...it should be kept very quiet, because irrespective of the value of that in the overall picture, the Rosenbergs deserved to hang...." (449). This admission reminds us that at the time of the "atomic spy" case's events, "the fantastic [was] beginning to be accepted as fact," as the novel's "Prologue" notes, quoting *Newsweek* (18)!

Thus in the novel, against this backdrop of events, Uncle Sam—the blustering bully and crudely arrogant superhero personifying the nation—reveals to Dick Nixon and others the contrived nature of the spy case he is using to dramatize the "facts" of history. Impatiently dismissing Nixon's qualms about the doubtful "evidence" used to convict the Rosenbergs, Uncle Sam angrily exclaims, "So all that courtroom splutteration was a frame up...what trial isn't?... Hell, *all* courtroom testimony about the past is ipso facto and teetotaciously a baldface lie, ain't that so?... Like history itself—all more or less bunk, as Henry Ford liked to say...the fatal slantindicular futility of Fact! Appearances, my boy, appearances! Practical politics consists in ignorin' facts! *Opinion* ultimately governs the world!" (86). Having been thus tutored in the niceties of statecraft, Uncle Sam's future Incarnation reflects, "Times Square, the circus atmosphere, the special ceremonies: form, *form*, that's what it always comes down to! In statemanship get the formalities right, never mind the moralities..." (91). Just so, when Uncle Sam furiously confronts Justice Douglas about the stay of execution the latter has ordered due to uncertainties regarding the Rosenbergs' guilt, he says, "Ain't no such thing as cold truth, hoss...the law and your bleedin' heart be *damned*! Watch out, my friend, morality is a private and costly luxury" (76).

Indeed, at this moment of critical struggle against the disorder and dangers posed by the Phantom, America will admit no uncertainties about *its* version of truth, for it sees the Phantom as the very "Creator of Ambiguities" (336) undermining the mythic guarantee of ultimate star-spangled supremacy. Morality must be forgotten as a "costly luxury" because it blocks the nation's pragmatic demand for a comforting catharsis reassuring *all* that evil has been overcome. So complacency about its vision of history convinces the nation of its right, as well as its need, to burn the Rosenbergs. As a result, the people ironically ignore a production of Arthur Miller's *The Crucible* in a nearby theatre as they swarm toward Times Square for their great national show (489-90). Meanwhile, their leaders gaily joke about the imminent event, such as when Dirksen convulses a crowd of Senators when he quips about the Rosenbergs' taking the Fifth Amendment in their trial, "they refused to answer on the grounds that it might tend to incinerate them!" (51). Similarly Vice-President Nixon chuckles in admiration over the way Prosecutor Saypol had been able "to make what might later seem like nothing more than a series of overlapping fictions cohere into a convincing *semblance* of historical continuity and logical truth—at least long enough to wrest a guilty verdict from an impressed jury" (122; italics mine).

Not just Coover's extensive research as a basis for his fictional treatment of the Rosenbergs' fate, but important nonfictional studies of the case as well, underscore the invalidity of conservative reviewer Podhoretz's charge that the novelist's re-creation of the historical episode—showing a lack of respect for "the evidence" and "known facts"—is "a lie." Actually, as parts of the foregoing discussion have already indicated, the core of Coover's vision of early 1950s America and the case itself is quite consistent with the "known facts." And examination of two key historical discussions of the Rosenberg case reveals that the fundamental facts in them are complementary to, rather than in conflict with, the essential "truths" informing *The Public Burning*'s satiric political art. Underlying the inception of the historical episode, after all, were not only a climate of political hysteria, but also fantastical characters upon whom the strange times conferred a credibility and power otherwise unbelievable—characters such as FBI Director J. Edgar Hoover and crucial prosecution witness Harry Gold. The novel's Prologue slyly suggests the unreality of Hoover's worldview both by echoing his famous pronouncements and by noting that his career "as America's Top Cop" was "contemporaneous with that of Mickey Mouse": As news of Russia's first atomic bomb test spreads, Hoover reflects, "Of course it's a spy ring, has to be, it always is. I *mean*, there's only one secret, isn't there? We had it, now they've got it, it's that simple. He's been warning them this would happen since 1937. The enemy within. Now, just look! Jumping Jehoshapat!" So he "whacks the intercom with his thick fists and cries: 'The secret of the atom bomb has been stolen! Mobilize every resource! Find the thieves!' " (15) Later in the novel, narrator Nixon confides, "I had a lot of contacts over at the Bureau, and I knew what kind of crazy and dangerous place it was—Hoover was in many ways a complete looney, arbitrary in his power and pampered like a Caesar, and if he dreamed up a spy network one day, then by God it *existed*. Doubt was out" (370-71). And Harry Gold (whose testimony led the government to David Greenglass and then Julius Rosenberg in its hunt for the atomic bomb "thieves") was a perfect pawn in the game to establish the spy network a Hoover "dreamed up," given his own extraordinary skills in fabricating facts from fantasies. The novel readily portrays this quality of Gold's from fact, not fictional flourish, in dealing with a man who played "weird baseball games with decks of cards, inventing a whole league of eight teams with all their players, playing out full seasons, keeping all the box scores and statistics, even taking note of what they looked like!" (124) When initially questioned by the government as the alleged "courier-link" between Rosenberg and Greenglass, in the bomb theft plot, he made "no mention of Greenglass or A-bomb sketches either—all this had come later after Gold had had several helpful sessions with the FBI. But even after Gold had begun to 'remember' Greenglass, there had *still* been no Jell-O box [the supposed signal that Gold was authorized by Rosenberg to receive the bomb drawings] and no Julius..." (125). But thanks to the government's effective use of this amazing witness, notes Nixon, "More than once what had looked like a complete Gold fantasy had resulted in arrests and confessions, almost as though he were dreaming the world into being. Maybe *he* was the real playwright here. And maybe the Rosenbergs quite reasonably feared some irrevocable casting" on Gold's part (126).

Despite the strongly liberal bias from which Coover clearly writes and despite his lack of access (while doing research for the novel) to much factual evidence (long suppressed by the government in FBI secret files), two major non-fictional studies of the Rosenberg case, both of which reveal and discuss newly released evidence, reach conclusions congruent with the main thrust of the political "fiction" now before us. In an edition of their *Invitation to an Inquest* updated with facts drawn from the previously unavailable FBI files, Walter and Miriam Schneir conclude that: Harry Gold was a notorious liar and unreliable witness whose testimony was carefully shaped by FBI questioning and coaching (see 363-70, 420, 422-24); Gold and David Greenglass (Ethel Rosenberg's own brother), incarcerated together in the months before the March, 1951 trial, collaborated with the government to make possible the "fantastic hoax" of the case (422); and the case as a whole was a premeditated frame-up based on no real evidence of espionage against the Rosenbergs (see 430-31 and 467-78). The Schneirs' research in the newly opened files leads to their labeling Hoover and the FBI—crucial contributors to the prosecution of the Rosenbergs—as "masters of deceit" in suppressing and manipulating facts.[1] Of course, the Schneirs' interpretation of evidence may be somewhat suspect in view of their emphatically pro-Rosenberg slant. Yet the more moderate *The Rosenberg File*, in its own way, also significantly validates the view of the case underlying *The Public Burning*. For even though Radosh and Milton have quarreled sharply with the Schneirs over interpretations of the case's facts[2] and by no means see the Rosenbergs *merely* as innocent victims, they nonetheless conclude that the Rosenbergs were *fundamentally* "scapegoats, condemned to death less because of the nature and seriousness of their crime than because at a particular moment in time their deaths served a cathartic function..." (448). Strikingly like Coover in this view of the case, the historians also share his perspective on the highly equivocal nature of all the facts involved. Indeed, they stress the many problems of an attempt to find the "truth" of the historical episode; as their volume's subtitle asserts, only an informed *"search for the truth"* is possible. However, enough certainties emerge from their objective research to convince them (in essential agreement with the novelist) that "the fate of the Rosenbergs remains a blot on America's conscience" (453) because of many violations of legal justice in the prosecution of "the spies." And in a remarkable analogue to a fictionalizing of the case in terms of the political mythology incarnate in Uncle Sam (opposing the evil Phantom), *The Rosenberg File*'s "Epilogue" closes with this somber judgment: "But if the Rosenberg case has an ultimate moral, it is precisely to point up the dangers of adhering to an unexamined political myth" (453). Thus it is ultimately clear that Coover's treatment of the case, far from being "a lie," is instead a searching fictional *response to* the essential lies with which we are troublingly confronted by the historical fact of the Rosenbergs' fate.

At last, then, Coover's commentary on the American transforming of fantasies into "facts" in the Rosenberg case finds particularly telling expression through his metaphoric use of a 3-D movie. In a very symbolic chapter punningly entitled "Third Dementia,"[3] we observe the odyssey of an anonymous man who, emerging from a darkened theatre ironically named "Trans-Lux" (beyond light) where he has seen the scary "House of Wax," and still wearing the weird 3-D glasses he has forgotten to remove, views outside reality in an irrationally distorted manner: "One man, still somewhat possessed by the images of famous historical persons going up in flames, their waxy faces melting horrifically, their stiffened bodies crashing forward into his lap, is disoriented by this new swirl of pictures out in the street" (283). It becomes evident that this anonym is Everyman, an emblem of America's vision of fearful fantasies experienced as facts, as if the horror film's illusions are mere metaphors for the contemporary world; the nation's paranoia about atomic attack is imaged forth on the screen as "the whole room explodes, strewing the audience with burning debris. He reaches, his clothes smoking, feeling like one molten in the furnace, hit by the winged shaft of fate, and run over on the tracks of history, a curb" (284). His mind controlled by illusions, this symbolically typical citizen cannot distinguish a movie lobby from the stage set with an electric chair, in the wanderings that lead to the public burning:

It's all coming together—the stampeding masses, the creeping socialism and exploding waxworks, the tracks of history and time-lapse overviews—into the one image that has been pursuing him through all his sleepless nights, the billowing succubus he's been nurturing for nine months now, ever since the new hydrogen-bomb tests at Eniwetok: yes, the final spectacle, the one and only atomic holocaust, he's giving birth to it at last. Like the mad artist [played by Vincent Price], we're all going to die horrible fiery deaths, and there's nothing we can do to stop it...it's in the script.... (286)

Obsessed by these grotesque images of the birth of a monstrous destructive force of death, like the rough Beast of Apocalypse in Yeats's "The Second Coming," the man finally staggers into the electric chair himself, as if compelled to identify with both victims and executioners in an attempt to save the nation by supreme sacrifice. But policemen soon subdue and remove him, and "he passes out" (having been drugged) "thinking: well, that does it. I've done everything I can, and what's come of it? A few bruises. A few laughs for the condemned. A misspent Friday, a curious episode on the way to Armageddon, nothing more" (288).

Likewise, when the vast throng in Times Square recovers its calm moments before the execution ceremonies, after an apparent descent by the Phantom in the form of a power blackout, the viewpoint of the people of light is that of very relieved moviegoers: "Nothing has really happened.... It's like coming out of a scary movie—nothing but camera tricks, the illusory marvels and disasters of Cinerama and 3-D, th-th-that's all, f-folks! Lights up and laugh!" (496). And so one show evolves into another, as, with "lights up" and the crowd figuratively laughing with the joy of rites of salvation, the Rosenbergs enter the stage (of history) and die. Thus Coover's portrayal of the epiphany involved in the moment of Ethel's death: as the electric charge hits, her body

is whipped like a sail in a high wind, flapping out at the people like one of those trick images in a 3-D movie, making them scream and duck and pray for deliverance. Her body, sizzling and popping like firecrackers, lights up with the force of the current, casting a flickering radiance on all those around her, and so she burns—and burns—and burns—as though held aloft by her own incandescent will and haloed about by all the gleaming great of the nation— (517)

In the light of this all-too-real vision summing up the temper of the times and Coover's overall illumination of a haunting political episode made from literally fantastic facts, the most apt final words for *The Public Burning* are those of narrator Nixon, that quintessential man of the age, in the Epilogue: hours after the epoch-making event in Times Square, he reflects, that it "was like something out of *Fantasia* or *The Book of Revelation*" (526)—which are apparently about the same in the worldview here exposed.

Notes

[1] This essential premise is developed in Chapter 34 of the Schneirs' study (432-66), which is pointedly called "Masters of Deceit." This ironic chapter title is borrowed from the title of FBI Director Hoover's own 1958 book.

[2] See the detailed, heated 1983 argument between these two pairs of historians in " 'Invitation to an Inquest': An Exchange," in *The New York Review of Books*.

[3] For an extensive discussion of this chapter in the novel, with a focus largely different from my own, see Louis Gallo, "Nixon and the 'House of Wax': An Emblematic Episode in Coover's *The Public Burning*."

Works Cited

Caute, David. *The Great Fear: The Anti-Communist Purge Under Truman and Eisenhower*. New York: Simon and Schuster, 1978.

Coover, Robert. *The Public Burning*. New York: Viking Press, 1977.

———. Rev. of *The Implosion Conspiracy*, by Louis Nizer. *New York Times Book Review* 11 February 1973: 4-5.

Gallo, Louis. "Nixon and the 'House of Wax': An Emblematic Episode in Coover's *The Public Burning*." *Critique: Studies in Modern Fiction* 23 (Spring 1982): 43-51.

Hume, Kathryn. "Robert Coover's Fiction: The Naked and the Mythic." *Novel* 12 (1979): 127-148.

" 'Invitation to an Inquest': An Exchange." *The New York Review of Books* 29 September 1983: 55-63.

Podhoretz, Norman. "Uncle Sam and the Phantom." Rev. of *The Public Burning*, by Robert Coover. *Saturday Review* 17 September 1977: 27, 34.

Radosh, Ronald, and Joyce Milton. *The Rosenberg File: A Search for the Truth*. New York: Vintage Books/Random House, 1984.

Schneir, Walter, and Miriam Schneir. *Invitation to an Inquest*. New York: Pantheon Books, 1983.

Yeats, W.B. *The Collected Poems of W.B. Yeats*. Definitive Edition. New York: Macmillan, 1956.

Grace Paley's Community:
Gradual Epiphanies in the Meantime

Barbara Eckstein

> ...I live now
> not as a leap
> but a succession of brief, amazing movements
> each one making possible the next

> Adrienne Rich, "From a Survivor"

1

The form of Grace Paley's stories is innovative, avant-garde, some say.[1] The technique of her conversational stories drives them by means different from the narrative of Henry James, the epiphanies of James Joyce, the drama of Ernest Hemingway, or the severe irony of Flannery O'Connor. Her omission of quotation marks is more than an incidental choice. The absence of quotation marks draws dialogue together with details of thought, character, and place. All are one with conversation, and conversation is the form of Paley's stories. Conversation creates a community that defies the kind of alienation which inhabits much twentieth-century fiction, especially that from the United States, and that eschews the accompanying romantic self misunderstood by a hostile world. Paley's community does exist within a hostile world where characters are sometimes alone, sometimes misunderstood, but their thoughts, their tables and chairs, their very selves are a part of an ongoing conversation which is necessary, evolving life. Often conversation is with the reader made confidante. But even when the characters share their stories among themselves, the reader is not the observer of drama—as in the conversations of Hemingway, or even James. Paley's reader is not a guest in the house.

The form of Paley's stories resists alienation, romantic self-absorption, and a sense of epiphanic change. Over the course of her thirty-year career as a writer of short fiction, her stories demonstrate a consistent distrust of the wounded, alienated self and develop an understanding of the evolutionary nature of change. Change often recognized in a moment happens in a lifetime or lifetimes of days: a

Paley character occasionally finds herself changed one day, but she is never in a moment devastated or reborn. This evolutionary change has a domestic quality usually considered feminine. It is, for example, a sense of change born of housework always undone simultaneous to its doing. Housework requires patience, persistence, modest expectations, but a vision of some tangible improvement. A sense of gradual change also arises from child-rearing. Only if a parent persists in certain daily repetitions will a child's inevitable change be in a direction the parent desires. The evolutionary change evident in nature and domesticity is not the change usually associated with politics. But in Paley's fiction personal and public survival come to depend on the persistence and patience inherent in this sense of gradual change.

From the beginning of her writing career, Paley has said that she writes stories out of her concern for women, women and children, women and men (Lidoff 5-6). The subject of women and Paley's reputation as a devoted anti-war activist have made her a particular favorite of feminists and peace activists who find in her fiction confirmation of their assumptions.[2] Though both feminism and pacificism are plural ideologies, Paley seems comfortable in their company. (For example, in a reading in New Orleans, she proposed on stage what many feminists and pacifists would, that the leadership of women is the world's best hope for humane life.) Without questioning the author's integrity as a political being in the world, I would like to look at the development of her fiction from 1959-85 and consider just exactly what it does suggest, over time, about women, peace, politics, and gradual epiphanies in the meantime.

To discover the politics and the plots of Paley's fiction, I ask of the stories how they define love and community,[3] two entities which, for Paley, may be very nearly the same thing. I question the nature of sexual love—both in and out of marriage—love among women, and the love of children and parents. And I want to know in what ways love creates or maintains a community, the parameters of that community, the characters' expectations of the community, and their responsibilities to it. Inherent in *The Little Disturbances of Man* (1959), *Enormous Changes at the Last Minute* (1974), and *Later the Same Day* (1985) is the development of a love, a community, surviving through its defiance of alienation and self-absorption and its skepticism about epiphanic change.

2

The sexual love of women for men is a significant motivation in a large number of Paley's stories, and yet her characters' sexual desires are almost free from the romantic expectations that accompany desire

in most Western fiction by women and men both (from the Brontes
to Gilbert Sorrentino). Nevertheless, the roles of women and men do
change over the thirty years of Paley's canon. "A Woman, Young and
Old," in the early collection *The Little Disturbances of Man*, introduces
a romantic mother pining for her French husband who deserted his family
because the children's noise ruined their love affair. She assures the
children they would have loved their father even as she tells them that
they drove him away. Like her mother before her, "she never could call
a spade a spade. She was imagination-minded" (25). In this atmosphere
of male-adoration, her pre-adolescent daughter throws herself at a young
soldier, declaring, "I know exactly what I want" (33). This daughter,
the narrator of the story, tells it straightforwardly from a distance of
years and apparently of wisdom so that neither mother nor daughter
seem to suffer for their obsession—as they would in Hawthorne, Faulkner,
or even Wharton. In fact, the mother finds a new husband who knows
enough French to satisfy her Francophile desires.

Like "A Woman, Young and Old," "Good-bye and Good Luck"
ends, as romances do, with marriage, but again the temporal distance
of the narrative from the events dissolves any pain of longing. The opening
story of the collection, it is told by a middle-aged, unmarried aunt to
her niece and, instead, celebrates the vicissitudes of life. In the first
paragraph she tells the girl, "Change is a fact of God. From this no
one is excused" (9); only her sister, the married woman, ignores such
a fact. Other facts, such as that Rosie, the aunt, was the mistress of
an actor; that he was married; and that, in middle age, after his divorce,
he asks her to marry him are material for another romantic plot that
is turned to wry comedy by distance and a narrator's strong will.

In "The Pale Pink Roast" and "The Contest," romance is not foiled
by narrative distance but by actions of the women characters in the
moment of the story. "The Pale Pink Roast" is a pretty ex-husband
seduced by an ex-wife whose new marriage he knows nothing about.
When he, appalled, does discover this information, she insists she seduced
him for love, not for power or out of regret. Their love-making and
this explanation serve his narcissism and her desire. In "The Contest,"
narrated by a man, he resists the woman's requests to turn their affair
into a preface to marriage. But rather than be a victim of romantic—
what he calls "greedy" (69)—tradition, she lures the man into helping
her win a contest for which the prize is $5,000 and a trip for two to
Israel and Europe. Then because he refuses to marry her, she takes the
trip without him.

The story, "An Interest in Life," in subject and narrative technique,
could easily present the tale of women's alienation and victimization.
A poor, young woman with three small children is left for an indefinite

period of time by a husband sure of his sexual powers. This woman, the narrator of her own story, could make the reader pity her entrapment, fear its power over all women. But instead an old beau, now a father in the suburbs, comes to her aid, attending to her and her children. He tells her that her problems are "the little disturbances of man," not true "suffering" (99). It is in response to this statement that she decides it is time they were lovers. If she is to be perceived as not truly suffering, she might as well not suffer. And yet, after two and a half years, she maintains a vision of a happy sexual reunion with her husband. Like the other women in *The Little Disturbances of Man* she accepts her sexual desire for men, even calls it love, but does not recognize, acknowledge, or even feel it as victimization—even when it might be reasonable to do so. Paley asserts connection to community and survival over time in contrast to the suffering of the self isolated from the context of others.

In Paley's first collection, either the characters themselves or the narrators avoid any equation of sexual desire and romance, particularly romantic obsession for a single individual. Paley, like the male narrator of "The Contest," seems skeptical of the desirability or simply the ability "to breathe eternity into a mortal matter, love" (70). Nevertheless, the women of these early stories pursue the roles of mistress, mother, wife, and live with the consequences of placing the sexual love of men at the center of their consciousness.

Love among women is more implicit than expressed in these early stories of the fifties. The aunt does share her life with her niece in "Goodbye and Good Luck" but, at least in part, because she cannot share it with her married sister who does not understand her and whom she does not understand. Though the household in "A Woman, Young and Old" is a female one, much of the affection is directed at men, even to the extent of luring men-friends away from Aunt Liz. At the story's end the two young sisters are closer, but only because the younger one is in awe of the older one's exploits with a man.

In these stories love of children is earnest but ambiguous and usually subordinated to the sexual love of men. This is certainly true in "A Woman, Young and Old" but also in "The Pale, Pink Roast" in which a young daughter, clearly much loved by both parents, is nevertheless left in the park with a woman whom the child has not seen in some time. This enables the divorced parents to go off alone and have sex. Virginia, the mother in "An Interest in Life," also worries about her children and appreciates her old beau's interest in them, but her sustenance comes from her sexual activity with her old beau and, even more, her sexual vision of her husband's return.

The centricity of men and subordination of children changes with the two stories "The Used Boy-Raisers" and "A Subject of Childhood," joined together in *Little Disturbances* under the title "Two Short Sad Stories from a Long and Happy Life." In the first of these two stories about Faith (who reappears throughout Paley's work), Faith's ex and current husbands, called only Livid and Pallid, complain about the food and take a passing interest in the education of Faith's sons (also Livid's sons). Their elliptical dialogue is part of the story's short-hand of suggestion. Livid tells Pallid

I'm so much away. If you want to think of them as yours, old man, go ahead.

Why, thank you, Pallid had replied, air mail, overwhelmed. Then he implored the boys, when not in use, to play in their own room. He made all efforts to be kind. (128)

The ironic, staccato style undermines any credibility the men's attempts at being fathers might have. In the meantime the children are lively and warm, and Faith is domestically engaged. When the men leave for the day, they are only vaguely appreciated for being "neat" and "shiny"; mostly they "are"—narrator Faith's phrase—"not my concern" (134). Nothing is really expected of these men, as fathers or husbands or lovers. It seems they are worthy not even of Faith's anger, only of the narrator's wry understatement.

Finally, in "A Subject of Childhood," a man is worthy of anger, ash-tray-throwing anger, not because he has deserted Faith or disappointed some expectations, but because he tells her she has been a lousy mother. He, a lover with a key, has roused her sons to a wild wrestling frenzy and blames her when he, and they, get hurt. She, who has "raised these kids, with one hand typing behind my back to earn a living" (139), comes vehemently to her own defense. The bewildered lover retreats, and Faith finds herself alone with the difficult love of children. She sees "through the short fat fingers of my son, interred forever, like a black and white barred king in Alcatraz, my heart lit up in stripes" (145). In this story the woman becomes more mother than lover, but the difference does not set her free. Also, she expresses only an inchoate awareness that her work as a mother must go on both in and outside the home.

The community of *The Little Disturbances of Man* is not yet a society of women. Its space is largely interior, single apartments, and its primary unit the family or a solitary pair of lovers. Most of the action that matters is at home. Except for Aunt Rosie's apartment in "Good-bye and Good Luck," home is the place where women cook and make love, where children play, and from which men leave, either for Africa, like Faith's first husband, or for the neighborhood streets, like her second husband. Women speak mostly to lovers, some to children, and some to women relatives—aunts, grandmothers—but not to women friends.

They value their own sexual desire more than marriage or the company of men, who, nevertheless, largely comprise their world, of which these women expect very little. They assume the responsibility for survival is theirs and so work to feed and educate their children. In this they value the children but not the work *per se*. Furthermore, nothing transcendent, neither God, nature, nor romantic love, much interests these women. Narrative distance, irony, and humor provide Paley's women characters with integrity, but they lack a kind of love and community necessary for a political vision to arise from the gradual, domestic change they experience.

Faith does surprise herself and her husbands when she expresses one opinion whose subject resides outside the walls of her apartment.

I'm against Israel on technical grounds...I believe in the Diaspora. After all, they *are* the chosen people.... But once they're huddled in one little corner of a desert, they're like anyone else... Jews have one hope only—to remain...a victim to aggravate the conscience. (131-32)

After this outburst Faith reflects,

I rarely express my opinion on any serious matter but only live out my destiny, which is to be, until my expiration date, laughingly the servant of man. (132)

This one opinion about the larger world is apparently also one about the smaller world inside her apartment. As a woman, Faith suggests, she too is a victim. But whether she grants herself and women in general the power "to aggravate the conscience" of their various corners of the globe is less clear. Because she expects nothing of her husbands, she seems to regard them as beneath moral law, unworthy of her prodding conscience.

The one story in this first collection which goes outside onto the neighborhood streets is also the one which pursues ideas about the larger world. "In Time Which Made a Monkey of Us All" is the first of two inventor stories with male protagonists. (The other is "This Is a Story about My Friend George, the Toy Inventor" in *Later the Same Day*.) Inventing, for Paley, is a sign for scientific research and the zeal for progress. Eddie, the inventor, tries to concoct a gas so foul-smelling that everyone would run from it but no one would be hurt by it. Thus it could be used as a peaceful weapon of war. But when he experiments with the gas by pumping it into basements all around the neighborhood, though no people are hurt, the gas kills all the animals in his father's pet store, including a beloved monkey. The story, which resonates with

the holocaust of gas chambers and the holocaust of nuclear explosions—
in war and in tests—skillfully raises questions about the culpability of
scientists.[4] Women have noticeably little to do in this story; they are
a minor sexual diversion for the "scientists." They must wait for
publication of Paley's second collection to become political beings outside
the home, much more than sexual creatures complicit with men's
activities.

3

Enormous changes have taken place in the women of Paley's fiction
when they appear again in *Enormous Changes at the Last Minute* (1974).
However, "Wants," the first story in the collection presents those changes
not as sudden but as given—as though the reader has looked up an
old friend after a long hiatus and finds her very different while she,
who has been steadily living her life, sees herself simply as she is. "I
don't understand how time passes," the woman narrator says to the reader
(3). Change occurs at moments of epiphany only in recollection but
not in fact. In fact, time passes.

In "Wants" twenty-seven years of marriage have come and gone
and the woman narrator meets her ex-husband, by chance, on the library
steps. (The action is conspicuously *outside*.) As though it is an accusation
defining the failure of their marriage, he tells her, "You'll always want
nothing." The reader might think he is accusing her of an anti-material
virtue, and yet his statement harkens back to the women in *Little
Disturbances* who expect neither responsible nor moral action from men.
Tolerance can be a failure of love. "It's true, I'm short of requests and
absolute requirements," his ex-wife silently admits in response (5).

But then she tells the reader—not her ex-husband, now departed—
what she does want:

> I want...to be a different person.... I want to be the effective citizen who changes the
> school system and addresses the Board of Estimate on the troubles of this dear urban
> center.
>
> I *had* promised my children to end the war before they grew up.
>
> I wanted to have been married forever to one person, my ex-husband or my present
> one. Either has enough character for a whole life, which as it turns out is really not
> such a long time. (5)

Within the passage of time, this woman has become a citizen of her
neighborhood, of the world at large. As she describes her past, motherhood
prompted active citizenship (an idea repeated in this second collection).
She even had, as it turns out, expectations for her marriage which she
now can admit—at least to the reader.

Time does not, of course, make every woman an active citizen though it does result in change. Mrs. Raftery in "Distance" laments the loss of youth and recognizes change, that is, aging, but not choice, not since she became pregnant long ago and had to marry. Her bitterness about all change in her husband, her son, and her neighborhood follows her assumption that only a narrow destiny can result from certain sexual facts. It seems that interest in neither children nor citizenship has resulted from the sexually of Mrs. Raftery's youth. And though she resents change, time still passes. In resisting evolution with her community, she finds only decay and confusion in old age.

Most all of the women of *Enormous Changes* discover themselves in the midst of change of which sexual desire and marriage play a part. But that desire is no longer the center of consciousness for these women. Even docile, pregnant Kitty in "Come On, Ye Sons of Art" is as warmed by "her friend Faith's grandmother's patchwork quilt" (72) as she is by Jerry, her wheeler-dealer lover. Faith of "Faith in the Afternoon," though unreservedly sad about the loss of her beloved husband Ricardo, accompanies her unhappiness on a visit to her parents at the Children of Judea home where all the material for change resides: her father's poetry and political idealism, her mother's stories of hardships endured by Faith's childhood friends, and love. Faith now articulates the felt loss of a sexual love that an earlier Faith would not admit, but she is not alone with the loss. Furthermore, the acceptance of one change and the possibility of others await her.

The love of parents, children, and women friends are the rising stars in *Enormous Changes*. In "Debt,s" "Living," "Politics," "Faith in a Tree," and "Northeast Playground," the long, sound friendship of women is assumed *a priori*. In "Debts" it is the stories of women friends the persona feels she must tell. In "Living" it is a woman friend whose death Faith mourns with the unceasing loss of her own blood. In "Politics" it is a group of women who act together for the neighborhood. In "Faith in a Tree" it is a community of women in the park who are Faith's family. And in "Northeast Playground" it is a younger generation of women who are the park community. Just as in *Little Disturbances* the reader did not see that women were friends, in *Enormous Changes* we do not see women become friends. They simply are. The recognition that these friendships matter, matter a great deal, is not the epiphany of a single story. Such an enormous change is the slow discovery of what has always been true.

Little Disturbances prepared us more for a devotion to children than to women. About this devotion to children, *Enormous Changes* leaves little doubt. Children are important not only as they are loved by Faith or Kitty but also as creatures in their own right living in a dangerous world. *Enormous Changes* presents three gloomy tales of children destroyed by the intersection of unsuccessful upbringing and a violent world: "Gloomy Tune," "The Little Girl," and "Samuel." We do not see these children through the eyes of parents or friends but through the eyes of an active citizen sympathetic to the fate of children in the larger world.

But the primary role of children in *Enormous Changes* is in the idea that parents become citizens of the world through the impetus of their children. One story, "Faith in a Tree," emphatically demonstrates this idea with which some readers have so whole-heartedly concurred.[5] Though reservations about this idea would be healthy—e.g., many people who are not parents are active participants in ecological struggles or electoral campaigns—it is difficult to argue with one critic's description of this story as Faith's awakening to political activism (Mandel). Faith herself sees a turning point:

I think that is exactly when events turned me around, changing my hairdo, my job uptown, my style of living and telling. Then I met women and men in different lines of work, whose minds were made up and directed out of that sexy playground by my children's heartfelt brains, I thought more and more and every day about the world. (99-100)

Faith's son's insistence that she object when a policeman imposes undue restrictions on demonstrators in the park is an instance of the child being the father of the woman. This is a romantic belief, a more romantic idea of children than any that appears in Paley's first collection. Taken to an extreme, it can be a destructive belief in the inherent goodness of innocence, which is often ignorance. And yet in Faith's description of her son's influence, there is also some appreciation for her own concern "more and more and every day about the world," the thinking which changes a person's "style of living and telling" and loving over time.

A wise child also appears in "The Long-Distance Runner," a story of Faith's foray into a world beyond her personal community. Faith places herself in the hands of a small black girl scout who guides her through a black neighborhood, once Faith's own.[6] Though Paley's women have not believed in romance or God, and have embraced the community of women without needing to believe in it as an idea, they do believe in the moral vision of children. This view is attenuated somewhat by the gloomy-tales children who are subject to the worst of society's influence. Nevertheless, the power of the moral child prevails. At the end of the book, the end of "The Long-Distance Runner," Faith returns home where her sons, now grown, engage in no-nonsense political activity. And Faith reflects on her visit to her old childhood home this way: "She learns as though she was still a child what in the world is coming next" (198). The "as though" is crucial here for it must separate the wonder of childhood from the responsibility of adulthood.

The secularized belief in the leadership of children does encounter complications in a couple stories. The younger generation of mothers in "Northeast Playground" may be another tough generation of female survivors, but this group of prostitutes and drug addicts does not seem to be especially enlightened. And the young hippy, quite full of ideology, who impregnates forty-year-old sociologist Alexandria in "Enormous Changes at the Last Minute" learns from the *older* generation that individual fatherhood warms the cockles in a way communal fatherhood does not. Nevertheless, it is the birth of baby Dennis, fit nicely into the sociological work of his middle-aged mother, that is the cause for celebration. But the celebration *is* of a mortal event within the continuity of father's songs, mother's work, and grandfather's aging, ailing life. Even an enormous change at the last minute like pregnancy at forty has a place prepared for it on the continuum of change.

The community of *Enormous Changes* is one of continuity, one in which choice is always possible but change is never *really* sudden. In the community are precious, old parents, including father of "Conversation with My Father," loyal women, and moral children. The disappointments of sexual love diminish in this context of love. This context, over time, allows for innovation and political action.

The parameters of the community are no longer the family or lovers within the walls of an apartment. Only Mrs. Raftery in "Distance" has stayed in her apartment, and she is jealous of youth. The neighborhood is the locus of action, dramatic and political. From it characters see the past and contemplate the future. They see the nations and neighborhoods they have come from ("Immigrant Story," "Faith in the Afternoon," "The Long-Distance Runner") and the nations and neighborhoods they can affect ("Wants," "Politics," "Faith in a Tree.") They can act to change the larger world only out of the context of their community. Faith, for example, sees the blacks in her old neighborhood ("The Long-Distance Runner") within the context of her remembered childhood there. Though this memory blurs her perception, it does not blind her. She sees that the distance between self and other, like past and present, has been short on reason, long on cruelty. But she tries to run the distance just the same.

Faith's son may have instigated his mother's political action, but the groundwork for Faith's political consciousness was laid by her parents, devoted to a Jewish socialist tradition and to the memory of their own parents' immigration to the United States. In "Faith in the Afternoon" their tongues are occupied with Yiddish and their minds with "severed Jerusalem," "the Second World War," "atomic energy," and "anti-

Semitism" (33-34). Faith, who already hears in her dreams "her grandfather, scoring the salty sea" (31), need only take another step to share her parents' concerns. However, "Faith really is an American and she was raised up like everyone else to the true assumption of happiness" (33), which she has not felt since her husband left her. An expectation of personal happiness which America promises obstructs Faith's progress toward concern for a world community.

And yet the woman in "The Immigrant Story," who describes her childhood as aflutter with American patriotism, finds a moral use for her optimism, her adherence to her American dream. Having informed her optimism with a substantial understanding of history, she feels justified in saying, "Rosiness is not a worse windowpane than gloomy gray when viewing the world" (174). Nevertheless, rosiness is not the most significant value of the story. The form of the story focuses on two anecdotes the woman's angry husband tells about his immigrant parents. The story ends, without further comment from the woman, with one of these tales. In the husband's telling of them the reader sees what the woman has implied: the man's passion and anger limit his interpretation of memory. The pains of childhood have become belief. His gray frustration and alienation do not provide a clearer picture of history than her "rosy" sense of survival and possibility. "The Immigrant Story" implies that the enormous changes which are history may best be managed by continuity, community, and a resistance to self-isolating despair.

4

Characters who explicitly seek understanding of time and space beyond the details of their own lives populate *Later the Same Day* (1985). But what answers they find derive from and apply to the immediate experience of their everyday lives in the community. The questions challenge the way love of men, women, children, and parents is practiced, but the questions have no existence apart from those loves.

In fact, these aging loves now sustain one another more than they compete. The noisy love of children no longer destroys the love affairs of men and women, nor is women's or parents' love the sustenance for sexual love of which nothing whatever can be expected. In this collection's first story, "Love," the woman narrator shares poetry, remembered love, political concerns, and enacted love with a husband whose personal history is as diverse as hers. She leaves this intimacy for the grocery thinking, "the heart of the lover continues" (6) and returns to it with an anecdote of an encounter. In the grocery she has met Margaret, a woman with whom she disagreed about the U.S.S.R. two years ago, a woman who "took away...to her political position" the protagonist's best, pacifist friend. Her smile at Margaret is returned so she kisses Margaret's hand because "so foolish is the true lover when responded to" (7). Love of one kind permits love of another.

Absence of love of one kind also can stymie love of another. In "Dreamer in a Dead Language," Faith, still a divorced mother of two boys, again visits her parents in the Children of Judea home. But her bitterness toward her ex-husband whom her father now likes and her father's desire to leave the home, and thus his wife, incite Faith to angry confrontation. She taunts her father with her multiple sexual affairs. Neither will accept the sexual necessities of the other's experience and place in time. The love between parents and children, demonstrated by Faith and her sons, does not successfully compensate Faith or her father for the sexual desire they still feel they need. For sex, in a moment, appears to forestall death while love exists in mortal time. Whether the ability to integrate loves is a function of character or of age is a question about community Paley raises in these stories. Whether knowledge of this integration can be achieved through the aging of movements (feminism, pacifism) or only individuals is a question Paley implies.

The community of women activists in these stories has aged. Mothers of adults now, the women of "Friends" and "Ruth and Edie" remember their childhood beginnings, celebrate their political actions, lament wayward children, praise successful ones, rejoice in grandchildren, and mourn the death of a friend. They exist in time and, among their peers, can accept that fact. When faith's son interrupts her private mourning to remind her of the vulnerability of the world into whose "softer parts" "living and dying are...stuffed," she reflects,

He was right to call my attention to its suffering and danger...to harass my responsible nature. But I was right to invent for my friends and our children a report on these private deaths and the condition of our life-long attachments. (89)

Concern for the ecological dangers provoked by Union Carbide does not exist apart from mourning for a dying friend. Political action without the personal feeling of every day life lends itself to violence against the other. Personal feeling without political action lends itself to an isolated self angry at an unknown other.

Moral guidance from children is more tempered in *Later the Same Day* than it was in *Enormous Changes*. As Faith tells the reader, "Hindsight, usually looked down upon, is probably as valuable as foresight, since it does include a few facts" (89). Those few facts gleaned from days lived just may have the ability to save youthful ideology from destructive rigidity. Also, parents of adults, unlike parents of babies, must look into those crevices where their children or their child-rearing failed. This is true for the dying Selena in "Friends," and it is even true for Faith and her new Chinese acquaintance in "The Expensive Moment." While Faith and Xie Feng ask one another, "What is the best way to help [children] in the real world?" Ruth, the mother of an exiled, young radical, has nothing to say (195). In the expensive moment of history, a few young people "are chosen by conscience or passion or even only love of one's own age-mates" to take radical action against the world's oppression. Then they go underground. And Faith, a mother, wonders if as much good could have been done "healing or defending the underdog" by a child who had become a doctor or lawyer (187). Moral guidance from children is not necessarily more wise than any other human advice.

Still, the women of *Later the Same Day* persist in their belief that starting anew with babies is a source of important hope and joy. In "The Story Hearer" and "Listening" middle-aged women express a desire to have a baby, remembering the middle-aged Sarah and her promising baby, Isaac. And in "The Expensive Moment" Faith and her friend Ruth imagine it would be wonderful if Ruth's radical daughter had a baby way off in her place of exile. Though the belief in babies seems a grandmother's nostalgia, more specific questions about childrearing in this 1985 collection create a universal *concrete* concern as a counterweight to youth's heavy, abstract ideology.

In *Later the Same Day* a community of love exists somewhere in the dialogue between the neighborhood and the world outside it. In several stories with characters who have been to China, ones who have studied China, or even Chinese characters themselves, information of the outside world must be understood through the prism of the local community. (The lens of ideology may seem clearer, but it provides for no peripheral vision.) "Think globally, act locally" is the slogan of the U.S. peace movement. But Paley's characters act a little differently from this: they can think and act globally only when they struggle to understand relationships locally.

In "Somewhere Else" American tourists in love with China, its revolution, and its people are caught taking pictures without permission although warned not to. Accused by a Chinese official, Paley's touring narrator writes, "we hoped we were not about to suffer socialist injustice, because we loved socialism" (48). Later the man who took the illegal picture in China has his camera confiscated by a gang in the Bronx because he was taking pictures there. Though this gang finally is persuaded to return the film and camera, the photographer then urges them to keep his camera. His friends later tell him that he does this because he has learned a man with a camera does not own the world. However, he then demonstrates that he at least has more precise memory of China than any of them. Every idea, local or global, stubbornly implies its opposite. Nothing makes this clearer than the paradoxes of human relations.

Global issues, in all their ambiguity, also penetrate the family. In "Zagrowsky Tells" a shopkeeper once accused of racism is now the adoring grandfather of a black child, Emanuel, the son of his schizophrenic daughter and a black gardener. The progressive women who once picketed Zagrowsky's store are pleased to see this change which, nevertheless, required of Zagrowsky a lifetime of troubles. The story Zagrowsky tells is the long, sympathetic tale of his change of heart—a change so slow he does not recognize it as such—and not a sudden change in ideas. Nevertheless having changed, he finds the world a different place, a place, for one thing, where the neighborhood women now rise to his defense.

Questions about Israel, communism, science, and Pinochet are more explicitly addressed in especially conversational stories such as "The Story Hearer" and "The Expensive Moment" than they are in stories of the earlier collections. And though they arouse arguments between young and old, men and women, or among virtually any group of characters, the stories offer no particular political ideology. One may well grieve over "the bad world-ending politics" as the character Jack does (181), but this does not seem to hurry understanding or change. And so one may seek a belief in the Cultural Revolution or some other idea. But Faith's mocking little poem implies the limitations of this adoration of ideal innocence:

> On the highway to Communism
> the little children put plum blossoms
> in their hair and dance
> on the new-harvested wheat (184)

Like the Czechoslovakian children in Milan Kundera' *Book of Laughter and Forgetting*, these children in innocent belief and absence of memory may be hastening the destruction of their culture. Even with conviction, it is not easy to bring the larger world home. It requires patience, persistence, and a sense of evolution as long or longer than life.

5

In a review of *Later the Same Day* Adam Mars-Jones writes,

The world which Grace Paley in most of these stories puts all her energy into saving is not a shared and vulnerable planet, but her private world of unified emotions and assumed politics, which she must perpetually repair without ever actually admitting that it has been exposed to damage. (1311)

Though I see no evidence that the emotions or politics of these characters are any more unified than they are for other kinds of communities, Mars-Jones does make an interesting assumption: that the vulnerable planet and one's private world are antithetical. The stories, which, I think, seek to prove otherwise, have not persuaded Mars-Jones. That he, a solitary British reviewer, is alone in this particular criticism suggests to me that he, unlike American reviewers, is impatient with the isolation of the United States from "the cruel history of Europe" (among other places).

Though I may misjudge Mars-Jones' motivation, the criticism of the United States is nonetheless important. Characters in Paley's stories, in fact, raise the same question. Zagrowsky, whose family were victims of Hitler, remarks "An American-born girl has some nerve to mention history" (*Later* 165); that is, the U.S. *has* no history to speak of. That Zagrowsky's wife, also an immigrant, says "we" and means Americans distresses him acutely. In "The Expensive Moment" Faith remembers herself at fourteen telling her father about her fear of aggressive Germany.

I'm the one that's gonna get killed. You? he answered. Ha ha! A little girl sitting in safe America is going to be killed. Ha ha! (*Later* 186)

Though the United States is geographically isolated from Europe, it does, of course, have a history of more than enough cruelty to teach a few things. Are non-Americans or immigrants to the U.S., nonetheless, the only possible sources of world memory and thus global conscience?

"An Irrevocable Diameter" in *The Little Disturbances of Man* and "The Burdened Man" in *Enormous Changes at the Last Minute*, stories of upwardly mobile suburban America, suggest the answer may be yes. The drama of these characters' sexual desires exists outside any community of women, children, parents and their mutual concerns. Though one might say this is because Paley does not know the suburbs as she does the city, the contrast to her urban stories merits some thought. Communities with some moral memory—of the Constitution and the Native American diaspora, of slavery and immigration, of Hiroshima and civil rights, of the arms race and women's pay—can exist within the United States, communities that do understand the responsibility of bringing the world home. But mostly they don't. Disconnection, not only in the suburbs, is more often the norm. Exploration of this failure is not often Paley's subject, but through the presentation of her developing urban community she at least shows it need not be so.

Paley's characters are sometimes naive about the feelings of men, the lives of blacks, or the promise of the Cultural Revolution. Outside of themselves and their own community, they are enthusiastic, bungling tourists. Paley lets them fumble and, in the meantime, maybe find themselves changed. Her characters are not, like Anne Beattie's, for example, paralyzed by private interests. Nor are they, like Nadine Gordimer's white South Africans, outside their author's sympathy. Paley's white American urbanites raise more questions than they find answers when they pursue responsible action, but they never stop talking to one another and the reader about what they should do for one another and their vulnerable planet. If Mars-Jones believes he sees in Paley some typical American isolation and naivete, I think he is wrong. Her wit does not sanction ignorance, but her compassion does affirm life's going on.

I have not attempted to distinguish the strongest from the weakest of Paley's stories or to show where her technique of seamless conversation succeeds and where it fails. Nor have I done justice to the primarily comic forms of any of the best stories in all three volumes. Instead what I have tried to do is articulate the development of values which make plausible Paley's moral community of separate but connected short stories. In thirty years of story-telling, Paley has developed a political ethic in her fiction which arises from its conversational form. In conversation is community. Over time, day by day, by trial and error, this community discovers its values. Paley's women discover that sexual desire is neither romance nor love. They discover that wry tolerance of men, even of irresponsible men, is not love or justice. They discover that motherhood is, if responsibly taken on, both a political and a personal activity. They discover that the friendship of women is an important political as well as personal community. Paley's women move from bedrooms and kitchens to meeting rooms and city streets. They extend their concern and their work from their relationships with lovers, children, parents, and friends in their neighborhood out into the political world of racial, economic, and ideological differences. This process of discovery is an evolution, which is imperfect and incomplete but continuous. Furthermore, over time, Paley's narrators come to use their humor and irony to reveal the foibles of the cohesive community rather than to divide self from other, for example, women from men.

From the beginning of her career, Paley has created characters who resist transcendental belief in romance or God or nature. The closest they ever come to such a belief is their faith in the moral vision of children. But Paley tempers even this idea in her most recent collection. Even as Paley's characters move out into the world as active citizens, her irony and her narration of trial and error undermine any adherence to ideological belief, be it Mao's Cultural Revolution in particular or socialism in general. This irony is not cynicism: Paley's characters are not nihilists. To the contrary, they play their role as active participants in their neighborhood and their world by resisting personal and political romantic expectations, which lead to large disappointments and hopeless cynicism. Because they maintain a community which extends across generations and through tenement walls, they are not isolated, alienated, or despairing. Thus, they do not mold their personal or political beliefs from the violent dichotomy of self and other.

If Grace Paley is considered a minor U.S. writer of the latter twentieth century, it is not simply because she writes short fiction rather than novels. It is because her politics of community in evolution runs against the grain of the major American tradition in fiction. The romantic individualist of the nineteenth century and the alienated, cynical self of the twentieth are offered love and responsibility in Paley's community. In the meantime contemporary feminists and pacificists are offered "hindsight" that "knows a few facts" and makes questions of assumptions.

Notes

[1] In an interview with Blanche Gelfant, Paley describes herself as a person with "antagonism...to prevailing fads" (290) while Marianne DeKoven describes Paley's fiction as "postmodern" (217).

[2] See, for example, Rose Kamel.

[3] These two large questions are, in part, derived from Austin McGiffert Wright's critical method in The American Short Story in the Twenties.

[4] Adam J. Sorkin notes that Eddie recapitulates the Nazis' efficiency. I see in the enthusiastic male coterie of Eddie and his assistants a recreation of the Manhattan Project's isolated male community. Also, the experiment's test time, shortly after 8 a.m., is reminiscent of the bombing of Hiroshima.

[5] Gelfant remarks, "Wise mother to be led by a child" (279).

[6] See John Crawford who describes the child guide as an archetype.

Works Cited

Crawford, John W. "Archetypal Patterns in Grace Paley's 'Runner.' " Notes on Contemporary Literature 11 (September 1981): 10-12.

DeKoven, Marianne. "Mrs. Hegel-Shtein's Tears.." Partisan Review 48 (1981): 217-23.

Gelfant, Blanche. "Grace Paley: Fragments for a Portrait in Collage." New England Review 3 (Winter 1980): 276-93.

Kamel, Rose. "To Aggravate the Conscience: Grace Paley's Loud Voice." Journal of Ethnic Studies 11 (Fall 1983): 29-49.

Kundera, Milan. The Book of Laughter and Forgetting. Trans. Michael Henry Heim. New York: Penguin, 1981.

Lidoff, Joan. "Clearing Her Throat: An Interview with Grace Paley." Shenandoah 32 (1981): 3-26.

Mandel, Dena. "Keeping Up with Faith: Grace Paley's Sturdy American Jewess." Studies in American Jewish Literature, 3 (1983): 85-98.

Mars-Jones, Adam. Rev. of *Later the Same Day,* by Grace Paley. *Times Literary Supplement* 22 Nov. 1985: 1311.

Paley, Grace. *Enormous Changes at the Last Minute.* New York: Farrar, Strauss, Giroux, 1974.

—— Fiction Reading. Loyola University. New Orleans, Louisiana, 6 Nov. 1986.

—— *Later the Same Day.* New York: Penguin, 1986.

—— *The Little Disturbances of Man: Stories of Men and Women at Love.* New York: Plume Books, 1959.

Rich, Adrienne. *Diving Into the Wreck, Poems 1971-1972.* New York: W.W. Norton, 1973.

Sorkin, Adam J. " 'What Are We, Animals?' Grace Paley's World of Talk and Laughter." *Studies in American Jewish Literature* 2 (1982): 144-54.

Wright, Austin McGiffert. *The American Short Story in the Twenties.* Chicago: U of Chicago P, 1961.

"Bringing the Corners Forward": Ideology and Representation in Updike's Rabbit Trilogy

Raymond A. Mazurek

I

In his review of *Rabbit Redux* for the *New York Times Book Review*, Richard Locke claimed that John Updike was "one of those wrestling most fiercely with 'the novel as history/history as the novel' " (1). From the perspective of over a decade and a half later, this is a surprising claim, as is Locke's association of the exploration of "the novel as history/ history as a novel" (a phrase taken from Mailer's *Armies of the Night*) not with the fiction of Barth and Vonnegut, whom he dismisses, but with the five contemporary U.S. writers he considers most significant: Mailer, Malamud, Bellow, Roth, and Updike. With the exception of Mailer (and to a lesser extent Roth), all of these writers are notable for their cautious approach to narrative experimentation and a traditional treatment of historical subject matter which pales in comparison to the experimental historical novels of Barth (*The Sot-Weed Factor*), Pynchon (*V, The Crying of Lot 49,* and *Gravity's Rainbow*), Coover (*The Public Burning*), and others.

However, while many critics would quarrel with his estimation of Updike's importance, Locke is right in suggesting that *Rabbit Redux* represents Updike's most direct entry into the sub-genres of historical and political fiction. Indeed, with the publication of a new *Rabbit* novel at the end of each decade—*Rabbit Run* in 1960, *Rabbit Redux* in 1971, *Rabbit is Rich* in 1981 and more Rabbits promised—Updike has clearly made the Rabbit novels a commentary on postwar America. The association of *Rabbit, Run* with the Eisenhower era is reinforced by the appearance of *Rabbit Redux* as a novel about the sixties and *Rabbit is Rich* at the end of the seventies, as Updike synchronizes the trilogy with the American habit of dividing time, or at least the surfaces of contemporary change, into decades—a habit so engrained that its artificiality often goes unnoticed.

However, I can hardly agree with the assertion of Donald Greiner that "Updike's Rabbit chronicles reflect the post-1950s United States with a combination of realistic and metaphorical accuracy not seen in other contemporary American fiction" (Greiner 98). Updike's style, with its meaphorical language that fuses images of America as lost Eden with images of sexuality and ideas from Protestant existential theology, is often more idiosyncratic than "accurate." But despite this stylistic idiosyncracy, it should be admitted that the Rabbit novels (especially *Rabbit Run*) do provide a critical reflection on contemporary America, but in a way that is more symptomatic than analytical. The limitations of the Rabbit novels as an imagination of history reflect the limitations of many of the prestigious novels in the contemporary period (with which Updike's trilogy shares far more than Greiner indicates) and the ideological limitations of some of the ways in which history is felt, imagined, and represented elsewhere in contemporary culture. Updike's Rabbit novels—and the prominence that many critics have given to novels like them—tell us as much about the postwar U.S. by their limited ability to tell our story as by those moments when their portrayal of the passing decades *does* appear remarkable for its accuracy.

Both the apparent accuracy and the limitations of Updike's trilogy can be partially explained by the extent to which the Rabbit trilogy conforms to what Richard Ohmann has called the "illness story." As Ohmann has argued in "The Shaping of a Canon: U.S. Fiction, 1960-1975," the dominant kind of story in the prestigious novels that are in the process of becoming canonical for the contemporary period is one in which "social contradictions were easily displaced into images of personal illness" (Ohmann 212). According to Ohmann, many of the most prominent novels of the period (including those of Bellow, Salinger, Heller, Plath, Kesey, Roth, and Updike) portray a protagonist essentially unable to adjust to available social roles or to understand the nameless causes of his (or sometimes her) maladjustment. The nameless malaise which troubles the protagonist is therefore interpreted as a sign of his or her personal inadequacy, instability, or illness—with the pervasive metaphor of society itself as "sick" in the late sixties a further development of the way of seeing embodied in the illness story. Ohmann suggests that this type of narrative is not an autonomous development in fiction but should be understood in terms of the needs and perceptions of the professional-managerial class that comprised the bulk of the readership for serious fiction in the period. In the era of the "end of ideology," the class of professionals and managers (and to a lesser extent, U.S. society in general) were led to believe that serious social conflict had ended and that problems that persisted could now be dealt with as technical problems. Difficulties were signs of the need for adjustment in two senses: adjustment of the controls by experts, or psychological adjustment on the part of the individual. However, since social conflicts over class, gender, the family, race, and the lack of satisfying work continued, one logical result was a predisposition for stories of maladjustment, which conveyed a sense of *something* definitely gone wrong but which placed that sense within the individual.

Following Raymond Williams and the increasingly sophisticated Marxist criticism of recent decades, Ohmann identifies the illness story as a "structure of feeling" in the contemporary period, associated with the needs and desires of a particular class but not reductively identified with the ideology of the ruling class or owners of the major economic resources of U.S. society (see Williams, 128-35). Thus, he indicates that the "illness story" provided a critical representation of society but was also a reflection of dominant ideological tendencies: individualism, and the tendency to displace the analysis of social conflicts and their causes with a focus on their effects on individual consciousness. The illness story's portrayal of social problems, sometimes focusing on individual malaise and other times depicting a generalized social sickness, consistently tended to displace social analysis.

Both Updike's ability to say "something that sounds right about where we are now" (Alter 49) in the Rabbit trilogy and his lack of analytical depth in writing about U.S. society reflect the extent to which Updike has mastered the illness story as a way of seeing. Although Ohmann makes only passing references to the Rabbit novels in his essay (most of them to *Rabbit Redux*), Updike's trilogy—especially *Rabbit, Run* and *Rabbit Redux* but also to a lesser extent *Rabbit is Rich*—is a paradigmatic example of the illness story. In *Rabbit, Run,* Rabbit's alienation and maladjustment become a metaphor for America at the end of the fifties, although this alienation is conceptualized in terms which reflect the individualistic assumptions of the dominant culture; in *Rabbit Redux,* the "illness" Rabbit experienced at the end of the fifties has expanded into the generalized malaise and widely celebrated maladjustment of the late sixties. In neither book does Updike provide an authorial or other perspective that is very convincing in analyzing this social alienation; *Rabbit, Run,* which focuses on presenting Rabbit's alienation, is a better novel than *Rabbit Redux* in part because *Redux* tries too unsuccessfully to explain the sixties through the endless but often superficial discussions of Rabbit and his black alter-ego, Skeeter. In *Rabbit is Rich,* the illness story has lost some of its critical force as it becomes muted in the story of Nelson, Rabbit's son, whose maladjustment lacks the metaphorical quality of either his father's or the counterculture's alienation. Nelson's troubles become naturalized as part of a merely generational conflict, just as Rabbit's and America's problems are described as a natural winding down, a confrontation with cycles leading to death and the inevitable dissipation of energy. While

Rabbit is Rich contains some of the implicit critique of American society of the earlier novels, that critique is lost in its naturalized metaphors, as the "illness" it describes is less a social sickness than a sign of the inevitable coming of death.

All three of these novels indicate Updike's strength in conveying what U.S. middle class life feels like from the inside as well as his limitations in reflecting on recent U.S. history and his tendency to create metaphors that displace the exploration of social problems. Updike's predisposition toward the illness narrative helps to explain how he can be simultaneously praised for his ability to convey the sense of his times and faulted for his weakness "in fathoming causes and asserting judgments" (Samuels, "Updike on the Present" (64). For the illness story tends to be non-analytical, presenting a way of seeing dominant in middle-class America without the critical distancing that would reveal its own limitions as a narrative rooted in the ideology of post-1950s U.S. society.

II
Rabbit, Run

As Ohmann argues, the illness story reveals the protagonist's inability to adjust to available social roles, thus betraying a deep anxiety about the available roles which the individual confronts:

Within the configuration of social forces I have described, maturity is equated with independence, in fact with a kind of invulnerability to the intrusion of social tension, an invulnerability to society itself. But even though one may push social conflict and historical processes out of sight, one cannot really cease to be social: at a minimum, social *roles* are indivisible from selfhood. To put the contradiction another way: the ideal self calls for a self that is complete, integral, unique; but in actual living one must be *some*thing and *some*body, and definitions of "somebody" already exist in a complete array provided by that very social and economic system that one has wished to transcend. Society comes back at the individual as a hostile force, threatening to diminish or annihilate one's "real" self. (213)

Rabbit Run, the story of the impulsive flight of Harry ("Rabbit") Angstrom, centers on the issues Ohmann outlines above: the inability of Rabbit to discover his "real" self, to match the ideals he has grown up with, and to become a "responsible," independent adult in the 1950s America. The novel begins with the twenty-six-year-old Rabbit, on his way home from his alienating sales job, impulsively joining a group of boys playing basketball. Towering over them, the six-foot-three former high school star is both in his element as a "natural" player and outside of his role—an adult playing seriously with children, who are uncomforable and confused by his presence. Returning home to his pregnant wife Janice, whome he thinks of as "dumb" (17), Rabbit watches the Mouseketeers on television and hears the ideal of selfhood proclaimed: "God doesn't want a tree to be a waterfall, or a flower to be a stone.

God gives to each one of us a special talent.... So: Know thyself. Learn to understand your talents, and then work to develop them. That's the way to be happy" (14-15). The inconsistency of this ideal and Rabbit's life comes through to him, at a visceral rather than a rational level, and walking to his in-laws to pick up his two-year-old son, Rabbit impulsively takes the car and drives.

Stepping out of his life like Hawthorne's Wakefield, Rabbit echoes the quest of many protagonists in canonical American literature, seeking the open road and a confrontation with a nature that is imagined as a feminine counterpart to the masculine self. Rabbit seeks to go south and west and "his image is of himself going right down the middle, right into the broad soft belly of the land, surprising the dawn cottonfields with his northern plates" (35). However, "the farther he drives the more he feels some great confused system, Baltimore now instead of Philadelphia, reaching for him" (34). Rather than discovering the freedom of the open road and of his figuratively sexual dream of nature, Rabbit drives in circles, and he returns to Brewer, having found alienation in strange coffee shops, where he is an obvious outsider and asks himself, "is it just these people I'm outside, or is it all America" (36).

Updike provides a remarkable description of the alienation of the hopes of young men like Rabbit in fifties America, expecting to find the good life in young marriages and responsibilities but finding meaningless work, the tensions of traditional gender roles, and an ideology—by which I mean not just political beliefs, but basic ideas, values, and feelings about social reality, and the relation of those ideas "to the maintenance and reproduction of social power" (Eagleton 21)—incapable of helping them to comprehend what has happened. Rabbit's belief in the quest, and in his uniqueness, only leads him into a celebration of his alienation, like so many other protagonists who conceived life as a confrontation between self and nature.

The overlay of imagery that Updike uses to describe Rabbit's situation serves to intensify further the sense of Rabbit's quintessentially American isolation. Updike provides a visceral sense of the conflict between the alienated individual and a hostile social order. Updike's metaphors of America as a lost Eden still pursued by the male self in a sexual quest for identity, and the images from Protestant existential theology that supplement this metaphorical system in the later parts of the novel, provide a definition of Rabbit's conflict rather than an analysis of its social causes. Thus it is natural that Rabbit, at the end of the first novel, should appear to be again, and seemingly forever, on the run: the quest, and a social situation that has made it futile, is what defines Rabbit *Angst*rom, whose name connotes existential anxiety.

The language Updike uses to define Rabbit is simultaneously one of the novel's sources of power and one of its major flaws. Updike's prose, as Gilbert Sorrentino, among others, has noted, tends to be "overwrought" (77). The style of *Rabbit, Run* makes it appear to belong necessarily to the canon of American literature, with its images of American promise, self, and nature, and yet the style which appropriates those images is sometimes too literary in a bad sense, almost inviting parody. Updike's is a belated attempt to rework the central Americanist signs, as can be suggested by the fact that John Barth's *The Sot-Weed Factor*, with its merciless parody of the idea of the U.S. as "virgin land," was published within a few years of *Rabbit, Run*. Updike's use of language, whatever its virtues or faults, can be thought of as the opposite of metafictional self-consciousness: just as metafiction seeks to make the reader aware of the mystifications of literary language, of how silly the idea of "virgin land" is if we examine it as a metaphor, Updike's use of language seeks to mystify, to make the reader feel the power of the cultural myths his characters live within. While this technique can help the reader to understand the "structures of feeling" which are Updike's subject, it also helps define the non-analytical quality of much of Updike's prose. The language of *Rabbit, Run* and that of Rabbit's visceral vision of reality are almost coterminus with one another, allowing little space outside of Rabbit's vision from which it can be judged. This is because those who are exploited and offended by Rabbit's actions—Janice and her parents (the Springers), the Reverend Eccles who tries to intervene, and Ruth, the prostitute with whom he lives for a time—are all defined within the illness story. They are incapable of providing the meaningful roles that Rabbit seeks, for they are part of the same nameless malaise that infects him. The women Rabbit encounters are allied either with the hostility of society (Janice and Mrs. Springer are thus "bitches") or with the promise of nature (Ruth, whom Rabbit imagines as a virgin on their first night together, is an earth mother, like the teenage Janice he remembers).

Updike, to his credit, provides narrative space where the alternative voices of Ruth and Janice speak of their having been used by Rabbit and other men. Ruth is sickened by men's use of her as an object in their private fantasies—"They couldn't have felt much it must have been just the *idea* of you. All their ideas" (138)—while Janice complains of Rabbit's rude clumsiness in the bedroom. Rabbit's bold statement of selfishness—and of the ideal of the autonomous self—is clearly intended by Updike as ironic; when Rabbit says, "If you have the guts to be yourself,...other people will pay your price" (140), his words appear within Ruth's narrative of her mistreatment by men and their "ideas." But while Updike clearly has made Rabbit's actions appear morally questionable—he brings destruction and harm to those around him by his irresponsible behavior—the novel can present little alternative to the ideals from which Rabbit acts, for its central vision is one of a conflict between the "real" self and society's constrictions.

The Reverend Eccles, whose humanistic Christianity is "only a moralistic version of convention" (Samuels, *Updike* 40), fails to bring Rabbit back to respectable society or to represent an alternative to the vision of society as a hostile force. Eccles is fascinated by Rabbit, perhaps because of Rabbit's ability to "give people faith" (135). In their conversations when playing golf, it is Rabbit, not Eccles, who affirms a belief in a "something that wants me to find it" (120), and his association of "it" with his real self in a further underpinning, on a theological level, of the metaphorical language that structures the novel. Thus it is Kruppenbach, with his traditional theology based on faith, rather than Eccles, whom Kruppenbach upbraids as a betrayers of his profession, that is associated with Rabbit's idealism (see Samuels, *Updike* 40-41). Rabbit and the inner quest for "something" are contrasted with the "nothing" that life in society, and its conventional behavior without faith, present to him. Rabbit, the existential hero, faces the threat of blankness and annihilation, the nothingness that exists if there is no "something": "the sky in the windshield is blank and cold, and he feels nothing ahead of him, Ruth's blue-eyed nothing, the nothing she told him she did, the nothing she believes in. Your heart lifts forever through that blank sky" (93). While there is a serious theological content to this imagery (see Hunt 13-48), on the level of *Rabbit, Run's* social meaning, the theological imagery is a further confirmation of the starkness of the conflict between inner self and outward society. The vagueness of the "something" that Rabbit is seeking, while it can be named as Grace if we accept Updike's theology, also can be viewed as underlying the namelessness of the malaise that troubles him and defines his social world. The images of "nothing," holes, and openings also fuse with the novel's sexual imagery in disturbing ways, for they define women as part of the hostile other (either society or nature, depending on whether they are bitches or earth mothers) and further confirm the necessarily male identity of the novel's conception of the self. Rabbit's days of heroism as a basketball star, which provide him with memories of unalienated action, are described in unmistakedly sexual images: "there was you and sometimes the ball and then the hole, the high perfect hole with its pretty skirt of net. It was you, just you and the fringed ring, and sometimes it came right to your lips it seemed and sometimes it stayed away, hard and remote and small" (40). Juxtaposed with Rabbit's despair at "nothing" after sex with Ruth ("Nature leads you up like a mother and as soon as she gets her little price leaves you with nothing" [83]), with Rabbit's revulsion from women who "handle themselves like an old envelope" (84), and with the repeated evocation of the Adamic myth of a feminized nature, this use of phallic imagery for describing basketball is disturbing. While Updike can hardly be faulted for failing to be sensitive on feminist issues in 1960, today, after feminism, such imagery appears too exploitative to be passively accepted—just as after metafiction and Monty Python, it is too self-conscious to be convincing.

While not entirely convincing, *Rabbit, Run* comes as close as any other novel to conveying a sense of the U.S. at the end of the nineteen-fifties. However, this is less because of its realistic accuracy than its adeptness at defining one predominant "structure of feeling" of the period—the illness story. It is obvious that a great deal of American experience in the 1950s—including the McCarthy era, the civil rights movement, the Korean war, fear of the bomb, or simply the experience of Americans who are different from Rabbit in age, gender, class, ethnicity, or belief—is left untouched by *Rabbit, Run*. For this, Updike cannot be faulted. Any novel, or even any history, has a limited ability to "represent" an era. Novels represent ways of seeing: philosophical perspectives, aesthetic ideas, or, more commonly, ideologies—ideas, values, and feelings about the social world—and it is through their representation of ways of seeing social reality that they can be said to represent an historical period.

III
Rabbit Redux

The success of *Rabbit, Run* as a novel about the fifties also helps define the limits of *Rabbit Redux* as a novel about the sixties. For in *Rabbit Redux* Rabbit's malaise—his desire to run from the constrictions of a society conceived as a hostile force—has become generalized, as society is swept by widespread rebellion. However, Updike has no new analytical framework for comprehending this rebellion. Rabbit, a middle-American working man, has become an advocate of the need for rules, for social conventions. Others run: Janice, who has an affair with Charlie Stavros and, in a reversal of roles, leaves Rabbit alone with the adolescent Nelson; Jill, the runaway upper-class hippie whom Rabbit takes in and who becomes Rabbit's lover; Skeeter, the black Vietnam veteran to whom Rabbit, pressured by Jill, also gives refuge when Skeeter is fleeing a drug bust. While Updike conveys a sense of the surfaces of life and conflict in the sixties, and while, especially in the character of Skeeter, he clearly attempts to develop an alternative voice to Rabbit's, *Rabbit Redux* suffers by not getting beyond the illness story which *Rabbit, Run* helped define. Even Skeeter, despite his Black English, is too much a repetition of Rabbit/Updike, especially in his attempt to give people a new "faith." Thus, more than fifteen years after it was published, I find it impossible to read *Rabbit Redux* without being troubled by its superficiality as a novel about the period. *Rabbit Redux*, Updike's most directly social and political work, suffers more noticeably than *Rabbit, Run* from Updike's failure to develop a convincing social analysis. As Charles Samuels notes, "in *Rabbit, Redux* Updike absorbs into his fiction some of the chief sources of our discontent and distills them into characters realistically comeplled by conflicting motives. However, refusing to sort out the motives or explain the discontent, he leaves us as baffled and dispirited as the age itself" ("Updike on the Present" 67).

Samuels' comments notwithstanding, it is not entirely clear that Updike's characters are all that "realistic." *Rabbit, Redux* might be subtitled "Rabbit Meets the Sixties," but the sixties Rabbit meets are too stereotyped. As George Hunt notes, Jill and Skeeter, the representatives of the sixties whom Rabbit encounters, are "astract: shadowy figures like ghosts on a screen, disembodied models of a generation as 'far out' to Harry as the astronauts, so that their reality is also suspect" (171). In the early pages of *Redux*, dominated by the story of Rabbit's problems with Janice and images of the Apollo moon landing, Janice says of Rabbit: "He put his life into rules he feels melting away now. I mean, he knows he's missing something, he's always reading the paper and watching the news" (54). Updike himself has suggested that Jill and Skeeter "just come in off the set into Rabbit's lap" (qtd. in Hunt 172). But while it may be inevitable that the encounters between the middle-American worker (Rabbit), the militant black (Skeeter), and the hippie runaway (Jill) are mediated by popular images of these stereotypes conveyed in the media, it is unfortunate that neither Jill nor Skeeter ever attain the depth of characterization of some of Updike's other characters.

To the extent that their discontent is explained, Jill and Skeeter are reflections of the younger Rabbit, a man now clinging to Eccles' rules and complaining that "everybody now is the way I used to be" (162). Rabbit's earlier dreams of freedom and Adamic union with the land have shrunk to a defensive loyalty to a nation that has given him the trappings of happiness—a cheap house in the suburbs, a steady job— that he had once shunned. Janice complains, "you were a beautiful brainless guy and I've had to watch that guy die day by day" (71). Rabbit's loyalty to nation is in a part a loyalty to a remnant of his dream: "America is beyond power, it acts as if in a dream, as a face of God.... Beneath her patient bombers, paradise is possible" (49). But that Paradise has been reduced to the garish light of the local Burger Bliss, just as the open road has been expanded to something beyond mystery and beyond comprehension by the Apollo moonshot. The newscasters "keep mentioning Columbus but as far as Rabbit can see it's the exact opposite: Columbus flew blind and hit something, these guys see exactly where they're aiming and it's a big round nothing" (29).

The connectin between space exploration and sexual coupling and uncoupling is made throughout *Rabbit Redux,* and the moon shot, with its phallic aim at nothing, is connected to sexual imagery similar to that of *Rabbit, Run.* Women are associated with threatening openings, holes, and nothingness, contrasted with the "something" announced by the male self. Jill, who is both Rabbit's lover and a substitute for the infant daughter who dies at the end of *Rabbit, Run,* and who herself dies in the fire set by Rabbit's neighbors, is clearly associated with this imagery, which takes on an apocalyptic tone in *Redux.* Thus Jill says to Rabbit, "when you're over me, I feel you're an angel. Piercing me with a sword. I feel you're about to announce something, the end of the world, and you say nothing, just pierce me" (190-91). But the figure most closely associated with this apocalyptic tone is not the female sacrifice, Jill, but the black prophet, Skeeter. Skeeter is the strangest creation of *Rabbit Redux,* and his relationship with and power over Rabbit is one aspect of the novel that critics have had difficulty explaining. In part, Rabbit is drawn to Skeeter by the very otherness that blacks represent to him, as Robert Alter has suggested (47). But the relationship between Rabbit and Skeeter is more than a racial encounter. Skeeter, like the Rabbit of *Rabbit, Run,* is someone who gives others faith. A substitute for the ministers (Kruppenbach and Eccles) of *Rabbit, Run,* Skeeter is also a conduit of the book's religious imagery, and that imagery—with its connotations of apocalypse—is the vehicle for describing the spread of a general malaise throughout society in the 1960s. It is no accident that Skeeter resists political interpretations of events in favor of an apocalyptic religious rhetoric.

Skeeter sees the evil in America as a product of its misguided idealism which makes historical explanations beside the point. Complaining of the dehumanization of black people have been subjected to in the U.S., Skeeter say:

"The thing about these Benighted States all around is that it never was no place where this happens because that happens...no sir, this place was never such a place it was a *dream,* it was a state of mind....Some white man see a black man he don't see a man he see a *symbol,* right? All these people are walking around inside of their own *heads;* they don't even know if you kick somebody else it *hurts.*" (213)

But Skeeter himself identifies reality as what goes on in one's head, just as he identifies America with a state of mind and himself with the "black jesus" (217) come to announce the prophetic word, as he tells Rabbit:

"You just don't *know,* Chuck. You don't even know that now is all the time there is. What happens to you, is all that happens, right? You. Are. It. I've come down"—he points to the ceiling, his finger a brown crayon—"to tell you that, since along these two thousand years somewhere you've done gone and forgotten again, right?" (231)

According to Skeeter, if a "man don't like Vietnam, he don't like America"; unlike Rabbit, Skeeter appears to mean this ironically, for in Vietnam, America's essence is revealed: "Nam is the spot where our heavenly essence in pustulatin' " (232). However, Vietnam—about which Skeeter reminisces in realistic horror only once (228-29)—is also a metaphor for the apocalypse. Skeeter connects Vietnam to his theory of the universe, which finds religious imagery in the discovery of black holes in space. Vietnam

is the local hole. It is where the world is redoing itself...it is the end. It is the beginning. It is beautiful, men do beautiful things in that mud. it is where God is pushing through. He's coming, Chuck, and Babychuck, and Ladychuck, let Him in. Pull down, shoot to kill, Chaos in His holy face. The sun is burning through. The moon is turning red. The moon is a baby's head bright red through his momma's legs. (230)

Skeeter's imagery of apocalypse is associated with the total transformation many people felt was about to occur in the late sixties, but its metaphors of a feminized nature and threat of nothingness, and of a masculine self, God, and something beyond, are familiar from *Rabbit, Run*. Skeeter's sense of apocalypse, morever, displaces social explanations of the sixties. Thus Skeeter dismisses talk of revolution, suggesting that Huey Newton is the black equivalent of Spiro Agnew and similar "gangsters.... The problem is really, when the gangsters have knocked each other off, and taken half of everybody else with them, to make use of the *space*" (217). The familiar Americanist sense of the land (here, expanded, metaphorically, also to "outer" space) displaces identification with the leaders a black militant might be expected to identify with. The apocalypse itself is Skeeter's justification and explanation: "Chaos is God's body. Order is the Devil's chains. As for Robert Seale, any black man who has John Kennel Badbreath and Leonard Birdbrain giving him fundraising cocktail parties is one house *nigger* in my book" (241). When Rabbit drags on a joint and says to Skeeter's rhetoric, "I believe" (243), he is assenting to the antinomian impulse and pursuit of grace (now the apocalypse of the second coming) that he affirmed in *Rabbit, Run*. Skeeter offers Rabbit momentary faith in the apocalypse that is the sign of America's malaise and potential redemption, just as the Rabbit of *Rabbit, Run* provided others with a faith that transformed his maladjustment into a significant comment on fifties America. Although Skeeter appears to lack the positive qualities of a religious figure, given his "irresponsibility, cruelty, moral weakness, schizophrenia, and cowardice" (Hunt 179), his weaknesses are similar to those of the younger Rabbit and are what one would expect from a central figure in the illness narrative. However, there is an additional problem in *Rabbit Redux* insofar as Skeeter, a black outsider, comes to embody social sickness in Rabbit's world. Skeeter indirectly brings about the destruction of Rabbit's home and the death of the white woman, Jill, and the lack of social analysis in the novel leaves the impression that the blacks are in some sense the cause of the social sickness of the sixties, despite Updike's wishes to avoid this sort of racist interpretation.

In the final section of *Rabbit, Redux*, Rabbit and Janice are tentatively reunited after Jill has perished and Skeeter has fled along the open road that once beckoned to Harry Angstrom. This inconclusive ending and the novel's final words ("O.K.?") are cited by Ohmann as paradigmatic of the illness story, in which "nothing has changed 'out there,' but our heroes are now 'O.K.?' " (219). It is less the social world "out there" that is Updike's subject in *Rabbit, Redux* than the state of mind of his protagonists—a way of seeing so closely connected to the perspective of the novel that *Rabbit Redux* is itself a symptom of one of the prominent ideological configurations of the sixties. With the passage of time, *Rabbit Redux* appears less satisfactory a novel than *Rabbit, Run,* for despite the trappings of the political novel, it does not provide the understanding or analysis which is possible in that sub-genre.

IV
Rabbit is Rich

If *Rabbit Redux* is a repetition of *Rabbit, Run* in the guise of a historical sequence, this is even more true of *Rabbit is Rich*, the most formless of the three Rabbit books. *Rabbit is Rich* is full of details evocative of the surfaces of middle-class life in the seventies, but these details do not come together to promote any deep understanding of the period, and its central themes are for the most part a reworking of those of the earlier novels.

Rabbit is now managing Springer Motors, the Toyota dealership that he and Janice have inherited part of from Janice's father—although Rabbit is still under his mother-in-law's thumb, as she owns half of the business as well as the house they share with her. Toyotas function as a metaphor for the America of declining expectations, oil shortages, and gas lines. Rabbit's world is a world that "is running down fast" (248) in an onrush of death and decline that Rabbit is increasingly able to adjust to:

the years have piled on, the surviving have patched things up, and so many more have joined the dead, undone by diseases for which only God is to blame, that it no longer seems so bad, it seems more as if Jill had moved to another town, where the population is growing. (67)

However, while Rabbit and Janice have accommodated to events, and have even feasted as owners of a Toyota dealership on the economic troubles of the 1970s, others have not adjusted as well. "The world keeps ending but new people too dumb to know it keep showing up as if the fun's just started" (81). Rabbit's son, Nelson, is one of the less-than-satisfied latecomers. Bitter towards Rabbit for having made a mess of the family's life, Nelson has never forgiven Harry for Jill's death, or for his infant sister's death in *Rabbit, Run*. In *Rabbit is Rich*, Nelson provides the central conflict by returning home from Kent State with his degree unfinished and trying to establish himself, against Rabbit's wishes, at the Toyota dealership. Nelson, it turns out, has gotten his working-class Ohio girlfriend, Pru, pregnant, and it is this situation that precipitates his desire to "make it" in the adult world. Nelson and Harry argue bitterly throughout the novel, for while Nelson wishes to settle in Brewer and marry Pru, Harry keeps offering him money to go back to school and allow Pru to have an abortion. Eventually Nelson and Pru do marry, but Nelson is hopelessly maladjusted in his various roles, as indicated by the sections of the novel narrated from his point of view. As Greiner notes, Nelson is an imitation of harry but "without the grace. No one is going to say about Nelson that he has the gift of life or that he gives people faith" (94). Yet in *Rabbit is Rich*, Nelson, like Skeeter in *Redux*, carries forward the central story of maladjustment, and by confronting Harry in a violent argument that ends with Nelson's smashing two convertibles in anger on the car lot, Nelson makes Harry feel oddly alive, full of "choked hilarity...these strange awkward blobs of joy bobbing in Harry's chest" (158). If only by providing conflict, Nelson does, indirectly, give "life" to a Harry Angstrom gone too comfortable and bored—just as he and Pru provide the new life, the baby, in the Angstrom family.

But Nelson's own narrative, like Harry's words, reveal him as a "disaster" (197). Uncomfortable at Kent State, where he had gone because of the associations of the obscure Ohio campus with the late sixties, Nelson quickly becomes disillusioned with both the remnants of the counterculture and student life. "As far as Nelson was concerned they could have shot all those jerks. When in '77 there was all that fuss about Tent City Nelson stayed in his dorm" (294). He is attracted to Pru, a college secretary from a rough background in Akron, partly because she represents a negation of the pretensions of college. At Kent State, Nelson and Pru comfort themselves, not with the quest of Rabbit's youth for the American dream, but with cynicism:

They agreed about things, basic things. They knew that at bottom the world was brutal, no father protected you, you were left alone in a way not appreciated by these kids horsing around on jock teams or playing at being radicals or doing the rah-rah thing or their own thing or whatever. That Nelson saw it was all bullshit gave him for Pru a certain seriousness. (294)

But back in Brewer, Pru sees Nelson the way Harry does, as "spoiled" (312), telling Nelson that Rabbit didn't think he was ready to work at the lot "and you weren't. You aren't. You aren't ready to be a father either but that's my mistake" (312).

Although Nelson spends his time complaining and accidentally or intentionally smashing the Angstroms' various automobiles, his story is a version of Harry's story in *Rabbit, Run* and of the illness story in general: he is basically unable to take on the adult roles expected of him. Nelson's situation gives the story a new twist, however, because his dissatisfaction connotes nothing about America but the decline of its society and the belatedness of Nelson's arrival. Nelson's maladjustment seems narrower and more personal, a product of Nelson's unfortunate situation as part of a generational cycle: one in which he inherits some of Harry's traits—finally running to Ohio just before his child is born— but is born too late to share in the hope of an American promise which might give his situation meaning. Thus, while Nelson majors in geography, connotating some connection to the land and the hope of a special relation to it, the road on which he hitchhikes is without significance to him: "the country's the same wherever you go. The same supermarkets, the same plastic shit for sale. There's nothing to see" (70).

While Nelson is maladjusted, he is as disconnected from Skeeter's prophetic anger as from Harry's hope and grace. The novel as a whole barely hints at a judgment of Rabbit, sunk in a complacement mixture of conformity and energy, or of the middle-American, middle-class life he represents. It is ironic that Rabbit spends his emotional energy fantasizing about the girl who might be his illegitimate daughter with Ruth when he should, as Janice says, be concerned about his *"real* son" (66), whom Rabbit is only too eager to thrust out of his household. But the sense of a social world that might present a perspective from which to evaluate the narrow self-entrapment in material things rather than in relationships—either relationships to one's family, or relationships to a world that is more than a supplier of gasoline and other goods to the American middle-class—is barely mentioned in *Rabbit is Rich*. There are a few passages which make such historical perspective and moral judgment all the more noticeable for its absence in the novel as a whole. The most notable of these occurs when Rabbit and Janice are lugging the South African gold and the silver they have purchased between their safe deposit box and the precious metals broker in the desolate streets of downtown Brewer. Carrying the absurdly heavy precious metal and becoming

Solid citizens by this extra degree, then, the two of them walk out between the great granite pillars of the Brewer Trust into the frail December sunlight...past two blocks of stores doing a thin Christmas business. Underfed little Puerto Rican women are the only ones skuttling in and out of the cut-rate entranceways, and kids who ought to be in school, and bleary retirees in dirty padded parkas and hunter's hats, with whiskey loose jaws; the mills have used these old guys up and spit them out. (341)

Literally staggering under the unwanted weight of his wealth, Rabbit stares up at "Mt. Judge: in his eyes as a child God had reposed on that mountain, and now he can imagine how through God's eyes from that vantage he and Janice might look below: two ants trying to make it up the sides of a bathroom basin" (347). Rabbit also passes down-and-out blacks who ask him for money, and he thinks he sees a sign that reads "SKEETER LIVES," but he huddles under the "false sky" (348) of the bank vault with Janice. Unable to get all the silver coins in the safe deposit box, Rabbit leaves disheartened, weighted down with worries over Nelson's cost to him and with the weight of the extra coins:

He feels, as if the sidewalk now is a downslanted plane, the whole year dropping away from him, loss after loss. His silver is scattered, tinsel. His box will break, the janitor will sweep up the coins. It's all dirt anyway. The great sad lie that is Christmas stains Weiser end to end, and through the murk he glimpses the truth that to be rich is to be robbed, to be rich is to be poor. (350-51)

Were this the tone of *Rabbit is Rich* as a whole, it might have become a powerful comment on America in the 1970s, a time of increasing callousness towards the poor and homeless and chauvinism towards the rest of the world, whether the oil rich Middle-east or white-dominated South Africa, whose black majority provided America's middle-class with gold Krugerrands to hoard. However, such historical insight has nowhere to go in *Rabbit is Rich*, for there is no figure—nor any consistent authorial analysis—who can carry it.

Rabbit's insights quickly turn toward his traditional obsession—women. The sexual fantasies and conversations that clutter the novel tend to trivialize *Rabbit is Rich*, as Rabbit's voyeuristic fascination with young Cindy Murkett—the wife of an aging golf partner—is stirred by his accidental discovery of the Murketts' pornographic pictures of each other (a vignette worthy of *Playboy*, where it first appeared, but unnecessarily drawn out for a serious novel). It is the surfaces of contemporary life that Updike dwells on, with only a few moments that strive toward a deeper analysis, usually based on images from earlier novels. Thus, during the vacation in the Caribbean that Harry and Janice take with two other couples, a sexual encounter is the occasion for a replay of the familiar sexual-religious imagery. When the couples swap, Harry gets not the nubile Cindy, but middle-aged Thelma, who has fantasies about him. Thelma—significantly stricken with lupus, a terminal illness which people are able to live fairly normal lives with for years—tells Harry of the magic of his ability to believe and enjoy life. The encounter with Thelma is full of religious imagery. After anal sex "he can't take his mind from what he's discovered, that nothingness seen by his single eye...he trusts himself to her as if speaking in prayer, talks to her about himself as he has to none other" and recovers "his old inkling, now fading in the energy crunch, that there was something that wanted him to find it, that he was here on earth on a kind of assignment" (392).

Rabbit's ability to experience a sense of renewal might be more convincing if he learned something from this insight—or if Updike did not require that Rabbit have a sexual encounter with a woman associated directly with death to enlighten him. What Rabbit experiences again is his old notion that everything has been all wrong and somehow can be made right, by momentary grace or whatever, but it is hard to connect this insight to Rabbit's life, except by saying that he occasionally realizes (but cannot understand) the alienation that remains behind his outward riches.

Rabbit is Rich ends in as inconclusive a way as the earlier novels. Rabbit has an encounter with Ruth after intermittent spying on her property, trying to determine whether the tall young woman who has come to his Toyota dealership is his illegitimate daughter. Ruth denounces Rabbit for interfering and denies that the girl is his, telling him, after he offers her money: "I wouldn't give you the satisfaction of that girl being yours if there was a million dollars at stake. I raised her. She and I put in a lot of time together here and where the fuck were you?" (419) But Rabbit, who thinks "God has never wanted him to have a daughter" (421), has instead a granddaughter through Nelson, the son he has failed. Sitting in the new, empty house that he and Janice have just purchased in the poshest neighborhood in Diamond County, Rabbit holds her, "fortune's hostage, Heart's desire, a granddaughter. His. Another nail in his coffin. His" (437).

Rabbit is Rich is thus partly the story of middle-class life rendered natural as the story of cycles of birth, growth, decline, and death, but this naturalization of a specifically cultural way of life is interrupted by moments of insight drawn from the earlier novels and the illness story that they tell. *Rabbit is Rich* therefore hints at something fatally gone wrong in America society, although this too is presented (in the representation of Thelma's terminal illness, and the references to death and "running out of gas" throughout) as a natural process. Despite the indictment of wealth which occurs when Rabbit is weighted down by his South African gold, *Rabbit is Rich* contains less social critique than either of the earlier Rabbit novels. Without the energy of Rabbit's antinomianism or the furor of Skeeter's apocalyptic rhetoric, there is no perspective from which Rabbit's world can be critiqued, either by his example of difference from its norms or his encounter with others who represent such a difference. While hints of the illness story remain, they too are muted. Nelson is merely a maladjusted young man, who will grow up and adjust; God and grace have no spokesman, and speak not a social gospel but a judgment where Rabbit and Janice are mere "ants"; the illness of America is only the decline and decay of real illness, Thelma's fatal disease, the mortality from which we all suffer.

V

The Rabbit novels as whole are inevitably ideological, however much Updike may wish to avoid explicitly political themes in favor of an emphasis on theology, on the family, or on "ordinary" life. In the interview with himself (through his fictional alter-ego Bech) that Updike published in the *New York Times Book Review* when *Rabbit is Rich* appeared, Updike identified the purpose of his fiction as

bringing the corners forward. Or throwing light into them, if you'd rather. Singing the hitherto unsung. That's applied democracy, in my book. And applied Christianity, for that matter. I distrust books involving spectacular people or spectacular events. Let *People* or *The National Enquirer* pander to our taste for the extraordinary; let literature concern itself, as the Gospels do, with the inner lives of hidden men. The collective consciousness that once found itself in the noble must now rest content with the typical (35)

In the reprinting of this essay in the collection *Hugging the Shore*, the reference to "applied democracy" is removed, and the sentence after "unsung" becomes "That's applied Christianity, for that matter" (874). As this revision suggests, Updike has consistently tried to move away from political topics or to transpose the political into something else (often the theological), as he does in *Rabbit Redux*. Yet as his own comments reveal, his project is inevitably social in its intention and caught up in the problematic nature of representation. For while Updike is aware, as he put it in the *Times*, that "reality keeps a pace or two ahead, scribble though we will" (35), his fiction intends to bring forward the corners of reality that are "unsung" and yet "typical," helping to contribute to "collective consciousness" by revealing the lives of "hidden men." While the project of naming unsung parts of social reality, or ways of seeing that reality, is probably shared by most serious writers who view fiction as more than an autonomous field of linguistic play, it is apparent that the naming of the "typical" and the "hidden" is problematic. Whatever is named as typical will in turn function to exclude and hide other parts of reality which therefore remain "unsung," and which themselves need to be brought forward. As Hayden White has noted:

Every mimetic text can be shown to have left something out of the description of its object or to have put something into it that is inessential to what *some* reader, with more or less authority, will regard as an adequate description. On analysis, every mimesis can be shown to be distorted and can serve, therefore, as an occasion for yet another description of the same phenomena. (3)

The interesting point, then, to be made about any act of mimesis is not *that* it distorts but *how* it distorts. In Updike's case, we can see that the very impulse to suspend references to political conflict is a fundamental part of his appeal, for the narrative form—the illness story— that the Rabbit novels helped to shape necessarily involves the displacement of social conflict.

Admittedly, the project of the Rabbit novels is an interesting one: to write the story of contemporary America from the point of view of the "hidden lives" of one group of Americans outside the history of "spectacular events" portrayed in the images of newsprint and television. For the quiet working and middle-class lives of Updike's "middle-American" Diamond County, the events of history—moon landings and oil crises, black revolt and the counterculture, monetary crises and hostage takings—appear to be outside of an everyday reality lived at the rhythm of the family and of personal life, although those events impinge through the factories transformed to retail outlets, the gas lines and increased prices, the minorities in center city who represent both fear and exoticism to a middle-American consciousness that is, despite itself, racist. Updike's problem throughout the Rabbit novels is how to present a perspective from which the way of seeing embodied in these hidden lives can be understood and evaluated. Here is where Updike is weakest as a chronicler of recent decades. He has never found a sustained and convincing alternative to Rabbit's point of view in the Rabbit trilogy, and Rabbit's consciousness, like the illness narrative of which it is a part, is almost by definition unreflective and incapable of such evaluation.

In his 1981 *New York Times* interview with himself, Updike spoke of the desire of every writer to be a "secreter of images" (35) that might take hold in the culture at large. As a chronicler of the dissatisfaction of the middle class in post-1950s America, Updike has helped contribute to the imagination of that dissatisfaction in our "collective consciousness," although the Rabbit trilogy appears less and less capable of illuminating the collective life of the U.S. It is unfortunate that the writer of *Rabbit, Run*, who helped reveal the restlessness beneath the success stories of the American decade, should be increasingly involved in telling the American middle-class what it wants to hear, rather than "bringing the corners forward" that might shake the complacency of the nineteen eighties.

Works Cited

Alter, Robert. "Updike, Malamud, and the Fire Next Time." *John Updike: A Collection of Critical Essays.* Ed. David Thorburn and Howard Eiland. Englewood Cliffs: Prentice-Hall, 1979. 39-49.

Eagleton, Terry. *Literary Theory: An Introduction.* Minneapolis: U of Minnesota P, 1983.

Greiner, Donald. *John Updike's Novels.* Athens: Ohio UP, 1984.

Hunt, George. *John Updike and the Three Secret Things: Sex, Religion, and Art.* Grand Rapids: William B. Erdmans, 1980.

Locke, Richard. "Rabbit's Progress." *New York Times Book Review* 14 November 1971: 1.

Macnaughton, William, ed. *Critical Essays on John Updike.* Boston: G.K. Hall, 1982.

Mailer, Norman. *The Armies of the Night.* New York: New American Library, 1968.

Ohmann, Richard. "The Shaping of a Canon: U.S. Fiction, 1960-1975." *Critical Inquiry* 10 (1983): 199-223.

Samuels, Charles Thomas. *John Updike.* Minneapolis: U of Minnesota P, 1969.

_____. "Updike on the Present." Macnaughton 63-67.

Sorrentino, Gilbert. "Never on Sunday." Macnaughton 77-79.

Updike, John. *Hugging the Shore: Essays and Criticism.* New York: Alfred A. Knopf, 1983.

_____. *Rabbit is Rich.* New York: Ballantine Books, 1982.

_____. *Rabbit Redux.* New York: Ballantine Books, 1982.

_____. *Rabbit, Run.* New York: Ballantine Books, 1982.

_____. "Updike on Updike." *New York Times Book Review* 27 September 1981: 1.

White, Hayden. *Tropics of Discourse: Essays in Cultural Criticism.* Baltimore: John Hopkins, 1978.

Williams, Raymond. *Marxism and Literature.* New York: Oxford UP, 1977.

Myth, History, and Counter-Memory

George Lipsitz

> I will tell you something about stories, [he said]
> They aren't just entertainment.
> Don't be fooled.
> They are all we have, you see,
> All we have to fight off,
> Illness and death.
>
> Leslie Marmon Silko, *Ceremony*

In the opening paragraph of *Their Eyes Were Watching God*, the novelist Zora Neale Hurston draws a distinction between the lives of men and women.[1] According to Hurston, men watch the far horizon where ships at a distance carry their wishes on board. Some men, whose ships come in with the tide, see their dreams realized, while others, whose ships stay out at sea, find their dreams "mocked to death by Time." But women's lives, in Hurston's view, proceed by another process. "Now, women," she writes, "forget all those things they don't want to remember and remember everything they don't want to forget. The dream is the truth. Then they act and do things accordingly" (1).

The world of men, in Hurston's account, is a world of objectivity and action. It is the world of history, of events, and of progress. In contrast, the world of women, as she describes it, is a world of subjectivity and sentiment. It is a world of myth, of stories, and of cycles. Men confront their dreams as entities outside themselves, as stories with clear resolutions knowable to all. Women experience their dreams as created constructs, as stories subject to revision under the pressures of conflict between desires and opportunities.

The point of Hurston's distinction between men and women is not so much to promote invidious comparisons between the genders as it is to foreground a strategy of story-telling appropriate to her experience as an Afro-American and a woman. As subjugated groups, women and blacks find themselves relegated to the margins of the narratives fashioned by dominant groups. Excluded from a legitimate share of public power and victimized by male privilege in private life, women learn from both historical and fictional narratives that only men may look out to sea

161

for their dreams. Similarly, Afro-Americans know all too well that historical narratives relating stories of "human" progress all too often conceal the inhuman oppressions of race and class upon which the triumphs of "civilization" rest. Women, Afro-Americans, and other groups relegated to the margins of dominant discourse learn that the "truths" of society obscure unconscionable lies, while the "lies" of myth and folklore offer opportunities for voicing long suppressed truths.

But myth and folklore are not enough. It is the oppressions of history—of gender, of race, and of class—that make aggrieved populations suspicious of dominant narratives. The radical subjectivity that Hurston describes, where the dream is the truth and people act and do things accordingly, can only provide momentary refuge from the consequences of history. Story-telling that leaves history to the oppressor, that imagines a world of desire detached from the world of necessity, cannot challenge the hegemony of dominant discourse. But story-telling that combines subjectivity and objectivity, that employs the insights and passions of myth and folklore in the service of revising history, can be a powerful tool of contestation. Zora Neale Hurston advanced just such a strategy of story-telling in *Their Eyes Were Watching God*, and subsequent writers from marginalized communities have frequently followed her lead. Seizing upon the adaptive strategies of story-tellers from diverse oral traditions, these writers have advanced a consistent body of principles of communication and action in their battle against dominant narratives. These principles have privileged empathy over individualism, emotion over analysis, effects over intentions. Their efforts to transcend the boundaries of dominant narratives have led them beyond history and myth to explore the sometimes dangerous terrain of counter-memory.

Counter-memory is a way of remembering and forgetting that starts with the local, the immediate, and the personal.[2] Unlike historical narratives that begin with the totality of human existence and then locate specific actions and events within that totality, counter-memory starts with the particular and the specific and then builds outward toward a total story. Counter-memory looks to the past for the hidden histories of those excluded from dominant narratives. But unlike mythical narratives that seek to detach events and actions from the fabric of any larger history, counter-memory demands revision of existing histories by supplying new perspectives about the past. Counter-memory embodies aspects of myth and aspects of history, but it retains an enduring suspicion of both categories. Counter-memory focuses on localized experiences with oppression, using them to reframe and re-focus dominant narratives purporting to represent universal experience.

My inquiry focuses on five novels by authors from ostensibly marginal communities. *Song of Solomon* by the Afro-American female writer Toni Morrison, *Losing Battles* by the Southern white female writer Eudora Welty, *Ceremony* by the Native American Indian female writer Leslie Marmon Silko, *No-No Boy* by the Japanese-American male writer John Okada, and *Bless Me Ultima* by the Chicano male writer Rudolfo Anaya all manifest the sense of counter-memory invoked by Hurston's introduction to *Their Eyes Were Watching God*.

It is my contention that these works not only speak to the needs of oppressed groups grappling with the hegemony of dominant narratives, but that they also address the contradictions and confusions of our time with unrivalled clarity and coherence. In the modern world, the bi-focal and ironic sensibilities of marginal groups take on new meaning as they speak to the increasingly decentered and fragmented consciousness characteristic of the current era. The declining legitimacy of grand ideologies in both capitalist and communist countries, the capacity for the mass media to fragment experience by transcending time and space, and the loss of intimacy and identity engendered by bureaucratic mass societies have all contributed to a sense of alienation and displacement that previously affected groups on the margins of society more than groups in the center. But in our time, sensibilities nourished in the oral traditions of oppositional ethnic and racial communities, in the spheres of activity dominated by women, and in the subcultures of working class life contain extraordinary relevance. Thus in recuperating strategies of story-telling from the past, Morrison, Welty, Silko, Okada, and Anaya not only tell the story of particular oppressions, but they identify as well a use of the past that speaks to present-day intellectual concerns with time, history, subjectivity, and fragmentation.

Beyond History and Myth

Contemporary novelists from marginal cultures grapple with issues of consequence to everyone in the modern world when they address the tensions between grand historical narratives and lived experience. Jean-Francois Lyotard identifies "an incredulity toward meta-narratives" as the operative principle of intellectual life in the world today (xxiv), and that incredulity poses particularly serious challenges to the legitimacy of history and myth. History is nothing if not a master narrative, a grand story that includes everyone whether they know it or not. Historians believe that time and chronology have meaning, that knowledge of the past enables people to place their "commonsense" impressions of the world in a larger, and truer, context. As the social historian Warren Susman explains in a formulaic statement,

It is history that can more reasonably explain the origin, the nature, and the function of various institutions and their interaction. Further, history seems able to point the direction in which a dynamic society is moving. It brings order out of the disordered array that is the consequence of change itself. As a result, history is often used as the basis for a political philosophy that while explaining the past offers also a way to change the future. (8)

Susman realizes that his description undercuts any claim for history as trans-subjective or universal. For it is only in western industrialized societies since the Enlightenment that this concept of history as an instrument for progress has taken root. Traditional societies blur the distinction between the past and present, emphasizing the cyclical and repetitive aspects of human experience rather than its linear or teleological aspects. On the other hand, what Susman calls "contract" societies— a short-hand term for Western capitalist countries—produce historical narratives that posit active and atomized individuals detachable from tradition, family, and ascribed roles (12). Susman assumes that contract societies are superior to traditional ones; therefore he sees the decline of historical narratives in the west as a blow to progress and a barrier against positive future change. Yet Susman fails to acknowledge that the declining legitimacy of Western historical narratives is not just a reversion to a pre-modern consciousness, but rather it reflects an emerging critique of the inadequacies of contract societies and the consciousness they nurture.

Unlike Susman, Hayden White applauds the declining legitimacy of historical narratives in the modern world. In White's view, history is an insidious fiction, a fabricated text passing for reality. White argues that historians impose a linear narrative on what is essentially a plural and non-linear experience. He takes issue with Susman's formulation of history as a means of solving problems. On the contrary, White sees the thrall of history as a major barrier against action on immediate problems because the master narrative of history makes individual and local consciousness so insignificant. In addition, he sees in historical narratives a totalizing tendency, a compulsion to judge all actions by a single standard that in White's view can only encourage the powerful to impose their own self interest on others in the name of "humanity" (see Ch. 1).

Yet for all its sensitivity to the totalitarian effects of historical narratives, White's formulation does little to provide a true and useful means of accounting for the accumulated legacy of human actions from the past that historical narratives generally address. The logical alternative to history is myth, a form of story-telling that goes beyond verifiable evidence to provide a unifying ritual for understanding common experiences. Myths flourish in modern societies, as even Warren Susman reluctantly concedes, and in many ways they supersede history in the popular consciousness. Will Wright offers a useful explanation for the prevalence of myth in advanced societies in his exegesis of the Hollywood western film as modern myth. Wright argues that

For us the past is history; it is necessarily different from the present.... But for this very reason, history is not enough: it can explain the present in terms of the past, but it cannot provide an indication of how to act in the present based on the past, since by definition the past is categorically different from the present. Myths however, can use the setting of the past to create and resolve the conflicts of the present. Myths use the past to tell us how to act in the present. (187)

Thus Wright reverses Susman's argument about utility and problem-solving, claiming that it is myth rather than history that enables us to act in the present. But Wright also stresses the conservative nature of this kind of action. Because myth emphasizes the eternal and cyclical, it speaks more to reconciliation with existing power realities than to challenges against them. Myth provides legitimation for current actions; it reconciles people to the disparity between their desires and their opportunities. Roland Barthes contends that myth functions primarily as a means for rendering "natural" (and consequently inevitable) that which is social (and subject to revision). In this way, myth can explain the past and order the present, but it does so only by accepting the inevitability of the world as it appears (129). History, on the other hand, involves a search for truth, a look beyond surface appearances. History explores how things came to be, including all the roads not taken and all the blasted hopes of the past. It enables us to judge competing myths by a single standard, that of factual investigation into the accumulated consequences of past action. If myth enables us to live with our pain by naturalizing it, history encourages us to ease our pain by understanding it intellectually and analytically.

In an age of incredulity toward meta-narratives, neither myth nor history can adequately order or explain experience. History's connection to contract societies with their instrumental and utilitarian philosophies prevents it from fully airing the continuities of human striving masked by narratives of progress. But mythical constructs, with their emphasis on repetition and cycles, tend to account inadequately for rupture, conflict, and change. The sense of time foregrounded in the five novels that form the object of this study is neither historical nor mythical. Rather they draw upon oral traditions and historical experiences to fashion the time of counter-memory. They challenge traditional western historical narratives, but not out of an unwillingness to solve problems or because of a reluctance to see the ways in which human beings are connected to one another through the accumulated legacies of the past. On the contrary, they seek to expand the scope of history by reconnecting with experiences and emotions rendered invisible by the individualistic ideology and the privileging of power common to historical stories as they are told within contract societies.

The Burden of History

In *Song of Solomon*, Toni Morrison takes aim at the nature of historical evidence by means of a story about the giving of names. Her protagonist suffers from the embarrassing name "Macon Dead III." When the young man asks how his grandfather acquired such an unflattering appellation, his father explains that it came from a drunken white man representing the U.S. government. The father relates that

He asked Papa where he was born. Papa said Macon. Then he asked him who his father was, Papa said, "He's dead." Asked him who owned him, Papa said "I'm free." Well, the Yankee wrote it all down, but in the wrong spaces. Had him born in Dunfrie, wherever the hell that is, and in the space for his name the fool wrote "Dead" comma Macon. (53)

In this instance, the written tradition of historical evidence takes confusion and turns it into a fact, while the oral tradition of myth explains what really happened. Of course, Macon has no particular reason to trust his father's version of the story which comes from an oral tradition with a fanciful sense of invention of its own. But contemporary experience as an Afro-American encourages Macon Dead III to distrust authority and the written word on which it relies, while vital information about his past comes to him through the oral tradition throughout the novel.

Written historical evidence also emerges as unreliable in Eudora Welty's *Losing Battles*. Faced with the Enlightenment rationality of the local school teacher and the local judge, a rural Mississippi family clings to the subjectivity of their oral tradition. When the judge tries to read them a letter, they protest against the primacy he gives to the written word. "I can't understand it when he reads it to us," one of them complains. "Can't he just tell it" (298). Similarly, the family constructs a young woman's identity out of speculation and memory in defiance of the "evidence" presented to them by the judge. He complains that they cannot possibly know her true identity because there are no birth certificates or marriage licenses to confirm the family's claim. He ridicules their interpretation of a scrawled message on a postcard which they interpret as evidence of her patrimony. The judge says, "But a postcard isn't the same evidence as license to marry, or a marriage certificate, and even that—" but one of the relatives contradicts him, saying "It's better! There's a whole lot more...in that postcard, if you know how to read it" (322).

The argument in *Losing Battles* is not so much about the nature of evidence as it is about the necessity of interpreting it. Welty presents both oral and written sources as valid and invalid; each has strengths and weaknesses. Problems arise when individuals privilege one kind of evidence over the other, when they refuse to interpret information actively and creatively. Thus the rural family immerses itself in lies and rationalizations because their desires conflict with the facts of linear history. But on the other hand, the school teacher and the judge devote themselves so thoroughly to the primacy of written evidence that they cut themselves off from other people and their desires. Welty encapsulates the battle between linear history and non-linear myth in a conversation among members of the family circle concerning the teacher, Miss Julia Mortimer. In that exchange Gloria Short tells Jack that the teacher wanted "everything brought out in the wide open, to see and be known. She wanted people to spread out their minds and their hearts to other people so they could be read like books." Jack Renfro says that Miss Mortimer must have been wise like Solomon, but Gloria replies "No, people don't want to be read like books" (432). For to be read like books is to acquire a static and impersonal identity. The kind of history that gives each individual a separate and autonomous story that can be validated in marriage licenses and birth certificates is a history that denies inter-subjectivity—the ways in which people shape and transform each other through collectively authored stories. Yet Welty insists that non-linear histories presented through oral traditions also distort and demean the human condition. The myths and mappings of the Beacham family produce a localized tyranny of misunderstanding and misreading. Political allegiances become matters of kinship. Individuals become defined by their places in family narratives rather than by what they actually think and do. Life and death issues of survival become clouded by paralyzing myths rooted in ignorance and deliberate misreadings of evidence. As Jennifer Randisi shows in her extraordinary critique of Welty, there is no winner in the battle between myth and history in *Losing Battles*, but there is something to be gleaned from the strengths of each form and something to be salvaged from the clash between them. That something, a blend of myth and history, belongs to the category of counter-memory.

A similar conflict provides the operative tension in Native American Indian author Leslie Marmon Silko's *Ceremony*. In her story a Laguna Pueblo Indian works through his alienation from linear history and the scientific Enlightenment world view behind it. Much of Tayo's personal pain comes from experiences that we might consider historical—

service as a combat soldier in World War II, captivity as a prisoner of war, incarceration in a mental hospital after his service as he attempts to accept the death of his brother in combat and to re-adjust to civilian life. In addition, his identity as a Native American forces him to confront a monstrous historical crime—the conquest and settlement of his native land by Americans of European ancestry.

Tayo's cultural clash with Anglo society revolves around questions of citizenship, property, and self-respect, but he experiences the conflict most directly as a battle about which stories are to be believed—the mystical, mythical, and spiritual stories that order experience along empathetic lines, or the linear scientific and historical "facts" that keep the world divided. Tayo remembers being told that anything could be accomplished if one knew the stories from the past—"If a person wanted to get to the moon, there was a way; it all depended on whether you knew the story of how others before you had gone. He had believed in the stories for a long time, until the teachers at the Indian School taught him not to believe" (19). By teaching him not to believe in superstition, the school authorities take away Tayo's belief that his problems can be solved; they tell him that the stories of the past must yield to the hegemony of historical and scientific facts. In the world of the school, as well as in the world of Army and the mental hospital, Tayo encounters the forces of division, dividing the past from the present, animals from people, people from the land, and people from one another. As he recalls in thinking about school

The science books explained the causes and effects. But old Grandma always used to say, "Back in time immemorial, things were different, the animals could talk to human beings and many magical things still happened." He never lost the feeling he had in his chest when she spoke those words, as she did each time she told them the stories; and he still felt it was true, despite all they had taught him in school—that long ago things had been different.... (99)

Yet while linear history and scientific thought provide barriers to true understanding for Tayo, they are not irrelevant to his search for truth and empowerment. The consequences of history can not be ignored; the conquest of the southwest, the war with Japan, and the enduring racism of postwar America offer specific historical oppressions in need of historical understanding. To retreat into a localized world of magic and tradition offers no solution to Tayo, because that retreat would not explain or address the root causes of his pain. In addition, the Indian "ceremonies" have lost much of their power because they have not been changed to fit new circumstances. Only a medicine man outside of his own tribe can lead him to the truth, a truth which involves a critical stance toward both Indian myth and Anglo-European history. As Tayo realizes, "The liars had fooled everyone, white people and Indians alike; as long as people believed the lies, they would never be able to see what had been done to them or what they were doing to each other" (199).

Only by combining myth and history can Tayo create a useful synthesis for understanding and action. The very forces of science and rationality responsible for division in his world also provide the possibility for ending division. Tayo understands that science has created a peculiar kind of unity in the modern world because everyone is united in fear of a nuclear holocaust. The ancient minerals of his native New Mexico provide the elements for the epitome of scientific rationality, the atom bomb. Yet in creating a device with a destructive power to destroy the whole world, the scientists have also restored ancient unities. Silko explains Tayo's perception of this unity by telling us that

There was no end to it; it knew no boundaries; and he had arrived at the point of convergence where the fate of all living things, and even the earth had been laid. From the jungles of his dreaming he recognized why the Japanese voices had merged with Laguna voices, with Josiah's voice and Rocky's voice; the lines of cultures and worlds were drawn in flat dark lines on fine light sand, converging in the middle of witchery's final ceremonial sand painting. From that time on, human beings were one clan again, united by the fate the destroyers planned for all of them, for all living things; united by a circle of death that devoured people in cities twelve thousand miles away, victims who had never known those mesas, who had never seen the delicate colors of the rocks which boiled up their slaughter. (257)

The horrible power of the atomic bomb undermines the legitimacy of Enlightenment rationality and enables Tayo to understand his own history for the first time. Because he has been excluded and trivialized within the master narratives, he understands the evils of exclusion and trivialization as basic flaws in the system of western thought. Rather than celebrating and accepting his exclusion and trivialization through a "delight in difference" as the postmodernists might advise, he instead struggles for a real unity that will do justice to the many voices suppressed by centuries of division. When he was in the mental hospital, the white doctors had tried to cure Tayo by urging him to accept division, to adjust to his differences. Tayo tried to believe them, but he knew that "medicine didn't work that way" and instead insisted that "his cure would be found only in something great and inclusive of everything" (132).

A history that built it synthesis from the plural and diverse experiences of people like Tayo would be "something great and inclusive of everything." Tayo's desire to understand both his personal crises and the oppression of his people through the interaction of grand and small narratives embodies the principles of counter-memory. His way of thinking recaptures the totalizing imperatives of historical thought, but grounds them in the plurality of particular oppressions. Counter-memory in this sense is not a denial of history, only a rejection of its false priorities and hierarchical divisions. In the modern world marginal and excluded people like Tayo take on a particularly important role in reclaiming historical thought because their experience makes them uniquely sensitive to the diversities upon which a new unity might be built.

Marginal and excluded groups also understand the shortcomings of the categories and labels used within dominant narratives. Just as Macon Dead could not trust the name he had been given by the historical record in *Song of Solomon*, Tayo cannot accept the narrow range of identities open to him as a Native American Indian stereotyped and defined by the conquerors of his people. Barbara Christian points out that Afro-American female writers like herself see beyond existing categories because their lives are more complex than the available definitions and descriptions of them. Christian writes, "Our expression of our lives cannot be narrowly conceived, for we cannot change our condition through a single minded banner" (4). Learning the truths of history for marginalized groups demands a complex negotiation between the legacy of historical events that effect everyone and the partial and limited account of those events that makes up the historical record kept by dominant groups. Women writers, and authors from other aggrieved populations have particular resources for managing that negotiation. "Such complexity" Christian contends, "is not confusion. It is that feeling awareness which June Jordan expresses in her 'Declaration,' the interconnectedness of supposed opposites, of mental knowledge and feeling knowledge, of the self and of the other" (16).

The sense of counter-memory informing the work of women writers like Hurston, Morrison, Welty, and Silko also pervades the work of male writers from ethnic communities. The Japanese-American writer John Okada and the Chicano novelist Rudolfo Anaya provide particularly strong presentations of counter-memory as a way of reclaiming historical thinking from the contexts created for it by dominant narratives. In each of their writings, a complex search for identity includes an exploration of history that requires more information than can be provided by written evidence. Thus for Okada as a Japanese-American and Anaya as a Mexican-American, ethnicity is a story filled with ambiguities and contradictions, not a static fact. To be an ethnic-American for these authors is to be involved in a delicate set of negotiations among multiple identities, and those negotiations can only be understood through attention to the many competing stories that make up any one individual's story.

In Okada's *No-No Boy*, Ichiro Yamada is the son of Japanese immigrants who finds himself torn between two cultures. War between the U.S. and Japan presents him with difficult choices and underscores his uncertain relationship to both countries. The U.S. government sends him and his family to an internment camp, while his mother prays for Japan to win the war. Deferring to his mother's wishes in an exercise of filial piety Ichiro refuses the U.S. Army's offer to release him from the camp if he will accept service in the military. Thus he is a "No-No Boy," one who refuses to serve in the army. But still, he cannot accept his mother's view of Japan as a sacred homeland. Ichiro believes himself to be an American, even when his ethnicity and his own actions prevent him from being accepted as one.

The consequences of historical events—migrations from Asia to North America, the war between the U.S. and Japan, and the anti-Asian racism of the postwar years—combine to pose questions of personal identity for Ichiro. Where does he fit into these quarrels not of his own making? He cannot attribute his problems simply to Japanese ancestry; he knows that his refusal to serve in the armed forces brings him scorn from many other Japanese-Americans. Yet he also knows that Japanese-Americans face suffering no matter what their choices. Like Tayo's brother Rocky in *Ceremony*, all of the Japanese-Americans in *No-No Boy*, who volunteer for service in the army wind up destroyed. Ichiro's friend Bob Kumasaka goes into the army and gets killed in combat, while his friend Kenji serves gallantly but returns home to die of his wounds. Kenji even tells Ichiro that refusing induction was the right choice, but Ichiro wishes in some ways that he could change places with Kenji. The reality is that there is no uniformly good choice for any of them, because they are all subject to forces beyond their control. But, again like Tayo in ceremony, Ichiro survives and acquires wisdom by realizing that his marginality gives him a unique, and a true, perception of American identity.

Like Silko, Okada sees the solution to the pain of marginality and division resting in some kind of larger unity. But he does not call for assimilation into the dominant society or for an acceptance of its historical narratives. Rather he demands that society and history be restructured to acknowledge the truths to be found in the margins. Ichiro comes to critique the monolithic appearance of America as a lie: even though he suffers from his exclusion, he recognizes that more people are excluded from the dominant narratives than are included in them. At one point he asks

Where is that place they talk of and paint nice pictures of and describe in all the homey magazines? Where is that place with the clean white cottages surrounding the new, red-brick church with the clean white steeple, where the families all have two children, one boy and one girl, and a shiny new car in the garage and a dog and a cat and life is like living in the land of the happily ever after?...

He then answers his own question with a suggestion,

Maybe the answer is that there is no in. Maybe the whole damned country is pushing and shoving and screaming to get into someplace that doesn't exist, because they don't know that the outside would be the inside if only they would stop all this pushing and shoving and screaming, and they haven't got enough sense to realize that. That makes sense. I've got the answer all figured out simple and neat and sensible. (159)

But acting upon that answer proves more difficult than Ichiro anticipated. By the end of the novel he remains convinced that "the margins are at the center," as the Deconstructionists might say, but that it is dangerous to pretend that the center does not exist. Instead, he seeks to reconstitute the center, to build a new consensus based on the utility and wisdom of marginal perspectives. Using his own history of exclusion as a guide he begins to understand other excluded groups and individuals. He cannot accept the "history" that relegates him to marginal status, but neither can he escape its consequences. He can mix his subjective reactions to his own oppression with objective evidence about the pain suffered by others. In this way, memories are not barriers to understanding; rather they make him specially equipped to both understand his immediate experience and to move beyond it.

Like Okada, Rudolfo Anaya tells a story about ethnic American counter-memory in his novel, *Bless Me, Ultima*. Anaya's Antonio Marez confronts the same kinds of competing stories that puzzle the protagonists in *Ceremony* and *No-No Boy*. Antonio is Mexican and American, Catholic and pagan, Indian and Spaniard, promising student to his teachers and potential priest to his mother. The narratives surrounding his life force him to choose between languages, flags, religions, philosophies, and histories. Antonio's journey toward self-awareness revolves around his growing recognition that these choices are false, that he cannot give up any of them. Instead, he learns to step in and out of identities in order to fabricate a multi-layered consciousness appropriate to his true history as the product of many cultures.

Given the sensitivity to these issues of multiple identity among women novelists, it seems particularly significant that a male novelist like Anaya chooses to embody wisdom in Ultima, the female character in the book who teaches Antonio that the highest truths involve connections to other people. Ultima does this by reconciling magic and science, paganism and Catholicism, and even men and women. More than his mother or father, Ultima provides Antonio with moral guidance by teaching him how to live with the divisions created by history without succumbing to their oppressions. Ultima encourages Antonio to fashion a new synthesis by drawing upon the past. As Antonio relates

Ultima told me the stories and legends of my ancestors. From her I learned the glory and the tragedy of the history of my people, and I came to understand that history stirred in my blood. (115)

But like Tayo and Ichiro, Antonio cannot find the answer in difference and division. As Ultima says to him in a dream, "You have been seeing only parts,...and not looking beyond into the great cycle that binds us all" (113). It is in looking at the great cycle that counter-memory goes beyond history and myth, that it transcends the false closures of linear history and the destructive ruptures and divisions of myth to create an active memory which draws upon the plurality of the past to illumine the opportunities of the present and the future.

Counter-Memory and History

Thus counter-memory is not a rejection of history, but a reconstitution of it. As Barbara Christian says on behalf of black women writers, "It is the resonance of history that lets us know we are here. memory not only reproduces the past, it gives us guides by which to evaluate the present, and helps to create the future, which is an illusionary concept unless we know that yesterday we saw the present as the future. It is not surprising then that contemporary Afro-American women writers have spent so much energy on reclaiming their history, so disrupted and ignored by both black and white scholarship" (4). And what is true for Afro-American women in this regard also holds validity for white southern women, Native American Indian women, and men from marginalized ethnic communities. By dwelling on difference and disunity, by playing off myth against history, writers like Morrison, Welty, Silko, Okada, and Anaya have pointed the way toward a new synthesis, one that offers dignity interchangeably to all peoples without first forcing them into an imaginary identity constructed from a top down perspective on human experience.

In his extraordinary book on modernism and post-modernism, *All That Is Solid Melts Into Air*, Marshall Berman writes that

Modern environments and experiences cut across all boundaries of geography and ethnicity, of class and nationality, of religion and ideology; in this sense modernity can be said to unite all mankind. But it is a paradoxical unity, a unity of disunity; it pours us all into a maelstrom of perpetual disintegration and renewal, of struggle and contradiction, of ambiguity and anguish. To be modern is to be part of a universe in which, as Marx said, "all that is solid melts into air." (15)

Cultural conservatives like Christopher Lasch bemoan the declining authority of traditional history in such a world; they see the rise of counter-memory as a threat to knowledge and order. As Lasch writes, "The poor have always had to live for the present, but now a desperate concern for personal survival, sometimes disguised as hedonism, engulfs the middle-class as well. Today everyone lives in a dangerous world from which there is little escape" (Long 191). Lasch's fear is that the middle and upper classes have fallen to the intellectual level traditionally reserved for the poor and the exploited. In some ways he is correct, but his pejorative description of that level obscures many of its strengths. The modern world described by Berman does place a priority on the consciousness and perspectives developed over centuries by oppressed groups. They are the ones who have had to develop dual and triple consciousness, who have had to live with the consequences of history while remaining skeptical about the veracity of dominant historical narratives. Out of necessity they have been forced to understand both the pleasure and the pain of difference and division. But rather than impoverishing our understanding of the past, the traditions of counter-memory enable us to account for some of the complexities of collective experience for the first time.

There certainly are dangers connected with a radical subjectivity detached from traditional standards of historical evidence. But those dangers are no greater than the ones attendant to linear history rooted in written evidence, but oblivious to sedimented oral traditions. By combining linear history and orally-transmitted popular memory, counter-memory has the potential to combine the best of both modes. If counter-memory lacks the traditional truth tests of evidence basic to linear historical texts, it also subjects itself to an even more rigorous test—the standard of collective memory and desire. For these narratives to work, they have to resonate with the experiences and feelings of their audiences; for them to work fully, they must address the part of audience memory that relates to real historical oppressions and suppressed hopes. Authors take great risks when they draw upon oral traditions; they surrender some of their individual control over the text to the contours and demands of collective memory. But that very surrender of authority brings them closer to truth. As the interpretive anthropologist James Clifford asks, "If we are condemned to tell stories we cannot control, may we not, at least, tell stories we believe to be true?" (121).

Women's Time and Counter-Memory

When Zora Neale Hurston wrote about men who find their dreams mocked to death by Time (using the upper case), she implied that women confront another kind of time. In an essay titled "Women's Time," Julia Kristeva offers a contemporary reformulation of the uses of time propounded by Hurston fifty years ago. Kristeva asserts that women find themselves torn between two kinds of time—cursive time and monumental time. Cursive time, the time of linear history, is important to women because it is there that sexism and discrimination become inscribed in state policies. The first stage of the women's movement in Kristeva's view fought for inclusion in cursive time by demanding public action against juridicial and economic discrimination. Monumental time, the time of life cycles and private rituals, is important to women because it is there that private and personal spheres of autonomy are carved away within the constraints of male hegemony. Kristeva sees the second stage of the women's movement as oriented toward monumental time through demands for recognition for "the specificity of female psychology and its symbolic realizations" and through efforts to "give a language to the intrasubjective and corporeal experiences left mute by culture in the past" (193-94). Thus Kristeva argues that women must understand both the time of men and the time of women, a parallel to the efforts of novelists using counter-memory who want their audiences to understand both the history of contract societies and the oral traditions of aggrieved populations.

But this dual consciousness is not enough. Left separate, these two spheres cancel each other out. Exclusive focus on cursive time obscures the resources and institutions nurtured by ritual and myth. Exclusive focus on monumental time obscures the institutional and structural forces of oppression constraining local subjectivities. What Kristeva calls "women's time" is also the time of other oppressed or marginalized groups—it is the essence of counter-memory. Counter-memory understand the limits of historical time, but still tries to act within it. Similarly, counter-memory celebrates the subversive visions and stubborn *jouissance* of monumental time, while still insisting on relating those local oppositional practices to macro-social causes and consequences.

Literature plays a special role in the articulation of counter-memory. As public texts touching audiences with historical memories, popular novels have some responsibility for historical accuracy in order to be perceived as credible. At the very least, they cannot disregard collective historical memory. On the other hand, as works of art and imagination they are not bound by the constraints of public records and verifiable evidence as would be true of historical scholarship. They belong to a realm between myth and history and they present a world view that mediates between the two. It is literature that brings out the hidden resonances of collective historical memory. As Kristeva asks,

Is it because, faced with social norms, literature reveals a certain knowledge and sometimes the truth itself about an otherwise repressed, nocturnal, secret, and unconscious universe? Because it thus redoubles the social contract by exposing the unsaid, the uncanny? And because it makes a game, a space of fantasy and pleasure, out of the abstract, and frustrating order of social signs, the words of everyday communication? (207)

Kristeva's implied answer to her own rhetorical questions is an affirmative one, and her insights apply not only to popular literature but to the concept of popular culture itself.

In what sense are the novels by Morrison, Welty, Silko, Okada, and Anaya "popular"? They each appear in mass marketed paperback editions, although Okada's and Anaya's are published by small presses. None of them has been commercially successful enough to make the best-seller lists, and all have received critical acclaim from scholars and critics. Yet they do not fall into the realm of "high culture" either; they do not attempt to live up to the codes of transcendent truth, of embodying the best and highest that mankind may imagine, as was true of the elite culture of the nineteenth century. These novels, like so much else in popular culture, seem to lie in a sphere with no name. They are not folklore or disposable mass commercial art, but on the other hand, they are not works clamoring for admission to the rarified canon of civilization's great books.

Traditional categories of classification cannot encompass the structure and aims of novels employing counter-memory, just as they cannot encompass other forms of popular culture like the romance novel, the rock and roll song, or the "B" movie. These forms all share some aspects of counter-memory that give new meaning to the term popular. They can be considered "popular" not because of the sheer numbers of people who consume them, but because of certain sensibilities that occupy a central place within them. They all draw upon oral traditions, vernacular speech, and a focus on the immediate and ordinary concerns of everyday life. Most importantly, they tap sources of collective popular memory to identify the repressed and suppressed traditions of opposition to oppression. Finally, while originating in local, particular, and specific oppressions, they use modern means of communication to reach out to other groups and individuals with similar, although not identical oppressions.

The cultural conservatives like Christopher Lasch and Daniel Bell who bemoan the loss of historical consciousness in the modern world, seriously misread the subtexts of popular culture. Certainly dominant historical narratives have lost much of their legitimacy. But within the interstices of popular culture, a rich collective counter-memory carries on the tasks of historical thinking in new and significant ways. Frederic Jameson understands the presence of this sedimented historical tradition when he describes all works of popular culture as having utopian moments that function as a critique of contemporary power relations. But even Jameson relegates the historical dimension of popular culture to a "political unconscious"—an uncomprehending desire to give concrete form to the absent cause that might make sense out of the incoherence of a world without believable historical narratives. But in popular cultural forms as diverse as motion pictures, television programs, rock and roll music, and gothic romances, a strong strain of counter-memory evidences an already existing history and politics. The qualities that Kristeva attributes to literature exist within many forms of mass popular culture. These contain many limitations, shortcomings, and contradictions. But in their focus on counter-memory, they draw upon an oppositional cultural practice deeply rooted in art, in history, and in popular collective consciousness. In the midst of division and disunity they dare to imagine a world where everyone's wishes may come in with the tide.

Notes

[1] I wish to thank Betty Bergland, Wendy Kozol, Adam Sorkin and Barbara Tomlinson for their comments on an earlier draft of this essay. I also appreciate my many discussions about the books under consideration here with Lori Cegla, Carter Meland, Thomas Redmond, and John Wareham.

[2] I am using the term counter-memory here in a distinctly different sense than it is employed by Michael Foucault in *Language, Counter-Memory, Practice*. For Foucault, counter-memory "must record the singularity of events outside of any monotonous finality" (139), "cultivate the details and accidents that accompany every beginning" (144), and describe the "single drama" that is staged in the process of emergence as "the endlessly repeated play of dominations" (150). In my view, Foucault's perspective offers much as a critique of dominant notions of myth and history, but as intellectual and social practice it can too easily degenerate into a pessimism which is itself a form of collaboration. In the collective memory of the sources tapped in this essay, I find an emancipatory practice and perspective. yet despite his own definition of counter-memory, I find Foucault's term too good to pass up altogether. Instead I have chosen to appropriate the word for purposes that its author would certainly not endorse.

Works Cited

Anaya, Rudolfo. *Bless Me, Ultimate.* Berkeley: Tonatiuh International, 1986.

Barthes, Roland. *Mythologies*. Trans. Annette Lavers. New York: Hill and Wang, 1972.

Berman, Marshall. *All That Is Solid Melts Into Air*. New York: Simon and Schuster, 1982.

Christian, Barbara T. *From the Inside Out: Afro-American Women's Literary Tradition and the State*. Minneapolis: Center for Humanistic Studies, 1987.

Clifford, James. "On Ethnographic Allegory." *Writing Culture: The Poetics and Politics of Ethnography*. Ed. James Clifford and George E. Marcus. Berkeley: U of California P, 1986. 98-121.

Foucault, Michel. *Language, Counter-Memory Practice: Selected Essays and Interviews*. Trans. Sherry Simon. Ed. Donald Bouchard. Ithaca: Cornell UP, 1980.

Hurston, Zora Neale. *Their Eyes Were Watching God*. Urbana: U of Illinois P, 1979.

Jameson, Fredric. "Reification and Utopia in Mass Culture." *Social Text* 1 (1979): 1-39.

Kristeva, Julia. "Women's Time." *The Kristeva Reader*. Ed. Toril Moi. New York: Columbia UP, 1986.

Lasch, Christopher. *The Culture of Narcissism*. New York: Norton, 1978.

Long, Elizabeth. *The American Dream and the Popular Novel*. London: Routledge, Kegan Paul, 1986.

Lyotard, Jean-Francois. *The Postmodern Condition: A Report on Knowledge*. Trans. Geoff Bennington and Brian v. Massumi. Minneapolis: U of Minnesota P, 1984.

Morrison, Toni. *Song of Solomon*. New York: New American Library, 1977.

Okada, John. *No-No Boy*. Seattle: U of Washington P, 1976.

Randisi, Jennifer. *A Tissue of Lies*. Washington, D.C: UP of America, 1982.

Silko, Leslie Marmon. *Ceremony*. New York: New American Library, 1977.

Sussman, Warren I. *Culture as History*. New York: Pantheon, 1984.

Welty, Eudora. *Losing Battles*. New York: Random House, 1970.

White, Hayden. *Tropics of Discourse: Essays in Cultural Criticism*. Baltimore: Johns Hopkins UP, 1978.

Wright, Will. *Sixguns and Society*. Berkeley: U of California P, 1975.

Politics and Metaphors of Materialism in Paule Marshall's *Praisesong for the Widow* and Toni Morrison's *Tar Baby*

Angelita Reyes

If anything I do, in the way of writing novels or whatever I write, isn't about the village or the community or about you, then it isn't about anything. I am not interested in indulging myself in some private exercise of my imagination...which is to say yes, the work must be political.
Toni Morrison, "Rootedness: The Ancestor as Foundation"

There is the theory in linguistics which states that the idiom of a people, the way they use language, reflects not only the most fundamental views they hold of themselves and the world but their very conception of reality.
Paule Marshall, "From the Poets in the Kitchen"

I ain't good lookin' and I ain't got waist-long hair
I say I ain't good lookin' and I ain't got waist-long hair
But my mama gave me something that'll take me anywhere
Traditional blues verse

American writers of African descent write from social and cultural perspectives which invariably reflect aspects of the Middle Passage[1] and its complex aftermath of American racism, prejudice, and exploitation of people of color. The Middle Passage has become a paradoxical metaphor of progress and displacement in American literature and correspondingly the metaphor of El Dorado likewise represents an ideology of social enterprise and New World conquest.[2] El Dorado— that search for gold in the New World—was one of the most devastating treasure hunts in history. Decidedly, the quest for El Dorado meant the exploitation of indigenous peoples in the Americas and of people brought to the Americas in bondage.

The historical reality of the Middle Passage and El Dorado underscored the conquest of land and people. Despite the fact that El Dorado as an actual place remained a geographical illusion for the conquistadors and patriarchs, just having the image of an El Dorado constituted the potentials of material wealth, happiness, and success. The pursuit of gold and golden cities continued as all of the Americas expanded for Europeans and new frontiers opened. In North America, patriarchs such as Thomas Jefferson, Andrew Jackson, Tom Paine, and Walt Whitman were a part of the new expansions and helped to mold new surrogate El Dorados in the continuous European-American expansion of land, property, and eventual industrialization (Berry; Parrington).

Implicit as historical metaphors in literature, Middle Passage and El Dorado imagery is used to appropriate and define the traditional and contemporary African-American experience. That experience is one of an inevitable implied political nature considering the ramifications of the history of black people in the New World. The Black Power movement of the sixties and early seventies emphasized the politics of official history rather than the politics of personal and inner experience. As the more personal voice has gained momentum and popularity, so has personal narrative become one of the ways to present the influence of history on the African-American community. Contemporary American writing places concern on the inner experience as it connects to new definitions of religion and spirituality. Jane Campbell points out that:

> The belief in radical revolt, while still very much alive on some fronts, is less visible than a belief in electoral politics. Religious faith and spirituality reattain widespread legitimacy.... At the same time, Americans gravitate toward the family as a refuge and manifest a renewed interest in family history. (136)

Without doubt, there is renewed concern for the family unit and its traditional strengths. One way for the ethnic community to reconnect with its spiritual and cultural heritage is to know its history.

Two writers deeply concerned with personal experience as it illuminates external history are Paule Marshall and Toni Morrison. Marshall's *Praisesong for the Widow* and Morrison's *Tar Baby*, both published in the early 1980s, explore the relationship of personal and documented history and how that relationship affects collective cultural values. Personal history is translated through metaphors of myth and ritual. By using historical and personal metaphors, the authors imply that African-Americans need to connect to those aspects of culture and heritage which are psychologically empowering. Indeed, for both Morrison and Marshall, personal histories and extended cultural metaphors are paradigms of African-American history. Through the representation of metaphor and the presentation of history, the two authors write against the indiscriminate acquisition of Euro-American cultural values which allow African-Americans to forget African heritage, or as Morrison characterizes it, to forget their "ancient properties." The ancient properties are essentially rooted in the *connected* consciousness of the African past.

Social and legislative efforts at integration and the emergence of a distinct black bourgeoisie, in addition to the renewed consciousness regarding women's rights, have caused some blacks to be dominated by *Euro*-American, rather than *African*-American values. These Euro-American values are fundamentally middle-class operatives of capitalism, which means, in part, the attainment of happiness through the quest for and acquisition of "things." The [con]quest continues in that the objective is material wealth just as it was for the founding conquerors of the Americas. El Dorado now translates into a modern quest for owning things even if it continues to mean the preemption of place, property, and people. But displacement and preemption are not only on economic grounds—there is psychological and spiritual preemption as well. In the metaphoric context of El Dorado, people have their sense of worth only when they can own through [con]quest. And in some instances, they still want to own other people.[3] Throughout *Tar Baby* and *Praisesong*, we see how events rooted in history and mythic thought conflict with the social consciousness of bourgeois American materialism. Certainly, Marshall and Morrison do not reject economic progress. The problem is to reach and maintain a compromise between material excess and spiritual propriety. By assuming a balance between Euro-American culture and African-American heritage, the community can better attempt to keep its feet on the nurturing ground. As *womanist* writers, Marshall and Morrison deal with

a philosophy that celebrates black roots, the ideals of black life, while giving a balanced presentation of black womandom. It concerns itself as much with the black sexual power tussle as with the world power structure that subjugates blacks. Its ideal is for black unity where every black person has a modicum of power.... (Ogunyemi 72)

American womanist interpreters are dynamic feminists in that they believe that women and men are complementary—neither should exist mutually exclusive of the other.[4] These women are mother-women to themselves, to other women, and to their immediate family.[5] They have a commitment to the community and larger society in that they are aware of the social injustices and, according to their circumstances, actively participate in building the new order. This is simultaneously the difficulty and the richness of the womanist experience in America. Womanism emphasizes a certain continuity of strength as in Alice Walker's imagery of: " 'Mama, I'm walking to Canada and I'm taking you and a bunch of other slaves with me.' Reply: 'It wouldn't be the first time' " (xi-

xii). Womanist discourse sees an inherent empowerment in the heritage of the extended African-American family rather than in the Euro-American nuclear family. There is the need to acknowledge self and kin. As Marshall clearly indicates, the sustaining values come from the kin who still walk and breathe as well as from the ancestors who have passed on. Furthermore, these values are primarily sustained through the culture-bearer of the community, that is to say, the woman who is not necessarily a biological parent, but a "sort of umbrella figure, a culture-bearer in that community with not just her children but all children" (Stepto 488). As culture-bearers, women are primary transmitters of the culture and its traditions. In the same instance, much of the contemporary literature indicates that the culture-bearer is not an earth-mother stereotype. The womanist culture-bearer is actively *engage* and defines "walking to Canada" accordingly. From this perspective, Avey Johnson's ancestor-aunt in *Praisesong* is the culture-bearer who reestablishes Avey's spiritual relationship to family, community, and history. Contrasting with Avey, Jadine in *Tar Baby* rejects the notion of extended family and ancestral connections for her ideal of family: essentially that she does not have to bond with family and culture. Jadine refuses to come to terms with the nurturing ground and her ancestors' ancient properties. Not only does she limit her spiritual growth, but her geographical boundaries as well are not capable of including kin and community. She has no sense of spiritual or cultural place. As one critic states, we see that in *Tar Baby* "notions of bourgeois morality and attitudes concerning the proper education and role of women have created a contemporary 'tar baby': a black woman in cultural limbo" (Willis 264). Like El Dorado, place is elusive for Jadine. At best, intimate and sacred place are fleeting moments of history and myth. Her happiness lies in the pursuit.

Despite their all-encompassing regard for African-American cultural and spiritual properties, Paule Marshall and Toni Morrison employ distinctly different strategies to explore women's histories, myth, and contemporary values. While Marshall is explicit in her use of ritual and mythology in *Praisesong*, Morrison's use of the metaphoric other in *Tar Baby* baffles many readers. Cunningly enough, Morrison's employment of the other is in the first instance an African mode of storytelling. Among the techniques the oral historian or *griotte* uses is inverted paradox. She places emphasis on what is *not* said and what is *not* seen in order to convey meaning and purpose. Morrison's technique incorporates the African and African-American rhetorical device of saying one thing to underscore another. What is seen is really an illusion of what the narrator, story-teller, or *signifier* wants to be understood. The technique is a vehicle for the actual narrative. Henry Louis Gates, Jr. aptly maintains that the concept of implied meaning, of chiasmus itself, of signification in the context of the African-American literary imagination, arise out of a neo-African vernacular culture that predates Ferdinand de Saussure by at least two hundred years ("Blackness" 285). Avey Johnson at the end of *Praisesong* very obviously has her feet firmly on the nurturing ground of her African-American cultural identity, whereas Jadine takes flight from the nurturing ground not willing to grip her own spirituality and heritage.[6] In other words, by depicting a character who takes flight *from* the nurturing ground rather than flight to embrace it, Morrison speaks through the paradoxical voice of the other. She juxtaposes absence and presence in order to *signify* on meaning.

From that paradoxical position, Morrison amplifies the need for the African-American community to know and appreciate its mythic and spiritual inheritance. Paradox in Morrison's fiction underscores the difficulty of balancing the want for material comfort and the need for spiritual and cultural bonding in the context of day to day reality. Morrison further reflects reality in that she depicts how people cannot live in the past, but must know its history. Therefore, she fine tunes her creative dialogue with myth and collective history through implied echoes of the Middle Passage and quest motifs. In contrast, Marshall focuses directly on the obvious and attempts to provide solutions. Marshall is highly explicit about the ramifications of the Middle Passage as she attempts ideally to provide solutions to complex problems. Collective Middle Passage remembrance is ritually overt and systematically woven into the narrative converging on the site of immediate geographical/ historical reality (the annual excursion of the Carriacou islanders and the enactment of the Big Drum dance) and collective personal growth (the annual ceremony acts as a historical touchstone for the islanders and as a spiritual lodestone for Avey Johnson).[7] Nevertheless, both authors depict the interaction of myth and documented history in order to demonstrate that certain Euro-American values must not be exchanged for those modalities of the African-American connected consciousness. A knowledge of history and mythic heritage allows African-Americans to grapple with the politics of day-to-day living, survival, and collective inspiration without indiscriminately succumbing to another group's value system.

Both Paule Marshall and Toni Morrison illuminate a tradition which is not ashamed of being religious and spiritual in order to cope with social injustices and cultural dilemmas. Marshall's widow, Avey Johnson, experiences the final phase of her historical and mythic ritual process through the sacred invocation of her ancestors, the Old Parents, in the immediacy of the Big Drum's Beg Pardon dance. Cultural and spiritual values are reappropriated for Avey because of her ancestor, Great-Aunt

Cuney. Great-Aunt Cuney is not only one of the Old Parents, but she is also a *Great* Mother in that she provides archetypal guidance by returning to Avey through dreams. As I have indicated, the significance of mother is not limited to its biological meaning, but rather transcends biological expression to include woman as a parent of spiritual culture. Jadine is adopted by her aunt and uncle after the death of her parents. Yet, she does not have a daughter's kind of caring for them. Avey Johnson reclaims the rights of daughterhood (as the younger woman paying homage to the older woman, Great-Aunt Cuney) and spiritual womanhood.

Paule Marshall demonstrates that despite the many difficulties, Euro- and African-American values can be bridged. Marshall resolves the tensions. Avey is able to connect the bridges; Jadine chooses not to connect her two worlds. She is unable to mediate between the spiritual world of her ancestors and the contemporary materialistic world of Europe and America. By using paradox, Morrison shows that building cultural bridges is tenuous for some, and sometimes not even desired. *Praisesong for the Widow* and *Tar Baby* both explore how materialism and the need to control other people can block a person's and the community's spiritual and cultural visions.

*   *   *

Paule Marshall's literary nurturing began in the "Bajan" community of Brooklyn, New York. Marshall fully credits the Barbadian mother-women of her childhood for providing her with such a rich source of cultural inheritance: African, African-Caribbean, and American. Of her own mother, Marshall writes: "She laid the foundations of my aesthetic, that is the themes and techniques which characterize my work" ("Shaping the World" 105). Her childhood years were not only shaped by the "unknown bards," these mother-women, but marked by the materialism of the West Indian community. As she depicts in her first novel, *Brown Girl, Brownstones*, the community is caught in the materialistic web of "this white man country." Their El Dorado is expressed through the determination to accumulate consumer commodities and to own "de house" (if not several) at any human cost. Their brand of materialism is an extension of Middle Passage denials and attempts to legitimize their worth. Selina, the central figure in *Brown Girl*, rebels against those values. Although she claims herself as a child-product of America, she also affirms herself as a child of the Caribbean, and by spiritual consciousness, of Africa. Her coming of age is testimony to being an American woman-child with a West Indian heritage. Marshall says of this representation:

The West Indies is so very important to me because it is part of a history that as a girl I tried to deny. I went through torture as a girl growing up in Brooklyn, going to school with those heavy silver bangles on my wrists, and when we went to the West Indies and came back with heavy West Indian accents, the kids used to laugh at us. It was dreadful. Now the West Indies represents an opportunity for me to fill in something I tried to deny, and it provides me with a manageable landscape for writing.... (DeVeaux 96)

With her third novel, *Praisesong*, Marshall continues to explore the dynamics of the West Indian cultural landscape, and its African heritage. The very title of the novel attempts to celebrate cultural transition and African continuity.

In traditional Africa the praisesong is a chant or poem-song which dramatizes the achievements of an individual or community within the realm of history and extended family. Performed by the *griot* or *griotte*, the oral historian, genealogist and musician, the praisesong is a highly developed "genre" in African oral literature. It is both a sacred and profane modality. In Marshall's invocation of praise-singing we see how the sacred overlaps with the profane reality. Avey Johnson's praisesong fulfills a vital function: it allows her to create a new opportunity for spiritual empowerment as she learns a new understanding of social propriety. At this point, some clarification is necessary as to how I am applying the concept of spirituality and religion, which is arrived at from within an African cultural matrix.

Traditional African philosophy and religion are characterized by sacred forces interwoven into the quotidian life of the community. Few valid generalizations can be made about a continent so vast and culturally diversified as Africa. However, among the few, it can be affirmed that religiosity as a pivotal force among African peoples. In his comprehensive study of African religions and philosophy, theologian John Mbiti maintains that, "Africans are notoriously religious....Religion is the strongest element in traditional background, and exerts probably the greatest influence upon the thinking and living of the people concerned" (Mbiti 1). For many non-Western peoples in general and African peoples in particular, there are no distinct boundaries between the sacred and profane. Historian of religions Mircea Eliade formulates the theory of the myth of the eternal return regarding the sacred: human beings can perpetuate enactments of the sacred and constantly share in a "trans-human" communication with the divine. Sacred activities are not reserved for "Sundays" and holy days only. African peoples consider all reality as potentially sacred. Furthermore, other worlds exist, but *in* this world. As Western cultures emphasize the *seen* experience in the material and concrete world, African peoples have traditionally acted as technicians of the *unseen*—the spiritual world.

When Africans were brought to the Americas, they brought with them their sense of religiosity: that human existence is fundamentally an ontological phenomenon and that religiosity is a central modality of that existence. The trauma of the Middle Passage did not sever New World Africans from their ancestral concepts of religiosity. In the New World, traditional religiosity shared its potentials and beliefs with New World Christianity. Attempting to survive their bondage, the neo-Africans incorporated their traditional beliefs into strategies for survival strength and psychological empowerment. Lawrence W. Levine states:

> The slaves' expressive arts and sacred beliefs were more than merely a series of outlets or strategies; they were instruments of life, of sanity, of health, and of self-respect. Slave music, slave religion, slave folk beliefs—the entire sacred world of the black slaves—created the necessary space between the slaves and their owners and were the means of preventing legal slavery from becoming spiritual slavery. (80)

Unequivocally they were legal slaves but not spiritual slaves. Out of an African spirituality and out of the Middle Passage consciousness, Morrison and Marshall write about the resilience of the oppressed by way of metaphor, history, and story.

A summary of *Praisesong* shows that Avey Avatara Johnson is a comfortably middle-class, self-conscious, elderly widow, who on a Caribbean cruise with two friends abruptly decides to leave the ship. When the ship docks for a few hours on the Caribbean island of Grenada, she disembarks and plans to fly back to her home, New York City. Significantly her trip has been jolted by recurring dreams of her long dead Great-Aunt Cuney of Tatem, South Carolina. Destiny intervenes and she misses the plane to New York only to get involved in the annual festival of the "out-island" people—people of the smaller island, Carriacou—who live and work in Grenada. The excursion back to their native land (Carriacou and by way of myth/ritual, Africa) is in fact their annual rite of rejuvenation, their rite of the eternal return, their trans-human communication with the African past and its sacred forces. The Big Drum ceremony is the enactment of their African past, their native land. The dance creates temporal space between reality and the spirit world. By going to Carriacou and experiencing the intensity of neo-African ritual dancing and music, Avey Johnson rediscovers her own sense of place as an American of African ancestry. She rediscovers what it means to bond with people and with the spirit, and not with *things*. As she leaves Carriacou, she resolves to renew her ties with her own ancestral and spiritual home, Tatem, South Carolina.

Avey Johnson's classical journey occurs on two levels: she is, in essence, the heroine embarking on a quest for spiritual enlightenment and renewed strength to deal with the human world. The journey becomes a validation of Avey's American social consciousness. By the middle age of life, Avey has settled for the illusion of El Dorado; that is to say, she has given in to the complacency of upper-middle class living and values. However, the spiritual void in her life began even before the death of her husband. By dividing the novel into four sections with the ritual-implied titles of "Runagate," "Sleeper's Wake," "Lavé Tete," and "The Beg Pardon," Marshall demonstrates how the journey motif is inherent to Avey's spiritual and social awakening. Through trans-human communication, Avey reestablishes order out of her own chaos. The reestablishment is of primary importance for Marshall:

I'm trying to trace history....To take, for example, the infamous triangle route of slavery and to reverse it so that we make the journey back from America to the West Indies, to Africa...to make that trip back. I'm not talking about in actual terms. I'm talking about a psychological and spiritual journey back in order to move forward. *You have to psychologically go through chaos in order to overcome it."* (my emphasis, DeVeaux 128)

One must undergo symbolic death in order to be reborn, in order to overcome the "difficult passage." Marshall is thoroughly aware of the rites of passage revisited among the Carriacouans. Moreover, *Praisesong* is obviously formulated on the structure of a ritual process (Van Gennep; Turner). From the outset of the novel, Marshall's ritual strategy juxtaposes images of whiteness and darkness to emphasize the themes of spiritual chaos and cultural loss. The luxury cruise ship, *Bianca Pride*, with its superficial elegance, explicitly represents Euro-America and the cruise-culture of affluent American widows. The very name of the cruise ship is purposely chosen by Marshall: it is a symbol of *white* pride. Despite the luxury and material order around her, Avey Johnson is confused because of the dreams she is having of her dead great-aunt who lived in the American south. Significantly, Avey dreams about the times when as a young girl in Tatem, South Carolina, her aunt used to talk about *her* grandmother who actually remembered seeing groups of Africans disembarking from the slave ships. With this focus on the Middle Passage, we immediately see that the old aunt represents that link with Africa, heritage, and history. The great-aunt's sense of place is historic and mythic because her own grandmother knew people who had made the Atlantic crossing.[8]

In keeping with the oral art of "recollectin'," Marshall interweaves history and myth. As a child, Avey visited her great-aunt (although called Great-Aunt Cuney for short, the ancestor is actually a great great aunt) during the summers and heard stories of the "stepping Ibos." The aunt had heard the legend from *her* grandmother who never lost sight of the Word, or Nommo, as empowerment. In this instance, Nommo is female energy, for "my gran" functions as a *griotte* (and in turn Great-Aunt Cuney) who preserves the memory of the Middle Passage and its meaning to her family by keeping the tale of the Ibos alive. Avey Johnson recalls this tale about a group of Ibos who were brought to the New World as slaves. However, they are technicians of the unseen and as they survey the new land *they look down into history* and see the calamities and atrocities that are to come. They decide to leave because:

they seen things that day you and me don't have the power to see. 'Cause those pure-born Africans was peoples my gran' said could see in more ways than one. The kind can tell you 'bout things happen long before they was born and things to come long after they's dead. Well, they seen everything that was to happen 'round here that day. The slavery time and the war my gran always talked about, the 'mancipation and everything after that right on up to the hard times today....Those Ibos...just turned...all of 'em...and walked on back down to the edge of the river here. Every las' man, woman and chile. And they wasn't taking they time no more. They had seen what they had seen and those Ibos was stepping! And they didn't bother getting back into the small boats drawed up here...boats take too much time. They just kept walking right on out over the river. (37-38)

Such is the story, in part, which Avey Johnson's great-great-great grandmother has told. The tale gives spiritual empowerment to those who have no political power. Believing in the story of the Ibos is one way of affirming heritage and resilience. The tale becomes a *touchstone* for the ability to cope and persevere. The tale is the empowerment of the Nommo. But as a child Avey Johnson never really understood the Ibo story. The dreams of her great aunt are disturbing, and it is not until she undergoes the complete rite of spiritual renewal that the significance emerges. But at this point the dream brings other memories and sorrows to the surface of her consciousness.

Avey Johnson was not always in pursuit of El Dorado. There had been a time in her life when, along with her spouse Jay, she had been in tune with those simple rituals of culture and heritage—the music, the empowering voices of African-American poetry, the dancing, and the visits to Tatem:

something in those small rites, an ethos they held in common, had reached back beyond her life and beyond Jay's to join them to the vast unknown linkage that had made their being possible. And this link, these connections, heard in the music and in the praisesongs of a Sunday...had *both protected them and put them in possession of a kind of power....*(my emphasis, 137)

When as a couple, they began to attain the realities of the American dream—material wealth and upward mobility—they forgot the sacred rituals of their past: Tatem, the tales, the music, their own sensuality. These were the folk materials which provided healing against the difficulties they faced as a black family struggling to overcome racial and economic pressures. Through years of hard work and fighting racial prejudice, Jerome Johnson becomes a man of status and property. However, in the painful effort to be an economic success in Euro-American terms, in the pursuit of the dream of El Dorado, both Avey and Jerome forget the folk modalities which had enabled them to cope with life, which had given them that rich sense of cultural place and spiritual continuity. Through embedded flashbacks, we learn that "All this passed from their lives without their hardly noticing" (137). Jerome stops calling himself "Jay." As an accomplished businessman in the black community, he is "Jerome" to everyone. In showing how the Johnsons undergo a spiritual decline of their marriage and of themselves, Marshall demonstrates how the submission to indiscriminate acquisition of material possessions and success robs people of the inner strengths and traditional inner ability to empower self. Avey realizes that long before she became a widow, she and her husband had died spiritually: they had died on the killing ground of materialism and false cultural values. Marshall's metaphor of death decoded implies that material wealth can generate a false sense of happiness. The newly acquired power is superficial; it is a limiting power that mimics Euro-American materialism. Economic progress is necessary for all Americans. However, the tension lies between economic progress and spiritual maintenance. How do Americans sustain a balance? How do African-Americans bridge the desire for economic progress which has been historically denied, while they simultaneously keep in view the psychic-cultural principles of an African tradition? Economic progress is necessary, but not to the extent of being possessed by the material wealth it offers.

Marshall clearly presents the philosophical position that happiness certainly does not come from material wealth. The Johnsons imagine their joy and contentment as they "arrive" economically. However, their material gain provides only a fleeting sense of happiness. Moreover, their conspicuous progress inevitably grows into a specter and shadow of the past when, although they had very little materially, they at least had the rich capacity to love each other and not things. Undoubtedly, the acquisition of things is as transitory as El Dorado. Although material wealth has its seemingly limitless possibilities, just as it did in the early American conquests, its course proves its own inadequacy for happiness. Those who keep their feet on the nurturing ground can distinguish between transitory modalities of material power and the eternal sources of spiritual empowerment. Marshall demonstrates how happiness that is measured by and restricted to material gain leaves an inner void— a spiritual decadence. It causes Americans of African ancestry to *disconnect* from the Middle Passage saga of struggle, survival, and spiritual propensity. Happiness derived from material wealth may be translated into secular power, but it is not *empowering*. Along with other womanist interpreters such as Alice Walker, Gayle Jones, and Toni Cade Bambara, both Marshall and Morrison attest in their writing that when African-Americans share in the material wealth of mainstream American society, they seem to move away from the inner resources—spiritual, psychological, social and artistic—of empowerment and coping. As Morrison indicates, the pursuit of material wealth limits and defeats all people: Valerian Street, the wealthy American capitalist in *Tar Baby*, ends up not only physically and mentally out of sync with reality, but spiritually dead.

Through a series of carefully directed incidents situated by the author, we see how Avey Johnson returns to the nurturing ground. She must experience symbolic death in order to be rebirthed into a new awareness of self, myth, and history. The old man whom she meets in Grenada, Lebert Joseph, represents (like Great-Aunt Cuney) the African connected consciousness in the Americas. For Lebert Joseph is the African and African-American confluence of the mythic deity Legba. Lebert Joseph corresponds to Papa Legba in Haiti, Papa La Bas in the southern United States, Esu-Elegbara in Nigeria, and Legba in Benin. Brought to the New World during the Middle Passage, Legba is personified by an irascible old man who usually carries a cane and limps. One leg is shorter than the other because part of him is in the spirit world and part of him moves in the world of the living. In some instances, he manifests both female and male energy. As the Guardian of the Gate, the Crossing, or the Threshold, Legba is a force of destiny who mediates between gods and human beings (see Herskovits; Laguerre). In the context of *Praisesong*, Marshall employs Lebert/Legba to further the ritual structure of the novel: he becomes the messenger, the interpreter, leading the central character further along her journey and finally to the threshold of the spirit world in order to rebirth to the world of the living. It is essentially because of Lebert/Legba, this spiritual messenger, that Avey comes to an understanding of her great aunt's presence in her consciousness. As an interpreter, Lebert/Legba knows that Avey Johnson is one of the people who has lost sight of her spiritual "nation" and needs to be reincorporated.

Throughout the narrative, Marshall continues to juxtapose dreams into a fusion of the past and present. In some instances, the fusion of embedded flashback leaves the reader confused about the time sequence of events especially when Avey is thinking/dreaming of the immediate past of her childhood along with remote past of her ancestors. The symbolic significance of the events in the journey motif are eventually clarified when it is understood that Avey must experience a crossing over and must be led to the Threshold in order to be cleansed and rebirthed.

Led by Lebert Joseph/Legba, Avey Johnson moves closer to the Threshold of historic and mythic time, closer to understanding the implications of Middle Passage and El Dorado history. The excursion to Carriacou symbolizes this psychological return into history—it is the difficult passage for her. The actual turbulence of the excursion invokes not only a symbolic enactment of the middle crossing, but the turbulence of the excursion invokes not only a symbolic enactment of the middle crossing, but the turbulence of American [con]quest and preemption. Avey Johnson must be purged of the unnecessary self and experience the symbolic return to the womb, to the unconquered landscape of the New World and her native land. The women who assist Avey on the boat ride during this turbulence of mind and collective history are like the mother-women of Marshall's own life. They are also the historic culture bearers—the primary interpreters of culture and spirituality. Indeed, the women who help Avey are very much reminiscent of "mothers" in Baptist churches who help passengers who suddenly are possessed by the Holy Ghost from harming themselves. The women on the *Emanuel C* (again such obvious symbolic naming implies Marshall's didactic narrative position) assist the elderly widow like spiritual mothers. Like technicians of the unseen, the mother-women know that Avey needs to be protected and needs to be renurtured at this point in her life. They approve of Avey's seasickness. She must be purged of material comforts, make the symbolic return, if necessary even by literally defecating on herself. She is humiliated as an adult in order to regain honor:

she had the impression as her mind flickered on briefly of other bodies lying crowded in with her in the hot, airless dark. A multitude it felt like lay packed around her in the filth and stench of themselves, just as she was. Their moans, rising and falling with each rise and plunge of the schooner, enlarged upon the one filling her head. Their suffering—the depth of it, the weight of it in the cramped space—made hers of no consequence. (209)

The "depth of it" is the suffering and conquest of a people. Paule Marshall is such a politically engaged writer that at times her writing leaves little for the reader's imagination. She forces her audience to join that political engagement, leaving little space for anything else. In *Chosen Place*, Saul Amron, a Jewish development expert, dwells on the same issue of historical suffering, past and present, when he says: "It's usually so painful though: looking back into yourself; most people run from it....But sometimes it's necessary to go back before you can go forward, really forward. And that's not only for people—individuals—but nations as well...." (359). By using extended Middle Passage and El Dorado metaphors, Marshall explicates her recurrent theme of knowing one's heritage in order to move forward. Avey Johnson must remove the trappings of conquest mentality in order to move forward and build. *Praisesong* is about an individual figure, but in the larger context, the character of Avey Johnson is a vehicle for Marshall's socio-political engagement.

The novel climaxes with Avey Johnson moving into liminal space with the Carriacou islanders during the Big Drum Dance; she ceases to be a runagate running and stumbling in darkness. In the circle of the dance, we see the rituals and movements of neo-African people coming together: from the "nations" of Africa emerge the "Banda, the Cromanti, the Temne, the Congo" (238-39). The description of the Big Drum is the accumulation of embedded symbolism leading toward the meaning of history, myth, and story. The dance itself is both spiritual rejuvenation and a necessary relief from the everyday struggle of economic survival because undoubtedly, the people understand the reasons why they ritually return to Carriacou.[9] The ritual dance is a social and spiritual connection with friends and with culture. Moreover, it prevents the islanders' alienation. In other words, the dance is a touchstone of their cultural sensibilities and spiritual needs. As a collective group, the people are not possessed by conquest and materialism. The Big Drum presides, enabling them to keep the channels of trans-human communication open. These people do not have to search for an identity since they already know who they are. They make the annual return to the past—to their native land (the metaphor of the eternal return)—in order to live the present and future. Therefore, the Big Drum rite of passage is their spiritual affirmation rather than part of a spiritual quest as it is for Avey Johnson. For people who are close to their rich source of myth and history, such rituals are consciously necessary and unconsciously enacted. The richness of their cultural and spiritual ties attests to their wealth of inner resourcefulness.

The end of Avey Johnson's excursion to Carriacou marks the beginning of her being able to empower self through a rekindled knowledge of the self in relation to society. Until her trajectory into the past, Avey Johnson had succumbed to the bourgeois quest for modern El Dorados. Using Caribbean and African-American ethnological idioms, Marshall demonstrates how the Middle Passage and El Dorado become extended metaphors of history which can help the community to rebuild itself and move forward.

*   *   *

Paule Marshall was once referred to as a "writer's writer." This phrase was used in the most complementary way. Considering Marshall's socio-political consciousness, it would certainly seem that she would want to write for the so-called masses as well. Whatever audience Marshall had in mind as *Praisesong* was being created, the novel materialized with heavy doses of ethnology and social idealism. *Praisesong* reads as a forced palimpsest of metaphors—politics, religiosity, history, ethnic rituals, and myths—which leads to ubiquitous enlightenment and ritual salvation. The force of the "message" overshadows Marshall's style and her own sense of language. In general, Marshall insists on defining history by weaving the memories of slavery into contemporary patterns of American life. From Marshall's perspective, the Avey Johnsons of America cannot exist outside of Middle Passage history. The "unexpected" spiritual journey enables Avey Johnson to reappropriate her own set of values and return home (her home in White Plains, New York, represents those who have "made it"), with a renewed sense of cultural spirituality. Therefore, like Merle Kinbona in *Chosen Place*, and Selina in *Brown Girl*, Avey arrives at a neat and assured awakening of what has to be done in order to stay the course. If only everyone *could* stay the course. At least, however, Great-Aunt Cuney does not insist that posterity has to relinquish economic gain; she only dramatically insists on paying homage to one's collective history and spiritual heritage. Marshall's metaphors of materialism and spirituality lead to inevitable awakenings. Her characters consistently converge at the gate of absolute enlightenment, enter the ritual process, and *remember* how to invoke history and reconnect. From this perspective, Marshall compromises with her interpretation of history because such absolutism is a romantic approach to history, myth, and social-political issues. Decidedly, in the African-American/African context, spiritual reconnections can be powerful and all-consuming, as Toni Morrison's most recent novel, *Beloved*, depicts. But stylistically Avey Johnson arrives all too suddenly and completely to her climax of enlightenment as she makes the decision to return to Tatem and Great-Aunt Cuney's sense of place. Avey Johnson is reincorporated happily and neatly. Undoubtedly, Marshall is a womanist interpreter. However, in *Praisesong* Marshall becomes an idealist failing to recognize where prescribed mythic events end and social reality takes over.

On the other hand, Toni Morrison's strategy illuminates the precarious nature of bonding and bondage, the precarious relationship of myth and history. If we can agree that broadly speaking, myth is a historical reflection of a people's world-view, then myth is dynamic as opposed to being static in its relation to history. Indeed, in contrast to Marshall's concept of the nurturing ground, we have Morrison's metaphor of the other which demonstrates that historical reconnections are elusive for some and that, in fact, pariahs exist in order to constantly be a reminder that everyone will not come into a heroic awakening— or even desire it. Morrison comments:

There are several levels of the pariah figure working in my writing. The black community is a pariah community. Black people are pariahs. The civilization of black people that lives apart from but in juxtaposition to other civilizations is a pariah relationship. *In fact, the concept of the black in this country is almost always one of the pariah. But a community contains pariahs within it that are very useful for the conscience of that community.* (my emphasis, Tate 129)

Decidedly, the "useful conscience" is interpreted as the paradoxical other in Morrison's writing.[10] This is Morrison's way of "talking around a subject," her strategy of signification. As she demonstrates in her novel *Song of Solomon* as well as in *Tar Baby*, the other is the pariah, the *déclassé* in the community of contemporary El Dorados. There are certainly those of the exploited victims who voluntarily give themselves to the conquistadors of modern materialism and political exploitation. Morrison's novels in general reveal her interpretive perception of American reality:

If my work is to be functional to the group (to the village...) then it must bear witness and identify that which is useful from the past and that which ought to be discarded; it must make it possible to prepare for the present and live it out, and it must do that not by avoiding problems and contradictions but by examining them; it should not even attempt to solve problems, but it should certainly try to clarify them. ("Memory" 389)

Whereas Marshall attempts to heroically solve the problems of the community, Morrison makes clarifications and expounds the contradictions of the community. The contradictions are often viewed in terms of the community's sexual and social politics.

In *The Bluest Eye*, Pecola Breedlove, the community outcast, is culturally and sexually exploited.[11] She does not transcend her plight nor does she arrive at an *awakening*. Her eventual mental breakdown is a metaphor for social madness. Victims consent and are consumed to the destruction of some and to the benefit of others. Pecola eventually demonstrates her inability to cope with the imposed restrictions of her family, community and society. Yet she serves as a necessary communal scapegoat, enabling that community to nurture its own cultural and racial potential. It is through her precarious end that the community can hope to assess its own limitations and contradictions. As an extended metaphor of Pecola, Jadine Childs also depicts inadequacies and contradictions. In fact, Jadine is a paradoxical and metaphoric continuation of Pecola in that she symbolizes the blue eyes of Pecola's fantasy. While physical ugliness and the desire to be accepted are part of the narrative element in *The Bluest Eye*, physical beauty and the false security of being accepted highlight the narration in *Tar Baby*.

Jadine Childs makes the conscious choice to be something else— to live in other civilizations as an *anti*-Madonna who fails to recognize her own ancient properties. In *Tar Baby*, Morrison consciously uses the African-American idiom of saying one thing to really mean and highlight another—one of the acts of African-American signifying (Smitherman; Gates, "Blackness"). As a signifier, Morrison's literary idiom upholds traditions and community values through apparent contradictions and surface restrictions. However, Morrison is not having an exclusive and direct dialogue with the familiar tale of Brer Rabbit, Brer Fox, and tar baby. Of another tar motif Morrison writes:

I found that there is a tar lady in African mythology. I started thinking about tar. At one time, a tar pit was a holy place, at least as important, because tar was used to build things...it held things together....For me, the tar baby came to mean the black woman who can hold things together. The story [the novel *Tar Baby*] was a point of departure to history and prophecy. (Le Clair 27)

The narrative element of tar is decoded as both a sacred and profane metaphor for entrapment and material illusions on various levels. The motif has to be understood not so much as a character type, but as a vehicle for the narration itself. Morrison juxtaposes and signifies the importance of what is absent through the *illusion* of what is present. Her writing can be characterized as achieving "direction through indirection." One critic refers to Morrison's juxtaposition of absence and presence as the "metaphor of lack" (Willis 274-77). Tar signifies both false illusion (materialistic values of the Streets and the Childs) and cultural cohesiveness (the potentials of cultural-spiritual bonding through family ties and progressive female nurturing). At one level, Morrison's metaphoric use of tar expresses binding to material possessions. But because tar as a gel substance has the positive quality of building, it also symbolizes the potentials of self-empowerment and community cohesiveness.

The novel's setting is a Caribbean island called Isle des Chevaliers where Valerian and Margaret Street, a wealthy American couple, own an impressive tropical mansion, L'Arbe de la Croix. Sydney and Ondine Childs are their black servants—"Philadelphia negroes" of tradition.

Jadine is their adopted niece and protégé of Valerian Street. The narrative unfolds as these five people move about the mansion with false ritualistic ease. They pretend to glide through the barriers of race and class. Enter Son: an unkempt, Rastafarian-looking black man who embodies the African nobility of Sundiata, the political and racial victimization of Bigger Thomas, and the sensuality of Zora Neal Hurston's Tea Cake Woods. To the Street household, Son is uneducated, violent-looking, and a thief. What *he lacks* is clear to everyone at L'Arbe de la Croix. Ondine and Sydney feel threatened by Son's presence because he reminds them of their own blackness and servile position in the white household. Accustomed to being in authority, elegant Valerian assumes the role of Professor Higgins, which does not impress Son in the least. However, Jadine, also initially repulsed by Son, is slowly drawn to his cultural earthiness and sexuality. Son is just that: a son/sun of the earth.

As Son's story unfolds, we see it is connected to the Middle Passage saga of racism and economic displacement. Although he is able to put history into concrete perspectives more than Jadine can or cares to, Son loses his sensibility of place and meaning when he is lured by Jadine's beauty and values. But like El Dorado, having Jadine will remain an illusion and unattainable. Son comes from the sea (he has jumped ship) and he returns to the sea (Thérèse, the woman-sage, manipulates him back to the island of the blind horsemen) questing for Jadine. When he attempts to draw spiritual and cultural sustenance from her, reality disappears into the fog of the past and invokes the myth of the blind horsemen. Gideon, one of the islanders, tells Son to let Jadine go.

"Let her go?" asked Son, and he smiled a crooked smile. Let go the woman you had been looking for everywhere just because she was difficult? Because she had a temper, energy, ideas of her own and fought back?...Let go a woman who was not only a woman but a sound, all the music he had ever wanted to play, a world and a way of being in it? Let *that* go? "I can't," he said. "I can't." (298-99)

Jadine's sophistication has such an effect on him that she becomes an illusion of need, an illusion of womanism. She is a *shade* of blackness in pursuit of El Dorado. Son believes that he can exist in Jadine's world, that she can be life-affirming, when she can only affirm through symbols of material wealth and success. He mistakes Jadine's physical beauty and her attractive life style for integrity and admirable defiance. In this respect, he fails to recognize her as an *anti*-Madonna. At this juncture Son confuses illusion and reality. When his own sense of worth depends on Jadine's acceptance of him, when his focus turns to her physical beauty (as defined by Euro-American beauty standards), he gets caught in rootlessness and spiritual loss. Initially, Son can be seen as a son of the earth—a black sun and culture-bearer. But within the new circumstances involving his love for Jadine, he is not the achiever; he is not the trickster who personifies cultural strength and wisdom. Some critics have misunderstood Son as the personification of Brer Rabbit, the trickster. Son is not so much the trickster figure. Instead, the motif itself (at the levels of symbolic interpretation) is again the vehicle on which to use paradox and *signify*: "in this sense, one does not signify something; rather, one signifies in *some way*" (Gates, "Blackness" 288). On still another level of interpreting the motif, Jadine lacks the power to culturally and spiritually bond. Cultural and spiritual bonding are not even precarious objectives for this chic, beautiful, Sorbonne-educated woman. Like the tar baby, she has been molded (primarily by Valerian Street's wealth) into a commodity for someone else's consumption. Her quest is for other civilizations, as home and place are more illusive.

Through the metaphor of absence, Morrison also shows how the Streets themselves are victims of loss despite their tremendous wealth; they too lack the qualities of cultural bonding. Furthermore, Margaret Street suffers from mother-guilt: Ondine is the only member of the household who knows that Margaret did not love her son Michael and physically abused him as a child. (Morrison juxtaposes Michael, the biological son who never appears, with the presence of the cultural son who tries to embrace his heritage.) That is their secret (Morrison implies that Ondine is just as guilty for not trying to stop the child abuse) until racial tension finally explodes. Valerian is devastated when he learns what happened to his son—not only because of the actual abuse, but because he realizes that it was Margaret's way of retaliation against his conquest of her and his power over everything in their lives. Margaret is also a victim of the pain caused by the conquerers. Valerian's own patriarchal control of others eventually backfires on him. He ends up being a senile and powerless old man on his own island world.

Morrison uses Jadine as a signifier for what the community *lacks*. Progressive women are needed to build and at the same time nurture. There are no clear-cut solutions to the dilemma of balancing cultures and values. Morrison's politics are evident: Euro-American materialism usurps people of color particularly when there are so many who are the have-nots of society. Morrison recognizes that African-Americans are being tested in this era of stress, disillusionment, disappointment, and general social decadence. Yet by invoking the community's own sense of paradox, Morrison's writing depicts how that community may recognize its own inadequacies and its own loss as it becomes obsessed with acquiring material possessions. Susan Willis states that *Tar Baby* "registers a deep sense of pessimism" (270). On the contrary. With its representation of the other, its strategy of signification, *Tar Baby* attempts to clarify and confront reality. Morrison is decidedly conscious of this objective:

the text, if it is to take improvisation and audience participation into account, cannot be authority—it should be the map. It should make a way for the reader (audience) to participate in the tale. The language, if it is to permit criticism of both rebellion and tradition, must be both indicator and mask, and the tension between the two kinds of language is its release and its power. ("Memory" 389)

As I have maintained, there are no absolute heroes in Morrison's writing. Although Son is a community outlaw, he is able to connect back to the past through his love for Eloe—the rural town of his birth in Florida. Eloe symbolizes rootedness even though people who live there are a marginal community. Eloe certainly has its pariahs, its heroes and anti-heroes, but importantly it has its sense of history, for it *is* place. For instance, Eloe has women who have literally built their own houses and do not stand on welfare lines. These mother-women do not bask in, for example, feminist theory on the reappropriation of religiosity and language. They simply are resourceful as their circumstances permit and do what their foremothers would have done for survival. Eloe metaphorizes one's sense of spiritual place and cultural sensibility. Son tells Jadine: "Anybody ask where you from, you give them five towns. You're not *from* anywhere. I'm from Eloe" (266). Jadine is unable to identify with the women of Eloe, or any of her foremothers for that matter. She is the woman-child who does not want to be, cannot be, a mother-woman because the comforts of immediate history have made it all too difficult. Valerian, Sydney, and Ondine have made life easy, privileged, and uncumbersome. Contrasting to the mother-woman in Langston Hughes's poem, "Mother to Son," Jadine's life has been a crystal stair. Unlike mother-women, Jadine has not "suffered" history, nor has she attempted "walking to Canada."

Morrison presents suffering as a modicum of wholeness and inner strength. From this perspective, suffering is not martyrdom or a sentimental, romantic idea of the human condition. Rather, if one is intent on constructive survival, then suffering is viewed as a source of wholeness, detachment, and spiritual strength. Suffering is the difficult passage that has to be bridged in order to control the very fear of what may have to be endured. It can act as a touchstone for wholeness and perseverance, as a motivation for action. Or it can destroy. Jadine's indiscriminate submission to material comforts and Euro-American values has made her unable to appreciate her own heritage. Consistently at the core of Morrison's writing is thus the problematic balancing of progress in terms of Euro-American values (the comforts of El Dorado) and appropriating the Middle Passage saga. Jadine fears confronting history. She fears confronting racism and patriarchal power in America. Finally, she fears coming to terms with her own communal heritage. At twenty-five she has established her own vision of life and quest for happiness. Moreover, her Euro-American values

are repeatedly associated with death, [compared] to the uncertainties of her race, which Morrison consistently associates with life and nature...she chooses in effect to be a creation rather than a creator, an art historian rather than an artist, a model rather than a designer, a wife rather than woman. (Byerman 213)

Jadine subconsciously rejects identifying with womanist culture because it would mean that she would have to "settle for wifely competence when she could be almighty, to settle for fertility rather than originality, nurturing instead of building" (269). Morrison further says that:

Black women seem able to combine the nest and the adventure. They don't see conflicts in certain areas as do white women. They are both safe harbor and ship; they are both inn and trail. We, black women, do both. We don't find these places, these roles, mutually exclusively. (Tate 129)

Jadine denies the potentials of being harbor and ship since she defines these roles as being exclusive of each other. Jadine and the Streets are indicators of the quest for material wealth and power over others. However, they only have the power to control and manipulate the seen—the material world.

In contrast, Thérèse Foucault, the local servant of the Streets who befriends Son, is a technician of the unseen. Significantly, Thérèse is a descendant of Maroon slaves. Her personal history is connected to mythic history in that her people were known as the blind horsemen who roamed the island during slavery. Thérèse is *nearsighted.* (When she agrees to take Son back to L'Arbe de la Croix, she has to steer the boat by *sensing* the current because she is no longer able to see as night approaches.) From the mythic perspective she is, indeed, *blind.* She has the power to see with the third eye. Her nearsightedness/blindness is departure to insight and knowledge, hence her advice to Son regarding Jadine: "Small boy...don't go [back] to L'Arbe de la Croix...forget her. There is nothing in her parts for you. She has forgotten her ancient properties" (305). In the spirit world blindness is actually the sacred ability to be a *seer.* Susan Willis accurately maintains that:

Blindness is another way of giving metaphoric expression to social difference and freedom...the lack of sight, which in bourgeois society is the basis for an individual's alienation, is in the mythic world the basis for the group's cohesion and absolute alternality.

This is because blindness is portrayed not as an individual's affliction but rather as a communally shared way of being in the world. (276)

Thérèse deceives Son into thinking that she will help him find Jadine by taking him back to Valerian's house. She steers the boat to the part of the island inhabited by the blind horsemen. (Note how Morrison assumes the reader will suspend disbelief and really understand the historical and social implications of the individual's mythic consciousness.) The narrative voice changes into a mythic one when Thérèse tells Son that the horsemen are waiting for him. Is Thérèse leading Son into an awakening, or is she leading him to his death by sending him to the horsemen who do not welcome strangers? Is he a stranger, or is he to become one of the seers? Is he actually stumbling as a permanent runagate, or is he going to walk steadily into the consciousness of freedom and renewed empowerment? Son has been dazzled/blinded by Jadine. Unlike the horsemen, at one point his blindness is destructive to him, to his sense of family, spirituality, and Middle Passage history. Therefore, he has to somehow be freed either through physical extinction (being killed on the rocks) or by successfully making the difficult crossing (spiritually and politically understanding the Middle Passage myth of the one hundred horsemen). Rather than providing the solution, rather than compromising with history and turning community pariahs into sudden political princes, Morrison leaves it up to the reader to decide his fate.

In the character of Jadine, we see that Euro-American ideas of progress, education, and wealth assume certain denials.[12] Progress and material wealth still translate into conquest and the exploitation of the the other Americans. Furthermore, African-American women writers recognize the double jeopardy (racism and sexism) in history. Zora Neal Hurston's *Their Eyes Were Watching God* shows how Nanny, the grandmother who was born into slavery, well understands the act of the conquerer and this double jeopardy: "de white man throw down de load and tell de nigger man tuh pick it up. He pick it up because he have to, but he don't tote it. He hand it to his womenfolks. De nigger woman is de mule uh de world so fur as Ah can see" (16). Patriarchs like Valerian Street are certainly bound to Middle Passage and El Dorado history as they mold cultural expatriates who perpetuate their value system. Upon making the decision to marry her wealthy European lover, Jadine decides to expatriate herself *to* Europe. She leaves for Paris wearing a baby sealskin coat—an impressive symbol of materialism and a very political display of capitalism considering the much publicized movement against the slaughter of baby seals.

*   *   *

When material wealth and the acquisition of things control and overpower spiritual sensibilities, the community loses sight of its ancient properties of cultural bonding; the community loses its hold on traditions which kept it from falling apart. As Morrison demonstrates in *Tar Baby*, it is certainly not just the African-American community that is victimized by the politics of materialism. But African-Americans cannot afford to lose sight of the very forces which enabled their ancestors in slavery to persevere and to create their own empowerment and political survival. Both Toni Morrison and Paule Marshall understand the importance of economic security for all Americans. But values need to be reappropriated in terms of equitable economic achievement rather than in terms of modern El Dorados.

Out of Eurocentric definitions of happiness, progress, and new urban values, African-Americans disconnect from the meaning of family, history, and womanist spirituality. Euro-American feminists seem to be overwhelmed by *discovering* how religiosity can be incorporated into political and social change. African-American women have always acted out of spiritual awareness as they grappled with social injustices and tried to effect a new Being. African-American women have always possessed a *womanspirit*. Their womenspirit is, as Morrison and Marshall demonstrate, a synthesis of the African concept of the sacred and New World interpretations of Christianity. Part and parcel of historical metaphor, Thérèse Foucault believes in the myth of the one hundred horsemen, not out of mere superstition, but out of her own subconscious knowledge of the myth's sacred meaning—what it invokes and what it sustains. The Big Drum ritual of the Carriacouans acts as a touchstone and lodestone to ethnic and social-spiritual meaning. Paule Marshall attempts to show and pave the way for renewed spiritual and social consciousness. On the other hand, as Toni Morrison concentrates on how Euro-American materialistic values have *affected* African-American life in the name of progress, she recognizes that not everyone is capable of coming into an awakening—or even cares to. She therefore allows the community heroes and anti-heroes to make their own choices. Her literary strategy employs the community's own aesthetic idiom of signifying the paradox. Morrison highlights the impact of loss in order that the community may regain its ancestral richness.

Notes

[1]The term "middle passage" refers to the route across the Atlantic which the Africans experienced before being sent to slavery in various parts of the Americas. Lemuel Johnson writes that "the Middle Passage in literature is, at bottom, a metaphor for displacement and exile. Predictably, the historical trauma of the slave trade generates the metaphor's dramatic and often decisive points of departure or reference....The Middle Passage has remained an enduring, even necessary, motif in the literature of the black diaspora" (62).

[2]The belief that a city of gold existed in the unexplored (by Europeans) area of South America led to European conquest and the search for El Dorado (the golden man) during the fifteenth and sixteenth centuries. Gold was found but not as much as the conquistadors wanted. Their greed perpetuated the legend/myth. The quest became the misappropriated myth of El Dorado—a quest of cruelty, preemption, and its legacies of slavery. *El Dorado* in fact, was a sacred myth/ritual of the Chibchas which the Spaniards confused with secular stories they helped to create. El Dorado as a place remained an illusion. Naipaul writes in *The Loss of El Dorado*, "Always the Indians told of a rich civilized people just a few days' march away" (18). Also see Perez, *El Mito del Dorado: Su Genesis y Proceso.*

Surrogate El Dorados continue well into contemporary times. For example, the wealth that is generated from the illegal drug trade between South America and the United States is now referred to as an "el dorado." At one time, in some black and Hispanic communities in the United States, the Electra 225 (the Deuce and a Quarter) and the Eldorado were automobiles of prestige and conspicuous spending. The Eldorado in particular was a car signifying new and often instant wealth.

[3]In *Tar Baby*, wealthy Valerian Street manipulates his entire household to the extent that his ego is completely nourished by power and authority.

[4]In her essay on womanism, Ogunyemi claims that the philosophy of womanism is conservative. On the contrary, womanism is dynamic in that it attempts to acknowledge the sexism which exists in the African-American community while simultaneously realizing the need for the complementarity of African-American men and women in the resistance to racism and sexism.

[5]Kate Copin uses the term "mother-woman" in *The Awakening* to mean "women who idolized their children, worshiped their husbands, and esteemed it a holy privilege to efface themselves as individuals and grow wings as ministering angels" (19). That is not the meaning of mother-woman in this essay. Rather, the mother-woman is consciously and unconsciously a feminist as the term applies to her particular circumstances. The "woman" component of the phrase invokes Alice Walker's definition of womanism;

[6]At the end of *Tar Baby*, Jadine literally takes flight from kin and community (her aunt, uncle, and lover, Son) by airplane. This type of departure by flying interacts with the myth of flying Africans who, in African-American folklore and myth, hated slavery so much that they decided to and were able to fly back to Africa. Notice that Jadine's departure is appropriated through an industrialized and Westernized medium; she has refused to acknowledge the spiritual and psychological forces which would enable her to fly as her ancestors could—to psychologically empower themselves for survival. Morrison's well-known use of the flying African motif is also seen in *Song of Solomon* where Milkman's spirit takes flight in an embrace of his history

after he has undergone spiritual and cultural rebirth. For a discussion on the motif of flying in Morrison's fiction, see Blake, "Folklore and Community in *Song of Solomon.*"

[7]Indeed, Marshall's narrative becomes didactic in its efforts to treat history and myth as necessary parts of the African-American consciousness. McClusky states in his essay on Marshall's works that *"Praisesong for the Widow* is not Marshall's most successful statement as a novel" (332).

[8]In addition, the South Carolina tidewater or "low" country is associated with maroons who escaped from southern plantations. Maroons were often referred to as "salt water" Africans because many of them had actually been born in Africa and had made the crossing. Because of their geographic isolation and rural environment, these early African-Americans had very little contact with the development of the mainland states and plantation culture. For a comprehensive discussion of *marronage* and maroon societies, see Price, ed., *Maroon Societies: Rebel Slave Communities in the Americas.*

[9]In historical economics and politics Grenada dominates Carriacou. For additional cultural and historical information about Carriacou see Smith, Hill; and Asch and Pearse.

[10]For further discussion on the concept of the other and its relationship to Morrison's use of folklore see my essay, "Ancient Properties in the New World: The Paradox of the 'Other' in Toni Morrison's *Tar Baby.*"

[11]The theme of sexual politics is just as prevalent in Morrison's writing as the theme of political materialism. Woven into Middle Passage metaphors is the role of sexual abuse. Brutal sexual exploitation of black women was so much a part of the middle crossing that a name was given to the mass act of raping women just before the ships embarked: *la pariade.* Many of the women were already pregnant when they were sold to plantations owners. Morrison refers to this in *Beloved.* For another literary description of *la pariade,* see Schwarz-Bart's *La mulatresse Solitude* (46).

[12]Andrea Lee's *Sarah Phillips* also deals with the theme of African-American expatriation in Europe by a cultural runagate.

Works Cited

Asch, Moses and Andrew C. Pearce. *The Big Drum of Carriacou.* Folkways, FE4011, 1956.

Berry, Wendell. *The Unsettling of America: Culture and Agriculture.* New York: Avon Books, 1977.

Blake, Susan L. "Folklore and Community in *Song of Solomon.*" MELUS 3 (1980): 77-82.

Byerman, Keith E. *Fingering the Jagged Grain: Tradition and Form in Recent Black Fiction.* Athens: U of Georgia P, 1985.

Campbell, Jane. *Mythic Black Fiction: The Transformation of History.* Knoxville, Tennessee UP, 1986.

Chopin, Kate. *The Awakening.* New York: Putnam's, 1964.

DeVeaux, Alexis. "Paule Marshall: In Celebration of Our Triumph." *Essence* May 1971: 70-135.

Eliade, Mircea. *The Sacred and the Profane.* Trans. Willard R. Trask. New York:

Harcourt, Brace & World, 1959.

Evans, Mari, ed. *Black Woman Writers (1950-1980): A Critical Evaluation*. New York: Anchor Books, 1984.

Gates, Henry Louis, Jr., ed. *Black Literature and Literary Theory*. New York: Methuen, 1984.

———. "The Blackness of Blackness: A Critique of the Sign and Signifying Monkey." Gates, *Black Literature* 285-321.

Herskovitz, Melville. *Dahomean Narrative*. Chicago: Northwestern UP, 1958.

Hill, Donald R. "More on Truth, Fact, and Tradition in Carriacou." *Caribbean Quarterly* 20. 1 (1974): 45-59.

Hughes, Langston. "Mother to Son." *American Negro Poetry*. Ed. Arna Bontemps. New York: Hill and Wang, 1963.

Hurston, Zora Neale. *Their Eyes Were Watching God*. Greenwich, Conn: Fawcett, 1965.

Johnson, Lemuel. "The Middle Passage in African Literature: Wole Soyinka, Yambo Ouologuem, and Ayi Kwei Armah." *African Literature Today: Myth and History*. Ed. Eldred Jones. London: Heinemann, 1982.

Laguere, Michael. *Voodoo Heritage*. New York: Sage, 1980.

LeClair, Thomas. "A Conversation With Toni Morrison: The Language Must Not Sweat." *New Republic* 21 March 1981: 25-29.

Lee, Andrea. *Sarah Phillips*. New York: Penguin, 1984.

Levine, Lawrence W. *Black Culture and Black Consciousness: Afro-American Folk Thought from Slavery to Freedom*. London: Oxford UP, 1977.

Marshall, Paule. *Brown Girl, Brownstones*. Chatham, NJ: Chatham Bookseller, 1959.

———. *The Chosen Place, The Timeless People*. New York: Avon Books, 1976.

———. "From the Poets in the Kitchen." *New York Times Book Review* 9 Jan. 1983: 3, 34-35.

———. *Praisesong for the Widow*. New York: Putnam's, 1983.

———. "Shaping the World of My Art." *New Letters* 40 (1973): 97-112.

Mbiti, John. *African Religions and Philosophy*. New York: Anchor Books, 1970.

McClusky, John, Jr. "And Called Every Generation Blessed: Theme Setting, and Ritual in the Works of Paule Marshall." Evans 316-34.

Morrison, Toni. *Beloved*. New York: Knopf, 1987.

———. *The Bluest Eye*. New York: Holt, Rinehart & Winston, 1970.

———. "Memory, Creation and Writing." *Thought: A Review of Culture and Idea* 59 (1984):385-90.

———. "Rootedness: The Ancestor as Foundation." Evans. 339-45.

———. *Song of Solomon*. New York: Knopf, 1977.

———. *Tar Baby*. New York: Knopf, 1981.

Naipaul, V.S. *The Loss of El Dorado*. New York: Vintage Books, 1984.

Ogunyemi, Chikewenye Okonjo, "Womanism: The Dynamics of the Contemporary Black Female Novel in English." *Signs* 11 (1985): 63-79.

Parrington, Vernon Louis. *The Beginnings of Critical Realism in America*. New York: Harcourt Brace Jovanovich, 1958.

Perez, Demetrio Ramos, *El Mito del Dorado: Su Genesis y Proceso*. Caracas: Biblioteca de la Academia Nacional de la Historia, 1973.

Price, Richard, ed. *Maroon Societies: Rebel Slave Communities in the Americas*. New York: Anchor Books, 1973.

Reyes, Angelita. "Ancient Properties in the New World: The Paradox of the 'Other' in Toni Morrison's *Tar Baby.*" *Black Scholar* 17.2 (1986): 19-25.

Schwartz-Bart, André. *La mulatresse Solitude.* Paris: Editions du Seuil, 1972.

Smith, M.G. *Kinship and Community in Carriacou.* New Haven: Yale UP, 1962.

Smitherman, Geneva. *Talkin' and Testifyin': The Language of Black America.* Boston: Houghton Mifflin, 1977.

Stepto, Robert. "Intimate Things in Place: A Conversation with Toni Morrison." *Massachusetts Review* 17 (1977): 473-89.

Tate, Claudia. *Black Women Writers at Work.* New York: Continuum, 1983.

Turner, Victor. *The Ritual Process.* Chicago: Aldine, 1969.

Van Gennep, Arnold. *The Rites of Passage.* Trans. Monika B. Vizedom and Gabrielle L. Caffee. Chicago: U. of Chicago P, 1960.

Walker, Alice. *In Search of Our Mothers' Gardens.* New York: Harcourt Brace Jovanovich, 1983.

Willis, Susan, "Eruptions of Funk: Historicizing Toni Morrison." Gates, *Black Literature* 263-83.

"Pieces of Harmony":
The Quiet Politics of
Alan Dugan's Poetry

John Gery

Within the milieu of contemporary literature, the poetry of Alan Dugan appears so stylistically individual that Richard Ellmann and Robert O'Clair, the editors of *The Norton Anthology of Modern Poetry*, open their account of him so: "Alan Dugan is conspicuously unaffiliated—to other poets, to any affirmative creed, to life itself" (1089). But is he really so unaffiliated? Or may he not, in fact, belong squarely in the midst of those poets whose work is chiefly derived from contemporary American bourgeois life (poets as diverse as Robert Bly and James Dickey, Philip Levine and John Ashbery)? As one of his admirers, Donald Davie, has noted, "He can't avoid seeming to imply that when you come right down to it booze and sex and money are the only things that any of us care about in all seriousness" (11). True, like most educated, professional American males, Dugan does not seem to attach himself to any philosophic or aesthetic principle so much as to the pragmatic problem-solving of everyday life, despite his consciousness of grander things. Perhaps because of this lack of an explicitly stated philosophy or politics, Ellmann and O'Clair consider "Dugan's attacks upon comforting hopes and wishes" to be the antics of "the clown of nihilism" (1090). But in an interview Dugan himself has overtly rejected this charge: "I'm not a nihilist. If I were a nihilist, I wouldn't both to write poetry" (Heines 291). Rather than a vision of anarchy in Dugan's poetry, behind the polemical satire, behind the self-consciousness coupled with self-deprecation, and behind the ruthless portrayal of the failure of American culture lies a vision of the social

"Life Comparison," "851," "Teacher's Vacation Lament in the Country," "Adultery," "Rising in Fall," "Winter: For an Untenable Situation," "Jewels of Indoor Glass," and excerpts all from *New and Collected Poems, 1961-1983* copyright © 1961, 1962, 1968, 1972, 1973, 1974, 1983 by Alan Dugan. *New and Collected Poems, 1961-1983* first published by The Ecco Press in 1983. Reprinted with permission.

and political dimensions of the quotidian, a humane and, at bottom, Classical vision inherent not only in the sheer vitality of his verse but in its quiet ability to celebrate.

I

To be sure, Dugan is stylistically idiosyncratic. His poems often scavenge for their material, their diction can be oddly abstract or abstruse, and their mood may strike a reader as utterly despairing. J.D. McClatchy notes that Dugan finds "nourishment" for his poems "in lies, illusions, treachery, pretension, bad faith, and old-fashioned lust" (291). Behind such preoccupations, however, lies a sensibility keen to the possibilities of syntax and rhythm, as well as to the effects of the rhetoric of conventional discourse. Dugan's poems may appear to mock or decry both artistic and social conventions, but what they do, in fact, is to exploit those conventions in good faith as they serve the poet's ends. Tony Harrison, one of Dugan's early reviewers, once criticized his method as a "frantic, but dissipated logic" with a "confusion of tones" (167), but another early reviewer, Terry Eagleton, praised that same method as evidence of Dugan's "*confidence* in verbal reasoning, the trust in the language's capacity to master and process its subject, which he both enacts and implicitly satirizes" (68).

With whom might such a method be aligned? Dugan is not easily associated with any recognizable school of poets around him. He is not notably traditional, as Anthony Hecht and Richard Wilbur are, nor does he manage his subject matter in the terse, elliptical style of a Robert Creeley or a Denise Levertov.[1] He is comfortable neither with what we might call the "deep image" poetics of W.S. Merwin and Charles Wright, nor with the "New York style" of surrealism whose chief progenitors are Frank O'Hara and John Ashbery. His sardonic tone sometimes reminds me of O'Hara's or Russell Edson's, though O'Hara rarely seems as bitter and Edson lacks Dugan's ear for verse. A more useful comparison might be made instead between Dugan and Robert Duncan, a master in his own right of the language of logical discourse, but here Dugan would be clearly distinguished from Duncan by his lack of interest in exploring the process and limits of language itself; he prefers to use the language of reason simply as a way to explore ordinary social experience and conscious feeling—in other words, to explore familiar, though generally scatological, experience in a poetry accessible to the logical intelligence yet erupting with rhetorical surprises.

Take, for example, "Life Comparison" (50) from Dugan's first volume, *Poems*, which brought him such recognition when it received the Yale Series of Younger Poets Award in 1961 and the 1962 Pulitzer Prize for poetry (all of Dugan's early books are reprinted in sequence in his 1983 *New and Collected Poems, 1961-1983*). Though the rhetoric of this poem is complex and the rhythm "frantic," even "dissipated" in spots, its literal meaning is never lost to us from one line to the next. It begins with the image of a hermit crab, examines and meditates on that image, and works toward a bald statement about the crab's meaning for this poet:

> Picked up, a hermit crab who seems
> to curl up in a dead snail's shell
> from cowardice, attacks the thumb
> sustaining him in extraordinary air,
> regardless, and if he is attacked
> by borers or the other enemies of shells,
> he crawls out, raw at the rear!,
> to find a new place, thus exposed.
> So, he does what is appropriate
> within his means, within a case,
> and fails: oh he could not bite off
> the top whorl of my fingerprint,
> although he tried. Therefore, I put
> him back to sea for courage, for
> his doing what he thinks he has to do
> while shrinking, and to propitiate
> my own incommensurate enemies,
> the firms, establishment, and state.

This poem is both straightforward, even polished, in its dealing with its subject, and subtle in its use of syntax, rhythm, and diction. The image and the idea stand in a direct relation to each other: the poet is to the hermit crab as "the firms, establishment, and state" are to the poet. Because of the linear development of this "life comparison," though, we apprehend this relationship only after we arrive at the final line, yet at that point, because of the poem's neatly devised analogy, we also come to understand that the poet's concern with the familiar struggle of the powerless individual in American culture is less metaphysical or psychological than it is political.

But look more closely at the rhetorical forces working in this apparently unequivocal poem. In eighteen lines, Dugan uses only three sentences and five independent clauses, implying the expression of a fairly complex statement in his use of subordination. Also, he includes some unusual words (*borers, whorl, propitiate, incommensurate*), which he carefully contains by using the language of logical argument (*regardless, if, thus, so, although, therefore*). Still, the most remarkable syntactic feature here is how the enjambment, through the logical necessity of the grammar coupled with the rhythm (roughly iambic pentameter), gives the poem the feel of quatrains or sestets, a sense poignantly reinforced by the closure of the *propitiate/state* rhyme at the end.

Throughout "Life Comparison" Dugan characteristically wanders from conventional prosody, but he plays off embedded patterns of versification to create a resonance of meaning. For example, the most significant line of the poem, "his doing what he thinks he has to do," is its only clean pentameter line, giving it proper grandeur. In addition, in line three, the article *the*, when used instead of *a* or the anticipated *my*, inflates the prominence of the noun *thumb* by generalizing it (as in the statement, "*the* thumb is the most important digit on the hand" or "*the* sleeping fox catches no poultry"). Furthermore, that same article drives the sentence forward into the particularity (which thumb?) of the following lines: "the thumb / sustaining him in extraordinary air." Even a flat generality, such as the prosaic, "So, he does what is appropriate / within his means," is surrounded by such traditionally common lyric devices as the interjection *oh*,[2] an exclamation point, and the unsophisticated repetition of phrasing ("within his means, within a case" and "for courage, for / his doing").

Dugan's collected work abounds with examples where the writer approaches his subject directly, yet in a manner as delicately novel as in "Life Comparison." The brief piece "Morning Song" (44), for instance, begins with a plainness of speech in lines that William Carlos Williams might have appreciated:

> Look, it's morning, and a little water gurgles in the tap.
> I wake up waiting, because it's Sunday, and turn twice more
> than usual in bed, before I rise to cereal and comic strips.
> I have risen to the morning danger and feel proud.

The enjambment here between lines two and three, as before, rhetorically introduces the tension felt by one who is apparently used to tossing and turning in bed as a "usual" experience. But then line four forges through whatever tension has been created by commenting directly on it. The mildly surprising word in that line, though, is "danger," a word that *identifies* (rather than *describes*) the poet's feeling, yet not a word generally associated with a relaxed Sunday morning. At the poem's close, the idea of danger is reiterated in the line, "I shall walk out bravely into the daily accident." In similar poems, such as "On an Accident: On a Newspaper Story" (98) and "851" (99), the latter quoted here in its entirety, instead of describing an image Dugan narrates an incident, gleans from it a kind of lesson which he openly states, and then undercuts his own discovery through self-deprecation:

A flying pigeon hit me on a fall day
because an old clothes buyer's junk cart
had surprised it in the gutter: license 851.
The summer slacks and skirts in the heap
looked not empty and not full of their legs
and a baseball cap remained in head-shape.
Death is a complete collector of antiques
who finds, takes, and bales each individual
of every species all the time for sale to god,
and I, too, now have been brushed by wings.

An imagistic poet might end this poem after line five, a meditative poet somewhere around lines seven or eight. Dugan, in contrast, works at a level of self-consciousness that directs him through the event to the idea and, beyond that, to bracketing that idea; in the final line he alludes to the source of his idea in a manner that mocks his own grandiosity: he has been "brushed" not by the wings of death, which he parodies, but by the wings of a pigeon. In short, by exploiting the language of formal discourse for its ironic effects, Dugan simultaneously admits his own intellectual attachment to that language as appropriate to his poetry, even as its frequent breakdown in the poems themselves reflects a corresponding breakdown in the reason and sanity of contemporary American culture.

II

As commentary on American culture, Dugan's poetry works mostly as social satire, a mode largely out of favor among his contemporaries (with a few exceptions such as Allen Ginsberg and Edward Dorn). Not surprisingly, then, the poet himself, whose professed themes are "love, work, war, death, what the world is like outside this window tonight" (Ryan 97), enjoys great popularity among neither the broadly political journals nor the tightly knit poetry circles of his generation—as, say, Robert Lowell did and Ginsberg still does. As in the work of both those poets, however, the pose of his poems remains that of the outsider, like the Roman satirists he so often alludes to, especially in their invectives against the social mores of their time. As McClatchy puts it, Dugan "sits and watches,...and the letters he sends to the world...are a mix of Roman contempt, Swiftian irony, and Brechtian argument. Reason is both his balm and his bane" (291). Despite the self-enclosed nature of his work, though, it is exactly by striking this Classical pose that Dugan is able, at his best, to avoid nihilism and suggest a faith in humane principles without having a nostalgic or elitist devotion to them.

In his satiric poems, Dugan's concerns are mundane, not
transcendent. Of the fifty-four poems in *Poems 4* (1974), for example,
I count at least fifteen on making a living, twelve on overt class differences,
ten or more on the pursuit of women (but not on love), four or five
on drinking, seven on war, several on the pitfalls of living in the city,
and an indeterminate number on money, an abiding concern of this
poet. A few poems have the kind of titles we have come to expect from
a contemporary poet—"The Dark Tower" (216), "On a Professional
Couple in a Side-Show" (225), and "I Dreamed I Got a Letter from
Ezra Pound" (236). But even these poems take unexpected turns. More
prevalent are poems signified by "Untitled Poem" (there are twelve of
these) or those with self-conscious titles such as "Love Song: Class
Analysis" (224), "Portrait in the Form of an Extended Conceit" (213),
and "Death's Chicken, Named Amelia" (a poem about the Depression)
followed by "Two Comments on 'Death's Chicken, Named Amelia' "
(242-43). Typical first lines in the volume play off the sorts of statements
someone might actually say or hear said in conversation:

> I live inside of a machine
> or machines. (229)

> You can't win, you can't draw,
> sometimes you can't even lose. (198)

> God, I need a job because I need money. (200)

> It was a matter of life and death. (243)

Our reaction to such lines in poetry is immediate, because we can
hear them spoken even as we see them on the page. Similarly, our basic
comprehension of a poem's general theme, in most cases, is available
on a first reading. But as in the case of "Teacher's Vacation Lament
in the Country" (246), we must be careful not to let the glossy surface
of the language obscure the poem's subtle implications:

> To have a toothache and no competent dentist,
> poison ivy of the groin and an affair,
> a sprained ankle in walking country,
> and going broke vacationing—these
> are just occasions for cocktail party humor.
> What is decisively lousy is to be
> out of whiskey on Labor Day
> when the liquor stores are closed
> and the merchants fly the flag for blood,
> not solidarity, the labor movement, and stars,
> while having to go back to town to teach

what, to whom, how, and why, on Tuesday.

As most of his critics agree,[3] Dugan is an urban poet, and this poem opens with the familiar complaint of the city bloke in the country. But that theme is abruptly dismissed after line five, when the second sentence turns toward a larger problem—the hypocrisy of those Americans who celebrate Labor Day as a kind of Veterans Day or Memorial Day ("for blood"), instead of as a day of "solidarity" among workers. The teacher, though he or she might be, is in no position to alter this circumstance. After all, like any common laborer "having to go back to town" to muddle through who knows what "on Tuesday," the teacher worships the same gods everyone else does, and for Dugan, in America those gods are ultimately the gods of money, material comfort, and self-interest.

Another point critics agree on is that Dugan has failed to change his style or concerns over the course of his career. For instance, "Dugan continues to make more poems, rather than 'developing' or changing style with each new book," wrote Helen Chasin in 1974 (31). And the danger with such adherence to one style, added McClatchy eleven years later, is not only that later poems become mannered parodies of the earlier ones, but that the poet has "prevented access to larger, more complex areas of experience" (293). Maybe so. But why must a poet change styles when the social conditions to which his or her poems speak themselves remain unchanged? Might not the argument be made that poets forever developing their styles resemble lovers forever trying new sexual positions? No matter how many different ways they approach their project, the same ancient fears and desires play on them. Dugan is not one to change for the sake of change. He has tried his hand at experimenting with form—evidenced in *New and Collected Poems, 1961-1983* by just a glance at "Coat of Arms" (72-73), "A Trial" (191), or "Triptych" (58)—but since the beginning of his career his obsessions have been rooted in ordinary male experience, often summarized in such litanies as "the firms, establishment, and state," "a help, a love, a you, a wife" (915), "in safety / from himself, them, or other enemies" (234), "to beg for women, money, and pleasure" (240), and "my goods, / evils, money, laughs, girls and all" (235), obsessions for which he has fewer answers than questions: "What do you say, why bother, who's driving, what's right?" (255)

In his persistence in writing about these matters, Dugan reminds me of Juvenal, the Roman satirist who bitterly attacked those social institutions which oppressed him while his fellow poets fled those same institutions for the refuge of more "literary" subjects"[4]

Must I stick to the usual round
Of Hercules' labours, what Diomede did, the bellowing
Of that thingummy in the Labyrinth, or the tale of the flying
Carpenter, and how his son went splash in the sea?
Will *these* suffice in an age when each pimp of a husband
Takes gifts from his own wife's lover—if she is barred in law
From inheriting legacies—and, while they paw each other,
Tactfully stares at the ceiling, or snores, wide awake, in his wine?
. . . .
Don't you want to cram whole notebooks with scribbled invective
When you stand at the corner and see some forger carried past
On the necks of six porters, lounging back like Maecenas
In his open litter? (66)

While other poets praised the strength of Hercules or lamented the fall of Icarus, Juvenal assailed the social and political corruption of Rome. While other poets dwell among subjective images for their own psychic alienation or grief, Dugan writes about finding a job, wasting away a free Sunday, keeping the house warm in winter, discussing sex with a teenage girl, or visiting an oppressive college town. The difference is that Juvenal, with his private disillusionment and public conscience, is more scathing of his compatriots in his satires than Dugan is in his lyric poems. Even in his more recent poems which consciously allude to or employ Classical satiric poses, when Dugan mocks, reprimands, or attacks, he lacks Juvenal's vitriolic righteousness, and he always numbers himself among the fallen. "I have a philosophical basis without a philosophy," he says in one of his interviews (Ryan 91).

Unlike Juvenal, Dugan confesses to his own self-interests, even to the point of deriding himself. In "Poem ('Always prudent but unprepared')" (177), the poet, having brought no umbrella to work, meditates on staying behind at the office during a rainstorm after everyone else has gone home. He thinks to himself:

Once
I'd hoped to dream in the rain
for life, unbothered by
the economics of appearance,

but surrounded by the clamps of a steady job, "now / I'm pressed in the synthetics too," like the secretary whose fingernail polish is so thick it comes off her onto the keys of her typewriter. The poet wishes he could bemoan his alienation from a life of dreaming, but in the end he must admire the secretary's "device of getting on / beautifully for survival" and concede that "pacing an empty office after 5" is "not so bad" after all, because, as he finally admits, having a job has a major benefit:

I get rebellious for the truth
of outside weather often, but
my check is here each Friday.

Or, in contrast to Juvenal's vivid Sixth Satire, expressing his deep disgust
with the lurid sexual practices of Roman housewives, Dugan in
"Adultery" (146) draws a crucial distinction between private "crimes"
and public ones, yet the subtle irony here is that by drawing that
distinction satirically he is merging the consequences of adultery with
the consequences of waging war:

What do a few crimes
matter in a good life?
Adultery is not so bad.
You think yourself too old
for loving, gone in the guts
and charms, but a woman says,
"I love you," a drunken lie,
and down you go in the grass
outside the party. You rejoin
the wife, delighted and renewed!
She's grateful but goes out
with a bruiser. Blood
passions arise and die
in lawyers' smiles, a few
children suffer for life
and that's all. But: One
memo from that McNamera and his band
can kill a city of lives
and the life of cities, too,
while L.B. "Killer" Johnson and His Napalm Boys
sit singing by their fire:
The Goldberg Variations.
So, what do a few crimes
matter in a neutral life?
They pray the insignificance
of most private behavior.

The "passions" that "arise and die / in lawyers' smiles" and the
"few / children" who "suffer for life" may seem, at first reading, obviously
insignificant when contrasted to the murder of "a city of lives" and
"the life of cities." Still, the symmetrical repetition of the question, "So,
what do a few crimes / matter in a neutral life?" is then thrown off
balance by the last two lines of the poem, especially by the uncommon
usage of the verb *pray* as a transitive verb. As I read it, not only is
the act of genocide an outrage on the lives of its many victims, but

it is also an outrage on those not directly responsible or engaged in it, because such an act, simply by being ordered, "prays the insignificance," or *entreats the lack of importance*, of the private actions of any individual. In other words, large-scale *political* immorality undermines any *personal* sense of morality one might have. Dugan's speaker in "Adultery" seems to be saying that adultery is harmless, relative to war, but in fact the poem implies that any individual's freedom to exercise moral choice in a meaningful way is essentially coerced by any immoral act of the state. Such an act sacrifices not just public morals (which Juvenal decried the loss of) but private morality, whereby the individual feels that his or her own actions are meaningful enough to be taken seriously. The values expressed in this poem are not merely aesthetic, nor is it operating only as comic satire.[5]

III

Undoubtedly the best piece written about Dugan to date is a review by Denis Donoghue in a 1970 issue of the *New York Review of Books*. Donoghue remarks on Dugan's devotion to "ramification": "The secret is attention, refusing to give up even when the case seems lost," he says, later explaining, "In the best poems Mr. Dugan has worked up steam before the poem begins, and the first lines release it; thereafter the power drives through the language, nothing is allowed to rest until the whole work of syntax is accomplished." Donoghue goes on to develop two analogies for Dugan's poetics, namely, the poem as an oasis and "poetry as graffiti, the book as a latrine wall" (37). The reviewer Peter Stitt echoes the latter analogy to Dugan's irreverence when he claims that, at his worst, Dugan's poems are "proud of their cleverness but without much to say" (405), a criticism of Dugan which, as I have tried to demonstrate, overlooks his considerable skill as a craftsman. In the former analogy, Donoghue describes Dugan's poem "Oasis" (22) as "a desert, thirsting to be realized, the underground spring the imagination itself, freeing its way up into speech and form" (39). He then incorporates into this account his sense of Dugan's satiric perspective and self-mockery: "Ironic to heroes, he does not propose to join their ranks." Taken together, this "oasis-poetry" technique and its "acrid note" of "disgust at the defeat of the American Sublime" make up what Donoghue calls Dugan's "Romantic idiom":

When Mr. Dugan mocks himself, the common reason is self-disgust, that everything is possible but nothing is fatal; that is, nothing is required, nothing is worthy of a grand idiom, a tragic drama. It is a mark of Mr. Dugan's good taste that the predicament issues in poems not lugubrious but spry. (37)

What an intriguing analysis, especially in its final sentence! If Dugan is obsessively preoccupied by the "defeat of the American Sublime," why should he bother to express his concern in poems that exhibit "good taste"? The answer to this question, implicit throughout his work, is also the chief reason for acknowledging his overall achievement, which can be seen as expressing a single humane vision, no matter how understated and despite what the poet himself says to the contrary.[6] What reveres Dugan is precisely what Ellmann and O'Clair misperceive as his nihilism but what is, more accurately described, his Classical position, his refusal to be decadent in what he considers a decadent age, and his uncompromising desire to celebrate whatever life around him that he can.

Like other contemporary urban poets (O'Hara, Ashbery, Levertov), Dugan is a poet of self-consciousness and unpredictability. But he keeps these impulses from so overwhelming his compositions as to break down their formal integrity—a recurrent criticism of Ashbery, for example. Note here, in a slightly different vein, how Dugan's self-consciousness is handled during his interview with Donald Heines:

Heines: Do you like people?
Dugan: I do like people in certain circumstances and conditions.
Heines: For example?
Dugan: Well, for example, if I didn't like *you*, if we weren't friends from way back, I wouldn't consent to be interviewed in the presence of this goddamned tape-recorder, which unnerves me. (291)

This is the kind of exchange that an interviewer will usually edit from the transcript of a recorded interview. However suspect Heines's or Dugan's reasons for not editing it out, this self-conscious banter illustrates Dugan's general embarrassment in discussing his art or himself lightly, and it ironically qualifies, if not renders untrue, much of what he has said throughout the rest of the interview. The inherent paradox of an interview with a writer is what is addressed here. The pleasure of reading an interview is in catching a writer off his guard, at home with his shoes off and his feet propped up, relaxed; in fact, interviews are carefully edited and rearranged, usually in close consultation with the one being interviewed. What results is a strained effect of nonchalance, a highly formal informality. Dugan's self-conscious remark belies a noting of the relative hollowness of such a literary exercise, beyond the immediate end of increasing the celebrity of the writer and his interviewer. Reading this passage, we share in both the interviewer's and the poet's embarrassment, I think. Nevertheless, by their leaving it in, we forge through this uneasy moment with them and move on the rest of the interview, for whatever it is worth.

Dugan clearly trusts his own ability to forge ahead in his poems as well, no matter what their subject matter, and as Donoghue points out, "nothing is allowed to rest" until a poem finds its own closure (37). Such an effort often turns up the unexpected, as Dugan himself admits in his interview with Michael Ryan: "I have the notion...that there is some construct that wants to surface, and if I follow the process, both by dreaming and by intellectual work, then the poem will result in a surprise, an emotional charge. It will say neither my conscious intention, nor will it say what the unconscious speaker wanted it to say, but those several individuals will be blended in a common voice" (97). Though Dugan does not put all his faith in a muse ("the unconscious speaker"), he does not abandon the irrational either. With one eye on the world and one eye on his own psyche, he creates dialectically, mixing intellection with discovery.

Often reprinted Dugan poems, such as "Love Song: I and Thou" (15), "Funeral Oration for a Mouse" (39), "Tribute to Kafka for Someone Taken" (46), "For Masturbation" (93), and "On Rape Unattempted" (181), tend to follow this premise. All these poems, were it not for the energy of the technique that drives through them, might well be considered otherwise as poems of despair. A textbook case of such a poem is "Rising in Fall" (211), where Dugan characteristically begins with a scatological observation which he works over until he is able to break through it with "a surprise, an emotional charge":

> Rising in Fall,
> the mushrooms feel like stiff pricks made of rot.
> Oh spreading glans, what
> a botanical striving to butt
> hogberry branches and leaves apart
> to rise to fuck the sky so fast,
> six inches in, up IT, with dirt
> on top of each umbrella ribbed beneath,
> in one night after rain. Stars,
> there is life down here in the dark.
> It wants you, upward, but not much.
> The mushrooms die so fast
> in their external manifestations that
> their maggots working to be flies
> make moving liquid of their blackening heads.
> Oh you can see them falling downward for a week
> to dirt—that's when they really live—
> and then the flies take off.
> How high do they get to sting us?
> Not high. It's ridiculous. I ask
> a woman, "Do you get the point
> of all this pointless action?"
> She answers, "Naturally. Yes. Idiot."

Scrutinizing the resemblance of a mushroom to a penis (an obvious resemblance most writers would avoid as a cliché), Dugan examines it as he does the hermit crab in "Life Comparison" and the pigeon in "851" until he discovers in it its salient feature, namely in this case its meager size when measured against the sky. Suddenly, however, he is moved to praise it, when he shifts his attention to the sky, by way of addressing the stars: "Stars, / there is life down here in the dark." He then turns back to the mushrooms, and by reflecting on their eventual limp condition, he ends up ironically celebrating a life post coitus and without heroism, no matter how insignificant a life that may seem: "Oh you can see them falling downward for a week / to dirt—that's when they really live...." Rather than linger in this moment of nostalgia, however, the poem abruptly turns to the presence of a woman, structurally reminding us that this poem is, as Dugan describes his own work, "the expression of one personality at one time in one place" (Althaus 85). In other words, even when touching on a feeling of universal despair, the poet never forgets his social and, by inference, political context. These various directions taken by this poem are never predictable, yet each turn in itself is self-evident and we never fully leave the poet's conscious mind. I do not know that we can expect any more from a contemporary poet than that—a coherent vision in the midst of the depiction of quantum chaos.

What may well be the most apt metaphor for this dialectic tension in Dugan's poetry appears as the final poem in *Poems 2* (1963), "Winter: For an Untenable Situation" (130). This poem is an extended conceit about a married couple remaining togehter at any expense, but it is also an allegory for life in a society like ours in which we seem willing to destroy ourselves for the sake of preserving our values, even if those values become self-consuming:[7]

> Outside it is cold. Inside,
> although the fire has gone out
> and all the furniture is burnt,
> it is much warmer. Oh let
> the white refrigerator car
> of day go by in glacial thunder:
> when it gets dark, and when
> the branches of the tree outside
> look wet because it is so dark,
> oh we will burn the house itself
> for warmth, the wet tree too,
> you will burn me, I will burn you,

and when the last brick of the fireplace
has been cracked for its nut of warmth
and the last bone cracked for its coal
and the andirons themselves sucked cold,
we will move on!, remembering
the burning house, the burning tree,
the burning you, the burning me,
the ashes, the brick-dust, the bitter iron,
and the time when we were warm,
and say, "Those were the good old days."

Dugan is witnessing the self-destruction of American civilization—the burning of both house and tree, both you and me. Yet this poem does more than merely lament that self-destructive course; it further recognizes the characteristic vitality and industry with which we act on ourselves as a part of the process of collapse. The very style of this poem embodies that vitality in its crisp language and its enthusiastic, though self-deprecatory, tone ("We will move on!"). In fact, as so often in Dugan's poetry, the final line here is one of surprising *celebration*, with its sentiment that, after all, now are "the good old days," regardless that their demise is imminent.

Even as he seems "an irreverent, devil-may-care whirling dervish, ill at ease in the twentieth century but loving every minute of it," as Stitt believes (406), Dugan remains not only a poet of Classical celebration but one with a conscience. Neither a cynic, finally, nor a nihilist, he is less like Juvenal than like the Virgil of the Eclogues,[8] an urban poet, yes, but one who shares with the pastoral poet an immediate sense of his environment. In Dugan's case, that environment happens to be a culture in which the power structures best succeed by creating the illusion that the public and the personal are antiseptically separate, that political structures have nothing to do with the ordinary private life of individuals. Because of the poetic discipline, adept satire, and intensive concentration prevalent in his best poems, Dugan reestablishes the abiding, inevitable connection between those two spheres, reminding us of our individual vulnerability without dismissing our social responsibility. Like the "man who first saw nothing" (147), the hero in Dugan's "On Zero," Dugan speaks honestly for his own kind: "his eye is the condition of his flock / and his flock is his food and fleece" (150), expressing not only the integral bind between ideology and poetry but their interdependence. It is primarily *because* of his acute awareness of his political context that Dugan has broken through the narcissistic, ornate poetic veils surrounding so many contemporary poets into a more complex poetics, a "Dugan's Edge" (56) which includes both "a spit he has made his own" (McClatchy 291) and, more significantly, an incisive language for cutting into the heart of American culture.

Nevertheless, if, as Wordsworth believed, lyric poetry expresses the immediate presence of emotion, Dugan is also a lyric poet whose task is ultimately to sing of the beauty of the natural world, including that which is human. Without fooling himself into a false belief in his own artistic autonomy or importance, without dismissing the largely apathetic, antipathetic world around him, Dugan still informs his poetry at every level with the same music of celebration found in the poems of the Classical lyricists, as well as in the work of a Mayakovsky, a Rilke, or an Auden in our own century. By way of variation, though, while deliberately addressing himself to the follies, the failures, and the scatological fallout of American culture, Dugan celebrates whatever "pieces of harmony" he finds among the shards in the "Jewels of Indoor Glass" (192):

> The broken glass on the stairs
> shines in the electric light.
> Whoever dropped the beer
> was anti-social or too drunk
> to sweep it up himself.
> So the beauty goes, ground
> under heel but shining, it
> and the deposit lost. But
> by the janitor's broom
> it is still sharp enough
> for dogs' feet, babies' hands,
> and eyes pierced by its lights,
> that he should curse the fool
> and I should try to praise
> the pieces of harmony.

Notes

[1]In a review of *New and Collected Poems, 1961-1983*, Ashley Brown approaches Dugan by comparing him to those poets born in 1923, the same year he was (Anthony Hecht, James Dickey, Louis Simpson, Denise Levertov, and Daniel Hoffman), but finds him separate from all the others because he "makes no appeal to history or 'culture' or to a transcendent view of life" (601).

[2]Anthony Hecht has noted about Dugan, "I would bet there's not a poet writing today who uses the exclamatory 'Oh' more frequently" (214).

[3]For examples, see Eagleton 68-70; Quinn 302-3; Chasin 31; and Brown 601. Some of these reviewers criticize Dugan's "urbanity," while others praise it.

[4]The lines quoted here are lines 52-59 and 66-69 in Satire I.

[5]For another example of a poem that juxtaposes political morals and private morality, though not quite so effectively, see "Untitled Poem ('I live the way...')" (287).

[6]Note this exchange in Dugan's interview with Keith Althaus, where Dugan addresses his sense of his own work:

Althaus: Do you think of your work to a certain extent as all one poem?
Dugan: No. With luck it might seem to an outside observer to be of a piece because it's the expression of one personality at one time in one place, but my own sense of it is that it's fragmented because I have so many different selves and have been in so many different circumstances and the rest of it, that I have no sense of coherence in my own life. (85)

[7]For more recent evidence of Dugan's awareness of this sense of American culture, see "Untitled Poem ('One used to be able...')" (303).

[8]Unlike Frank O'Hara, whose work habits seemed to characterize him as a manic poet writing apace with the pressures of city living (with poems or fragments of poems left in typewriters or stuffed into drawers, as though ephemeral), Dugan has always taken a disciplined approach to composition, similar to the pastoral poet who has plenty of leisure time. He says that he keeps Virgil's motto, "Nulla Dies Sine Linea" ("No Day Without a Line"), posted above his writing desk in New York (Heines 294), a sign that he writes in a deliberate, maybe even plodding, manner.

Works Cited

Althaus, Keith. "An Interview with Alan Dugan." *Northwest Review* 20.1 (1982): 75-85.

Brown, Ashley. Rev. of *New and Collected Poems, 1961-1983*, by Alan Dugan. *World Literature Today* 58 (Autumn 1984): 600-01.

Chasin, Helen. "*Poems 4.*" *Village Voice* 22 August 1974: 31.

Davie, Donald. "Cards of Identity." *New York Review of Books* 6 March 1975: 10-11.

Donoghue, Denis. "Oasis Poetry." *New York Review of Books* 7 May 1970: 35-38.

Dugan, Alan. *New and Collected Poems, 1961-1983*. New York: Ecco Press, 1983.

Eagleton, Terry. "New Poetry." *Stand* 12.3 (1971): 68-70.

Ellmann, Richard, and Robert O'Clair, eds. *The Norton Anthology of Modern Poetry*. New York: W.W. Norton, 1988.

Harrison, Tony. "Poetry: Wonderland." *London Magazine* 11.1 (April-May 1971): 163-68.

Hecht, Anthony. "Writers' Rights and Readers' Rights." *Hudson Review* 21 (Spring 1968): 207-17.

Heines, Donald. "A Conservation with Alan Dugan." *Massachusetts Review* 22 (Summer 1981): 285-300.

Juvenal. *The Sixteen Satires*. Trans. Peter Green. Baltimore: Penguin, 1967.

McClatchy, J.D. "Weaving and Unweaving." *Poetry* 145 (February 1985): 291-306.

Quinn, Sister Bernetta, O.S.F. "Two Signatures." *Poetry* 119 (February 1972): 301-03.

Ryan, Michael. "An Interview with Alan Dugan." *Iowa Review* 4.3 (Summer 1973): 90-97.

Stitt, Peter. "The Circle of the Meditative Moment." *Georgia Review* 38 (Summer 1984): 402-14.

Amiri Baraka and the
Politics of Popular Culture

David Lionel Smith

Among contemporary writers, no one has been more provocative, politically and otherwise, than Amiri Baraka, formerly known as LeRoi Jones. In the political sphere, Baraka has been as notorious for his radical transformations as for his radical stances. Bohemian aesthete, new left polemicist, black cultural nationalist, and Marxist-Leninist-Maoist, Baraka has declared his politics uncompromisingly at every phase of his career. More importantly, in terms of the present discussion, he has always insisted on an integral relationship between political and aesthetic commitments. I have written elsewhere on the major phases of Baraka's career and how his politics have shaped his creative work.[1] The purpose of the present essay is to examine Baraka's use of popular cultural motifs and his understanding, at various points of his career, of how political meaning imbues the icons of popular culture.

The term "popular culture" deserves a bit of clarification. Fredric Jameson has attacked trenchantly the notion that culture can be legitimately divided into separate "high" and "popular" spheres.[2] Jameson's point seems to me valid, especially as a response to certain facile notions of what "popular" means. Nonetheless, this designation remains useful as a way of specifying a broadly recognized category of cultural artifacts. When I use the term "popular culture" in this essay, I refer specifically to the non-literary mass communications media: television, radio, comic books, recordings, etc. For my purposes, the common link among these media is not their content but their accessibility. These media make artifacts of culture available to virtually anyone, with an absolute minimum of ostensible literacy prerequisites. Literary media, by contrast, and books particular, demand at the least a basic competency in and ease with reading before one can experience

"In the Tradition" from *The Music: Reflections on Jazz & Blues* by Amiri Baraka and Amina Baraka. Text: Copyright © 1987 by Amiri Baraka. By permission of William Morrow and Company, Inc. Reprinted with permission.

a given work. In the visual medium of television or the aural medium of radio, one can enjoy a cultural artifact—the Three Stooges or the Metropolitan Opera, say—without even understanding the language.

From such observations one might infer, depending on one's biases, that the non-literary mass media are either lower (less sophisticated) or more democratic ("popular") than literary media. Neither of these dubious inferences is within the purview of the present essay. A related error, however, needs to be noted. Many commentators believe that because non-literary media are more broadly accessible, they are also more representative as repositories of common values. As Jameson forcefully argues, this claim is doubtful at best, and the exact opposite may indeed be more likely. In any case, this is an exceedingly difficult theoretical point. How one resolves it will depend upon what one accepts as fundamental. Like Jameson, one may privilege the psychological yearnings of the creative subject, torn between the reality which he confronts and the utopia toward which he aspires. In this case, one would likely join Jameson in finding the most highly wrought works of modernist and post-modernist literature as the best mirrors of our epoch. But one might also privilege objective factors, such as the means of cultural production, and therefore seek to locate fundamental values in the public forms of commerce, technological developments, and modes of communication which mediate all cultural production. Such a focus would probably follow the lines proposed by Raymond Williams over the past two decades and an inquiry of this sort would be much less likely to privilege one sort of artifact over the other as worthy objects of study. My own views are somewhat closer to Williams', though not to the point of complete agreement. Regardless of one's theoretical stance, this is a highly fraught and hotly contested issue on which claims ought not be made lightly.[3]

These theoretical ruminations do bear pointedly on Baraka's work, though their precise significance can be better understood from a retrospective than a prospective view. Since his earliest publications, Baraka has apparently regarded popular cultural artifacts as quintessential repositories of cultural values. In his early work he often regarded such icons with a reverential nostalgia, and in his later work he has more often treated them as deplorable manifestations of a depraved culture, which he, the poet, must expose. Whether his shifts in attitude represent a movement toward more or less sophisticated understandings of these artifacts will be among our points of inquiry. But regardless of what else we infer, it is clear that popular culture remains a major source of poetic inspiration to Amiri Baraka.

One reason for this fascination is that throughout his career, Baraka has struggled with a problem which has been perhaps the most characteristic dilemma for Afro-American writers: namely, the dichotomy between one's self as a talented, upwardly mobile person, at home in the elite and mostly white world of artists and intellectuals, and by contrast, common black folk, whom one lives apart from yet in some sense represents and wishes to serve. Individuals facing this dilemma have responded in various and often extreme ways. Baraka's response has been especially complicated. Intellectually, however, he has repeatedly turned to popular culture as a mediation between himself and common folk. Not surprisingly, his attitude toward popular culture has shifted with each major phase of his career, reflecting his own philosophical and aesthetic commitments.

Baraka's fascination with popular culture is apparent in "In Memory of Radio," one of his earliest and most famous poems. That poem begins:

> Who has ever stopped to think of the divinity of Lamont Cranston?
> (Only Jack Kerouac, that I know of: & me.
> The rest of you probably had on WCBS and Kate Smith,
> Or something equally unattractive.) (*Preface* 12)

From the outset, the poet asserts a kind of moral superiority for himself and his bohemian friend, who are presumably hip enough to recognize that the Shadow (Lamont Cranston's alter ego) is a god. The rest of us, in contrast to the tiny elite of hipsters, are dismissed as middle class, square, gullible and tasteless. The terms of this dismissal become clearer later in the poem, as the poet parodies a popular romantic song which tastelessly borrowed lines from Tennyson's great elegy, "In Memoriam" (" 'Tis better to have loved and lost") and invokes the ultimate bad taste of people who would "put linoleum in your living rooms." As the true *cognoscenti* worship the Shadow, who "knows what evil lurks in the hearts of men," the rest of us are misled by double-dealing TV evangelists, such as the faith healer Oral Roberts and Bishop Fulton J. Sheen, whose gospel is "how to get saved *&* rich!" (original italics). These false prophets the poet links to Hitler, which presumably makes us, the general public, into so-called "good Germans."

On one level, we can view the poet's posturing here as a typical bohemian gesture. As Werner Sollors has persuasively demonstrated, such self-righteous attacks on middle class culture by the rebellious children of the middle class have always characterized bohemian movements. It is worth noting, however, that the poet qualifies his self-righteousness. He does not claim that he knows the answer to that most profound of theological issues, the problem of good and evil, but that the Shadow knows. The poet only claims to recognize the difference between a true prophet (the Shadow) and a false one (Oral Roberts). Regarding his own knowledge, the poet persistently shrugs his shoulders: "What can I say?"; "Am I a sage or something?" Beneath the poet's generic bohemian gesture, then, we can read a commitment to faith over complacency. Even in conventional theological terms, this formulation shows the poet's attitude in a much more favorable light than our original reading.

But needless to say, the Beat Movement was an artistic, not a religious movement. Therefore, it is hardly surprising to find that even the most overtly theological concern resolves itself into aesthetic terms. The poet, recalling his childhood, asserts: "Saturday mornings we listened to *Red Lantern* & his undersea folk. / At 11, *Let's Pretend* / & we did / & I, the poet, still do, Thank God!" The aesthetic equivalent of faith is imagination, which the poet here links to innocence. Imagination, he implies, distinguishes him and Jack Kerouac from the rest of us and makes them, like the Shadow, good guys. And while the poet does not claim to share all of the Shadow's knowledge, he does recognize that "Love is an evil word," because turned backward, it becomes "evol." Evidently, unquestioning faith is good toward the Shadow but not toward evangelists. This, perhaps, is because the Shadow is an imaginary being. Hence, imaginary saviors are better than real ones. This conclusion is cynical, but it also corresponds closely to the skeptical strand in most of our religious traditions. The poet's aesthetic faith turns out not to be so different from religious faith.

What does this say about Baraka's attitude toward popular culture? Most obviously, Baraka regards popular culture as a heterogeneous, multivocal, and potentially bewildering repository of common values. It contains the values which make a Hitler possible, but it also contains the sources of artistic inspiration. It nurtures skepticism and gullibility simultaneously. This vision of popular culture is irreducibly complex. The poem is called "In Memory of Radio," not "In Memory of Lamont Cranston." The Shadow and Kate Smith occupy the same medium. Implicitly, then, the poem insists upon critical discrimination in the consumption of popular cultural artifacts, because these artifacts are not necessarily what they seem to be. It neither condemns nor glorifies popular culture out of hand.

Throughout *Preface to a Twenty Volume Suicide Note*, Baraka uses the icons of popular culture in a similar fashion, both as objects of criticism and articles of faith. The same is true in his second collection of poems, *The Dead Lecturer*, except that these poems express the central existential crisis of Baraka's life, and his formulations present polarized extremes with a tone more shrill and less coy. He still sifts through the artifacts of popular culture in search of adequate articles of faith, but the sense of satisfactory resolution expressed in "In Memory of Radio" eludes him here.

The poet's dilemma in these poems receives forceful, though abstract, expression in *"An Agony. As now"* (original italics). It begins:

> I am inside someone
> who hates me. I look
> out from his eyes. Smell
> what fouled tunes come in
> to his breath. Love his
> wretched women. (*Lecturer* 15)

Here, as throughout *The Dead Lecturer*, the poet expresses his concerns very obliquely. In essence, he feels torn between the black world and the white world (a problem exacerbated by his being a black man with a white wife), between bohemia and "the real world" (symbolized respectively by Greenwich Village and Harlem), between artistic expression and political action. These conflicts call the validity of his entire life into question. In particular, he fears that he will become like many of his artist friends:

> They speak of singing who
> have never heard song; of living
> whose deaths are legends
> of their kind. (31)

In short, he fears being a phony. Following the course mapped out in "In Memory of Radio," the poet again embarks upon a quest for moral absolutes, hoping to become unambiguously virtuous in a world where duplicity is the norm. Needless to say, such a quest can only end either in frustration or in glib dogmatism.

To ensure that the reader cannot over look the explicitly moral address of *The Dead Lecturer*, Baraka prefaces it with an oath from the Green Lantern comic book:

> "In brightest day, In blackest night
> No evil shall escape my sight!
> Let those who worship evil's might
> Beware my power...
> Green Lantern's Light." (8)

As we shall see momentarily, this manifesto provides a direct clue to how the poet will regard popular culture, both here and later in his career. Most immediately, however, this remorseless light of self-righteousness is turned upon the poet's friends and especially upon himself. It is hardly surprising, then, that he feels trapped inside someone who hates him. Disconcertingly, to reveal the hidden sins of his and his friends' hearts turns out to offer no solace, and even worse, to produce no constructive change. Perhaps the poet might have saved himself some scars by studying Nathaniel Hawthorne, our most meticulous commentator on the pernicious psychology of self-righteousness. And indeed, the poet recognizes to a degree the character of his problem. But as "I Substitute for the Dead Lecturer" indicates, his self-contemplation is horrifying:

> For all these wan roads
> I am pushed to follow, are
> my own conceit. A simple muttering
> elegance, slipped in my head
> pressed on my soul, is my heart's
> worth. And I am frightened
> that the flame of my sickness
> will burn off my face. And leave
> the bones, my stewed black skull,
> an empty cage of failure. (60)

These lines offer as powerful a statement of self-doubt as anything in contemporary literature. As I have argued elsewhere, Baraka's formulation of the issues constitutes a very inauspicious basis for his transition to becoming an explicitly political poet. The dead lecturer is his old self, and the self-inflicted violence that allows his new self to emerge is a sad foreshadowing of the extravagant rhetorical violence which subsequently mars his work.

In the context of this agonized and compulsive self-questioning, Baraka comes to regard popular culture as an objective correlative for his own psyche. Poems such as "Rhythm & Blues," "A Poem for Willie Best," and "Green Lantern's Solo" invoke familiar icons of popular culture, but what they actually express is the poet's own involuted anguish. Indeed, only a very canny reader will perceive any relationship at all between these titles and the poems which follow them.[4] The poems are exceedingly difficult and abstract, especially the first two, and furthermore, the intense alienation symbolized by the disjuncture between title and content is an essential meaning of the poems. "A Poem for Willie Best," dedicated to the actor who played a demeaning darky character named "Sleep 'n Eat," is especially memorable for its exploration of the relationship between the public guise and the inner self. All three of these poems evince an extraordinarily perceptive observer of popular cultural artifacts. Yet at the same time, they also present a writer who has completely detached those artifacts from their normal contexts in order to express more precisely his personal crisis of dislocation. The issue which these artifacts crystalize for Baraka is not politics but rather aesthetic and existential *angst*.

The Dead Lecturer was the last book of poems by LeRoi Jones. In 1965 Jones changed his name to Imamu Amiri Baraka and moved to Harlem, symbolizing his abandonment of Greenwich Village and his entry into "blackness" as a cultural, political, and existential self-definition. Baraka's use of popular culture changed during his black nationalist years (1965-74). Indeed, he seldom wrote about cultural artifacts during these years. Instead, he devoted much of his energy to polemical writing, and when he did address existing culture, he usually concentrated his attention on black folkways or modes of behavior: culture in a more broadly anthropological sense. Broadening his range of concern in this way might ideally have allowed Baraka's work to become more richly complex. Unfortunately, his widening of cultural address accompanied a narrowing of theoretical vision. In his earlier work, Baraka had regarded popular culture as a repository of diverse and often contradictory values, which required the viewer to exercise constant vigilance and skeptical caution. In his black nationalist poems, by contrast, Baraka began to treat nearly all established culture as reprehensible, embodying a heinous legacy of cowardly compromises, deceptions, and bad faith.

The perpetual refrain and explicit design of these poems is the need to destroy "Negro" consciousness and to replace it with a true, "black" consciousness. His "Poem for Halfwhite College Students" admonishes: "when you find yourself gesturing like Steve McQueen, check it out, ask / in your black heart who it is you are, and is that image black or white." (*Selected Poetry* 109) His most famous poem of that period, "Black Art," ends with the declaration:

> We want a black poem. And a
> Black World.
> Let the world be a Black Poem
> And Let All Black People Speak This Poem
> Silently
> or LOUD (107)

To offer one final example, Baraka's "Leroy" ends with a similar claim, though presented in this case as a testament:

> When I die, the consciousness I carry I will to
> black people. May they pick me apart and take the
> useful parts, the sweet meet [*sic*] of my feelings. And leave
> the bitter bullshit rotten white parts

alone. (134)

The questioning, skeptical observer of the early poems has yielded to a declarative, single-minded crusader in these black nationalist poems. The search for truth ends, and the assertion of truth ensues.

Several factors contribute to Baraka's narrow conception of popular culture during this period. The intensity of his own personal conflict and the general weakness of black nationalist cultural theory during the 60s would alone have been sufficient to move him in this direction. Two flaws in particular vitiated black nationalist cultural theorizing during those years: on the social level, a wholly inadequate understanding of how culture is transmitted through the process of historical experience (not to mention a dire ignorance of basic historical facts); and on the personal level, a philosophical idealism which falsely attributed a functional autonomy to consciousness as the determinant of behavior. The notion that consciousness can be created or altered merely at the level of discourse is implicit in Baraka's rush toward didactic writing and his flight from the perception of ambiguity. The role of the poet, according to this conception, is to teach the people the truth of their own blackness. (This reflects the significance of his name Imamu, which means "priest" or "prophet."[5]

In "state/meant," the epilogue to his first collection of essays, *Home*, (1965) Baraka articulates this concept succinctly:

> The Black Artist's role in America is to aid in the destruction of American as he knows it. His role is to report and reflect so precisely the nature of the society, and of himself in that society, that other men will be moved by the exactness of his rendering and, if they are black men, grow strong through this moving, having seen their own strength, and weakness; and if they are white men, tremble, curse, and go mad, because they will be drenched with the filth of their evil. The Black Artist must draw out of his soul the correct image of the world. (251)

One might, and perhaps should, quibble with several assumptions embedded in this manifesto. But in the present context, the essential point is to note how narrowly this statement defines the poet's role. It assumes that black men are weak, that white men are evil, and that the artist knows and must assert the truth about "the world." But the only "truths" which interest him are those which will strengthen black men or weaken white men. So much certainty and so much prescription leaves the poet little conceptual space for questioning or ambiguity. Furthermore, the truth of culture turns out to be a rather simple litany of false consciousness, given these definitions.

Ultimately, to see popular culture simply in terms of "blackness" and "whiteness" was a commitment not to see the specificity of cultural artifacts at all. Such a commitment necessarily entailed an *a priori* ahistoricism. In 1974 Baraka startled both his adherents and his detractors by publicly rejecting black cultural nationalism and adopting a Maoist version of Marxism-Leninism. He states the rationale for his change in the polemical introduction to his book of Marxist poems, *Hard Facts* (1975):

> Earlier our own poems came from an enraptured patriotism that screamed against whites as the eternal enemies of Black people, as the sole cause of our disorder & oppression. The same subjective mystification led to mysticism, metaphysics, spookism, etc., rather than dealing with reality, as well as an ultimately reactionary nationalism that served no interests but our newly emerging Black bureaucratic elite and petty bourgeois, so that they could have control over their Black market. This is not to say revolutionary Black nationalism is not necessary, it was and is to the extent that we are still patriots, involved in the Black Liberation Movement, but we must also be revolutionaries who understand that our quest for our people's freedom can only be realized as the result of Socialist Revolution! Our nationalism was reactionary when it focused on White people as the cause of our oppression rather than the system of monopoly capitalism. (*Selected Poetry* 238)

In this recantation Baraka embraces the distinction between "revolutionary nationalism" and "cultural nationalism" which had been asserted years earlier by Huey Newton, the leader of the Black Panther Party, and other left-wing black nationalists in their criticism of cultural nationalists such as Maulana Ron Karenga and Baraka. Newton wittily dismissed his opponents as "pork chop nationalists" (Newton 495). Thus, Baraka's change of position can be understood as a refinement rather than a complete reversal. He rejects one form of nationalism in favor of another.

In line with this political adjustment, Baraka also restates his aesthetic principles, insisting that art should be politically engaged and rejecting

> the unclarity, romanticism, sadness, & pessimism, the little tearful odes to weakness we write. The people don't need these. They need odes of strength, attack pieces, bomb, machine gun and rocket poems. Poems describing reality and methods of changing it. Rhythmic reading lists, objectivity, clarity, information, science, as well as love and concern. We should not act or write like we're crazy, but as impassioned revolutionaries aiming to help destroy the capitalist system! Be passionate, but disciplined enough to deliver the death blow! (238)

To a large degree this reaffirms the vision of a political aesthetic which Baraka had articulated during the 1960s in works such as "Black Art." But he also rejects some of his earlier positions, such as the admonition in his essay "The Revolutionary Theatre" that political art "should stagger through our universe correcting, insulting, preaching, spitting craziness—but craziness taught to us in our most rational moments" (*Home 210*). For the younger Baraka, an artist was above all an honest and forthright man, and in a society where "the denial of reality has been institutionalized," such a man would naturally appear "crazy," as he says in "LeRoi Jones Talking." At that time, he stated: "I am something like Kit Smart or Blake or Rimbaud or Allen Ginsberg. We're all ravers, in one fashion or another" (*Home* 183). In substance, Baraka's revised position may be virtually identical to this earlier one, but statements such as the latter provide too clear a reminder of bohemian—and white— associations from which Baraka had long since distanced himself. If his earlier emphasis on "craziness" exemplified his bohemian outlook, his new emphasis on "facts" and "rationality" reflect a different ideological stance and Baraka's understanding of Marxism as a "science."

Whatever else this transition may have achieved, it certainly did not bring Baraka into a more sophisticated relationship with popular culture. Indeed, the poems of *Hard Facts* are even more blunt, ahistorical, and reductive than his cultural nationalist poems. Works such as "A New Reality Is Better Than a New Movie" show flashes of Baraka's cruel wit, but they offer little else of interest. This particular poem is ostensibly a commentary on the natural disaster movies of the 1970s (e.g., "The Towering Inferno"), but it is neither effective as poetry nor cogent as analysis of the relationship between cultural artifact and cultural epoch. And failing in these crucial aspects, how can such work possibly forge a new consciousness and inspire people to take political action? In sum, Baraka by the mid-1970s still had not succeeded in formulating an aesthetic adequate to the challenge of popular culture.

The turning point for Baraka came with his reinvestigation of Afro-American history, which helped him to transcend the dogmatic cultural nationalist assumption that the past offers only a dreary chronicle of abject slavery, cowardly capitulations, and false consciousness. At the same time, his study of Mao and rediscovery of Langston Hughes made him recognize the existence of a long and powerful international tradition of politicized art. These discoveries made it possible for Baraka to reconceive the relationship between the artist and existing culture. As a cultural nationalist, Baraka had assumed that the artist must destroy the corrupt existing culture in order to create a new, more humane culture. Now, he began to recognize the tradition of struggle embedded within existing culture, and this recognition entailed the possibility of an art grounded in that tradition of struggle. Such an art could celebrate as well as criticize; it could embody the complexities of real historical experience. Perhaps most importantly, it would allow the poet to write as a voice within a tradition and not just as a lonely pioneer, attempting by the naked force of rhetoric to lead his audience away from reality and into the promised land of utopian "blackness."

Baraka explores these new possibilities most successfully in his poem "In the Tradition" (1981), a work which first appeared as a recording performed by Baraka and the avant garde jazz musicians David Murray, and Steve McCall. By issuing this work as a recording, Baraka demonstrates that he has reconceived the nature and potential of the poetic medium. He makes this point explicitly in his introductory comments to the album, reprinted in his 1987 book *The Music:*

The poetry of the dying epoch (racism and monopoly capitalism, imperialism) exists mostly on paper. It is print bred and bound, and actually intended for a particular elite....Black poetry, in the main, from its premise (unless the maker be considerably "bourgeoisified") means to show its musical origins and resolve as a given. (243)

In other words, traditional poetry as a printed form is inherently elitist. This work, by contrast, exists in a popular medium, where it is available to a much broader audience. It aspires to become an artifact of popular culture. Of course, it also comments upon popular culture.

"In the Tradition" takes as its point of departure a TV show, "The White Shadow," about the white coach of an inner city basketball team. The show's narrative premise and its iconography obviously invoke, to the critical viewer, the "tradition" of white dominance and black subordination, which is the same kind of relationship whether involving masters and slaves or missionaries and natives. Imperialism takes many guises. Even the opening lines suggest the richness and complexity of the poem's achievement:

> Blues walk weeps ragtime
> Painting slavery
> women laid around
> working feverishly for slavemaster romeos
> as if in ragtime they spill
> their origins like chillers (lost chillen)
> in the streets to be
> telephoned to by Huggie
> Bear from Channel 7, for the White Shadow
> gives advice on how to hold our homes
> together... (*The Music* 105)

Baraka links slavery to the contemporary mass media and the rape of black women to the destruction of black families by using the musical traditions of blues, jazz (the word "walk" refers to a style of jazz bass playing), and ragtime to suggest the continuity of Afro-American experience. The good liberal White Shadow is ironically compared to the "slave master romeos" (rapists who sexually abused their human chattel) to suggest how much the forms of oppression have changed without changing the fact of oppression. The tears of line one become the paints of line two, implying that the music itself makes visible and audible the history of African-American suffering. The transparent pun on "laid" sets up the implied pun on "working feverishly," which invokes the various meanings of labor for slave women: field work, domestic chores, sexual exploitation, and childbirth, to name a few. "Spill their origins like chillers" refers both to giving birth and to telling the story of one's life ("chillers" are horror stories or murder mysteries). By implication, blues, jazz, and ragtime all relate this same chronicle of oppression. Social, cultural, and political history merge. Baraka has never written lines of greater poetic density.

In the following stanza, Baraka extends the theme of oppression by drawing an analogy between the white coach of a black basketball team and the overseer of slaves. In this instance, however, Baraka views the attempted oppression as a failure:

> hey coah-ch
>
> wanna outlaw the drunk, cannot deal with skyman darrell
> or double dippin hip doctors deadly in flight
> cannot deal with Magic or Kareem...hey coah-ch coah-ch
> bench yrself in the garbagecan of history o new imperial dog
> denying with lying images
> our strength & African
> funky beauty   (105-06)

These lines invoke the styles of great basketball players, such as Dr. J., Julius Erving, who epitomized quickness and an acrobatic, gravity-defying elegance; Darrell Dawkins, whose backboard-shattering dunk shots earned him the nickname of "Chocolate Thunder"; Magic Johnson, the versatile, crafty playmaker, whose style combines extremes of passion and cool restraint; and Kareem Abdul-Jabbar, whose calm self-possession, reliability, and strength of character make him a regal presence. Rather than becoming mere cogs in some preconceived masterplan, these players redefine the nature of the game by the sheer force of their talents. For Baraka, the white coach symbolizes the attempt to contain and exploit black creativity—"African funky beauty"—under the guise of liberal benevolence: in effect, a reassertion of old-fashioned missionary strategies. Yet Baraka insists that despite the kind of neo-imperialism which The White Shadow represents, the strength of African-American culture, exemplified by its sense of style, has triumphed. In this vision, historical experience becomes a struggle for self-realization which sometimes succeeds, not merely a chronicle of abject suffering.

Furthermore, this poem encompasses some new political perceptions, which are expressed by the following lines:

> . . . Tradition of
> For My People Margaret Walker & David Walker & Jr. Walker
> & Walker Smith Sweet Ray Leonard Rockin in Rhythm w/Musical Dukes
> What is this tradition Basied on, we blue Black Wards strugglin
> against a Big White Fog. Africa people, our fingerprints are everywhere
> on you america. our fingerprints are everywhere. Cesaire told you
> that, our family strewn around the world has made more parts of that world
> blue and funky, cooler, flashier, hotter, afro-cuban james brownier
> > a wide panafrican
> > world   (107)

Here he links the poet (Margaret), political activist (David), and musician (Jr.) via their common name: Walker. Walker Smith, obviously a coy inversion of the structural motif, using Walker as a last name, is in fact doubly coy, since this is the real name of the boxer Sugar Ray Robinson. Baraka joins him here to another "Sugar Ray," his contemporary namesake. The rhythm of an Ellington tune ("Rockin in Rhythm") links the boxer Ray Leonard (famous for his flashy style and fast hands or "dukes") to the Duke himself. Count Basie, whose band played in a hard-driving, bluesy manner, becomes the bass line of the tradition; and the struggle against oppression links the 1960s playwright Douglas Turner Ward (himself named for two great revolutionaries, Frederick Douglass and Nat Turner) to his 1930s predecessor, Theodore Ward, author of a militant play called *The Big White Fog*.

On the other hand, the poet also recognizes that defeats and betrayals and other travesties are "in the tradition" too:

> in the tradition of those klanned & chained
> & lynched and shockleyed and naacped and ralph bunched
>
> hah, you rise a little I mention we also the tradition of amos and andy
> hypnotized selling us out vernons and hooks and other nigger crooks of
> gibsons and crouches had other assorted louses of niggers that turn from
> gold to shit proving dialectics muhammad ali style   (108)

In other words, one may deplore "civil rights leaders" such as Vernon Jordan and Benjamin Hooks, representatives of the Urban league and the NAACP, but one can hardly deny that they are part of "the tradition." Unlike in his nationalist poems, Baraka here declines to attribute political differences to inadequate "blackness." This change of attitude could be attributed to Baraka's Marxism. Indeed, he invokes dialectics at the end of this passage, and the struggle between opposing tendencies is fundamental to dialectical thinking. Baraka allots only a small space in this poem to his black opponents, but he does include them as real historical figures, not just as abstract whipping boys—e.g., the "negroleader" in "Black Art." (His long-time nemesis Kenneth Gibson, whom Baraka worked to elect as the first black mayor of Newark, is an important presence on this list. Gibson's betrayal—from Baraka's perspective—of the folk who supported his candidacy was a crucial factor in provoking Baraka to reject nationalism. Gibson forced him to recognize that blackness alone is no panacea.) The point here is not that Baraka deserves congratulations for becoming more "liberal." The true significance of this change is that including Gibson and his ilk makes Baraka's historical vision fuller and more accurate. One might contest Baraka's claim that triumphs have greatly outweighed defeats or his assessments of the relative influence of various figures for better and worse, but his account of history is certainly plausible—even persuasive. His nationalist works, by contrast, were rarely historical in any but the most perfunctory sense.

In the conclusion of the poem, Baraka reemphasizes his central theme: that the Afro-American tradition, properly understood, has always been one of politicized culture:

> ours is one particular
> one tradition
> of love and suffering truth over lies
> and now we find ourselves in chains
> the tradition says plainly to us fight plainly to us
> fight, thats in it, clearly, we are not meant to be slaves
> it is a detour we have gone through and about to come out
> in the tradition of gorgeous africa blackness
> says to us fight, its all right, you beautiful
> as night, the tradition
> thank you langston/arthur
> says sing
> says fight
> in the tradition, always clarifying, always new and centuries old
> says
>   Sing!
>   Fight!
>   Sing!
>   Fight!
>   Sing!
>   Fight! &c. &c.
>   Boosheee dooooo dee dooo dee dooo

dooooooooo!

DEATH TO THE KLAN!   (112)

The theme of Afro-American history, according to this poem, is singing and fighting: celebration and struggle. As the poem indicates, the struggle has not been futile, because Black fingerprints (music, writing, athletics, style, etc.) cover America. American music is "nigger music." This vision of continual struggle and partial triumph is quite different from the perspective of Baraka's earlier poems. Furthermore, the poet himself becomes reintegrated into the tradition rather than remaining a detached commentator. He becomes a participant in that struggle rather than a guru goading others on. The poem locates politics in the activities of everyday life—literally, in the cultural process itself—not just in isolated and specialized movements or events. This conception regards culture as a single continuum and explodes the dichotomy between high and low, elite and popular culture, by recognizing that these spheres interact constantly in real experience. Finally, the poem views revolution as a process long in the making, not just as some future cataclysm.

This is not to suggest that "In the Tradition" exhausts or settles all the important questions. One might still ask how Baraka understands the dialectic between continuity and change within a tradition. Is this work a celebration or an intervention, an expression or an enactment? How can the retelling of history facilitate new developments rather than repetitions? Such questions are crucial to a serious consideration of political art, but they are rarely the concern of poems. (The work of Yeats, despite his conservatism, offers perhaps the most conspicuous exception.) Since Baraka's literary essays over the past decade have tended more toward chronicle than toward theory, it is difficult to infer what his positions would be. Only his future work will tell.

Regardless, "In the Tradition" rejects the false dichotomy between culture and politics. It offers a sophisticated historical understanding, and at the same time it is aesthetically sophisticated and satisfying as well. This poem represents a significant advance in the debate about culture and politics by providing a vision of politicized culture. Whether other poets—or for that matter, Baraka himself—will recognize the importance of this model remains to be seen. Regardless, "In the Tradition" deserves to be recognized as a masterpiece of political art and a major statement on the interpenetration of culture and politics.

Notes

[1]Werner Sollors, *Amiri Baraka/LeRoi Jones: The Quest for a Modernist Populism,*

is an excellent source for discussions of the relationship between Baraka's writing and politics. My own article in *Boundary 2* traces Baraka's development but concentrates on his black nationalist phase, taking "Black Art" as his paradigmatic work from that period.

[2]"Reification and Utopia in Mass Culture" begins an inquiry into the theory of culture, which Jameson expands in "Postmodernism, or The Cultural Logic of Late Capitalism." The latter is especially notable for the variety of artifacts he examines in his anatomy of our present culture epoch.

[3]The hierarchical view implicit in the notion that "popular culture" is a "lower" realm is imbedded in the dominant sense of the word "culture," as it has been commonly used since Matthew Arnold. The opposition of "culture" and "entertainment" is among the most obvious derivations of such thinking. Much has been said against this effete and anthropologically naive conception, but hierarchical thinking and its inevitably repressive social consequences (as, for instance, in the form of "white supremacy") are integral aspects of the Western tradition. Jacques Derrida's "White Mythology" is a brilliant critique of this phenomenon. On the genealogy of the concept of culture, Raymond Williams' seminal *Culture and Society* remains unsurpassed. Jameson develops his cultural critique most thoroughly in *Marxism and Form* and *The Political Unconscious*; in his recent essays, he has turned his attention increasingly toward nonliterary cultural forms, such as architecture and film. Williams' collection of essays, *Problems in Materialism and Culture*, is probably the best overview of his work. *Marxism and Literature* provides a full-length elaboration of his cultural theory, and *The Year 2000*, a revision and expansion of his celebrated *The Long Revolution*, offers a compelling mixture of theoretical reflecting and specific analysis. *Television: Technology and Cultural Form* is a succinct and lucid examination of this popular medium and of the dialectical relation between culture and technology.

I find Jameson's readings of both texts and artifacts trenchant and altogether admirable. As a point of method, however, I think that he overemphasizes psychological factors and especially the dynamic between the artist's striving for self-expression and the limitations imposed by the cultural epoch. Such analysis is often illuminating, but it tends toward abstraction. Williams, by contrast, is far more empirical. But sometimes he extends his investigations into such minutely detailed elaborations of conflicting particulars that his analyses lose focus and rhetorical force. We need a methodology which combines Jameson's psychological subtlety and Williams' attentiveness to detail and wariness toward abstraction. Unfortunately, that synthesis is easier to invoke than to achieve.

[4]For excellent close readings of Baraka's poems, Kimberly Bentson, *Baraka: The Renegade Behind the Mask*, is especially strong on the early (pre-1965) poems. Sollors is also very useful, but his broader-ranging book tends to be less detailed on individual poems.

[5]Theodore Hudson's *From LeRoi Jones to Amiri Baraka*, though a bit dated now, is the best source of information on Baraka's biography. For accounts of Baraka's name changes, see Bentson (267) and Sollors (263n). Baraka collected his writings on black nationalist theory in *Raise Race*. His autobiography contains a lengthy and exceedingly harsh account of his nationalist phase and especially of his fellow nationalists. For a succinct and rather mordant critique of 1960s black nationalism from a Marxist perspective, Adolph Reed's "Black Particularly Reconsidered" is peerless.

Works Cited

Baraka, Amiri. *The Autobiography of LeRoi Jones.* New York: Freundich Books, 1984.

————. *The Dead Lecturer.* New York: Grove Press, 1964.

————. *Home.* New York: William Morrow, 1966.

————. *The Music.* New York: William Morrow, 1987.

————. *New Music, New Poetry.* With David Murray and Steve McCall. India Navigation IN 1048, 1981.

————. *Preface to a Twenty Volume Suicide Note.* New York: Totem Press//Corinth Books, 1961.

————. *Raise Race Rays Raze.* New York: Random House, 1971.

————. *Selected Poetry of Amiri Baraka/LeRoi Jones.* New York: William Morrow, 1979.

Bentson, Kimberly. *Baraka: The Renegade Behind the Mask.* New Haven: Yale UP, 1976.

Derrida, Jacques. "White Mythology: Metaphor in the Text of Philosophy." *New Literary History* 6 (1974): 5-74.

Hudson, Theodore. "From LeRoi Jones to Amiri Baraka." Diss. Howard U, 1971.

Jameson, Fredric. *Marxism and Form: Twentieth-Century Dialectical Theories of Literature.* Princeton: Princeton UP, 1971.

————. *The Political Unconscious: Narrative As a Socially Symbolic Act.* Ithaca: Cornell UP, 1981.

————. "Postmodernism, or The Cultural Logic of Late Capitalism." *New Left Review* 146 (July/August 1984): 53-92.

————. "Reification and Utopia in Mass Culture." *Social Text* 1.1 (Winter 1979): 130-48.

Newton, Huey. "Interview with Huey Newton." *Black Protest Thought in the Twentieth Century.* Ed. August Meier, Elliott Rudwick and Francis L. Broderick. 2nd ed. Indianapolis: Bobbs-Merrill, 1971. 495-516.

Reed, Adolph. "Black Particularity Reconsidered." *Telos* 39 (Spring 1979): 71-93.

Smith, David Lionel. "Amiri Baraka and the Black Arts of 'Black Art.' " *Boundary 2* 15.1 & 2 (Fall 1986/Winter 1987): 235-254.

Sollors, Werner. *Amiri Baraka/LeRoi Jones: The Quest for a Modernist Populism.* New York: Columbia UP, 1978.

Williams, Raymond. *Culture and Society.* 1960. New York: Columbia UP, 1983.

————. *Marxism and Literature.* New York: Oxford UP, 1977.

————. *Problems in Materialism and Culture.* London: Verso, 1980.

————. *Television: Technology and Cultural Form.* New York: Schocken, 1975.

————. *The Year 2000.* New York: Pantheon, 1983.

Contributors

Tom Dardis obtained his doctorate at Columbia University in 1980. Formerly editor-in-chief of Berkley Books, he is now Professor of English at John Jay College of Criminal Justice in New York City. He is the author of *Some Time in the Sun, Keaton, Harold Lloyd,* and *The Thirsty Muse.*

Barbara Eckstein has taught at Tulane University and the University of New Orleans. She writes comparative studies of contemporary literature and politics and is currently completing a book entitled *Internal Difference: Reading Politics as Paradox.* She also writes fiction. Barbara Eckstein is an active participant in the work of Educators for Social Responsibility.

John Gery is Associate Professor of English at the University of New Orleans. He is the author of a volume of poems, *Charlemagne: A Song of Gestures* (1983), and a poetry chapbook, *The Burning of New Orleans* (1988). His criticism on contemporary literature has appeared in *Concerning Poetry, Critique, Essays in Literature, Poesis,* and elsewhere.

George L. Groman is Professor of English at LaGuardia Community College of the City University of New York. A Ph.D. in American Civilization from New York University, he has won grants from the Woodrow Wilson and Andrew Mellon foundations. Publications include *Political Literature of the Progressive Era, The City Today,* and articles on political and literary subjects.

George Lipsitz is Associate Professor of American Studies at the University of Minnesota. He is the author of *A Life in the Struggle: Ivory Perry and the Culture of Opposition* (Philadelphia: Temple University Press, 1988) and *Class and Culture in Cold War America* (South Hadley: Bergin and Garvey, 1982).

Raymond A. Mazurek received his Ph.D. from Purdue University in 1980, and has published essays on Poe, Dickinson, John Barth, Thomas Pynchon, Robert Coover, and John Berger. Currently, he is an assistant professor of English at Penn State University, Berks Campus, in Reading, Pennsylvania, where he has also been active in Central America solidarity work.

Gabriel Miller is the author of *Screening the Novel* as well as books on Daniel Fuchs, John Irving, and Clifford Odets. He is currently editing a collection of critical essays on Clifford Odets and is a member of the English Department of Rutgers University, Newark.

Paul Orlov is currently Assistant Professor of English at Penn State University (Delaware County Campus) and has previously published articles on Dreiser, Whitman, and Frost. The present essay on Coover reflects his strong interest in American literature on modern socio-political themes—an interest also motivating his continued study of his "specialty," Dreiser's fiction.

Ruth Prigozy is Professor of English at Hofstra University. She has co-edited *Short Stories: A Critical Anthology*, and her essays on Fitzgerald, Hemingway modern literature and film have appeared in *Fitzgerald/Hemingway Annual, Commonweal, Twentieth Century Literature, Prospects*, and *Literature/Film Quarterly*. She is completing a book on director Billy Wilder, and is writing a book on Fitzgerald and popular culture for University of Mississippi Press.

Angelita Reyes is on the faculty of Penn State University in the Departments of Comparative Literature and English, and the Women's Studies Program. She was recently awarded a summer fellowship by the National Endowment for the Humanities to conduct research in Jamaica for a forthcoming book on Afro-American and Caribbean women's writing.

James Seaton is Associate Professor of English at Michigan State University. He is working on a book tentatively entitled *Cultural Conservatism, Political Radicalism*. He has published essays on cultural critics such as Dwight Macdonald, H.L. Mencken and Christopher Lasch. Professor Seaton has written one book, *A Reading of Vergil's Georgics*.

David Lionel Smith is Associate Professor of English at Williams College, teaches courses in American Literature. He is currently completing *Racial Writing, Black and White*, a study of how texts by black and white Americans construct "race" as a form of identity in particular historical moments.

Adam J. Sorkin is Associate Professor of English at Penn State Delaware County Campus. He has published numerous essays in journals including *American Literature, Modern Fiction Studies* and *Contemporary Literature*, as well as translations of poetry. A Carl Bode award winner for a 1986 *Journal of American Culture* article, he is currently working on a book on Cold War American writing.

Joseph J. Waldmeir is Professor of English at Michigan State University. He has published widely in modern and contemporary American literature, including *American Novels of the Second World War*, and essays on Hemingway, Steinbeck, Updike, etc. He edited *Recent American Fiction: Some Critical Views*, and books on Hemingway and John Barth.

ACA4807   1/25/90

PS
228
P6
P64
1989

PE1591 W38 c. 3
Ref +Webster's collegiate thesaurus.

0 00 02 0245398 1
MIDDLEBURY COLLEGE